HOW to Program

Visual Basic 5.0

Control Creation Edition

HOW *to* Program

Visual Basic 5.0

Control Creation Edition

JEFFREY · P. · McMANUS

Ziff-Davis Press
An imprint of Macmillan Computer Publishing USA
Emeryville, California

Publisher	Stacy Hiquet
Associate Publisher	Stephen Sayre
Acquisitions Editor	Simon Hayes
Development Editor	Angela Allen
Copy Editor	Candace Crane
Technical Reviewer	Vidya Bharat and John Kee
Production Editors	Barbara Dahl and Edith Rex
Proofreader	Jeff Barash
Cover Illustration and Design	Megan Gandt
Illustrator	Mina Reimer
Book Design and Layout	Bruce Lundquist
Indexer	Anne Leach

Ziff-Davis Press, ZD Press, and the Ziff-Davis Press logo are trademarks or registered trademarks of, and are licensed to Macmillan Computer Publishing USA by Ziff-Davis Publishing Company, New York, New York.

Ziff-Davis Press imprint books are produced on a Macintosh computer system with the following applications: FrameMaker®, Microsoft® Word, QuarkXPress®, Adobe Illustrator®, Adobe Photoshop®, Adobe Streamline™, MacLink®Plus, Aldus® FreeHand™, Collage Plus™.

Ziff-Davis Press, an imprint of
Macmillan Computer Publishing USA
5903 Christie Avenue
Emeryville, CA 94608

ISBN 1-56276-485-3

Manufactured in the United States of America

10 9 8 7 6 5 4 3 2 1

This is for my sister Jill,
who rubbed my shoulders
when they were sore and
served me cocktails when it
was time to stop working.
Thanks for everything.
You are the greatest,
and anybody who says
differently will have to suffer
my violent wrath.

Table of Contents

Acknowledgments

I'd like to thank Laura Lemay for her advice and support. Thanks to John Chen for his friendship and for his extremely valuable assistance in helping me navigate the sometimes Byzantine machinations of a certain software company over the years. And thanks to Mike and Laura Medina for their help and advice.

Thanks to my editors at Ziff-Davis Press for believing in me and for letting me keep the corny jokes in.

I'd also like to thank the following legion of truly righteous mental heavyweights for their technical help and hints: Tom Digby, Jim Huguley, Matt Luallen, Tales Normando, Marty Pavlovic, and Bob Rossney. Your generosity with your time and knowledge has improved this book greatly.

This book was written in San Francisco and Livermore, California in Fall of 1996 and Winter of 1997.

This is not a sexist cookbook.

Introduction

A world in which every piece of software has the ability to interact with every other piece of software ain't gonna happen anytime soon. But you can always dream. I personally hope to someday put a software chip in a small house pet—a cat, perhaps—and control it through the use of Visual Basic properties and methods.

But perhaps I'm sharing too much.

Windows developers have had the ability to use software components ever since Visual Basic first came out. People Who Know About These Things tell us that the Windows component market—formerly restricted to VB developers, now expanding to accommodate developers in applications as disparate as FoxPro, Access, Visual C++ and Microsoft Word 97—has grown to a sizable software subindustry that sells on the order of $250 million worth of products. That's a lot of widgets, whatzits, and data-aware ding-dongs by anybody's standards.

How to Hurt Uncooperative Users

With the advent of this kooky Internet thing, it's certain that this component technology will continue to grow and mature and eventually get to the point where it will become a part of every application, Web page, vibrating hotel bed, and house pet on earth.

However, it's not there yet. The idea of sending software components to users through a Web page is a compelling one–if your users are using a Web browser that supports the software component technology standard you chose.

Of course, if visitors to your Web site simply refuse to use "The Correct Browser," you have a number of options for remediation that you may wish to consider:

▶ Shoot them

▶ Garrote them

▶ Systematically buff their elbows with sandpaper until they howl with agony

▶ etc.

Only through the cooperation of Webmasters all over the world will the ActiveX assimilation of Planet Earth be completed in a timely and cruelty-free fashion.

Until Web browser support for ActiveX becomes as ubiquitous as the rubber insole, there are still plenty of reasons to develop ActiveX controls. You probably have at least a few of these in mind, or you wouldn't have bought this book (and I wouldn't have written it). It is my opinion that rapid development of ActiveX controls will be most prevalent in two areas: vertical applications (written in Visual Basic or any one of a number of other development environments that support ActiveX) and on private Web servers (also known as intranets).

It will be interesting to see what happens with ActiveX support in Microsoft Office 97, although I couldn't tell you exactly how it's going to work, because as I write this, Office 97 is exactly 24 hours away from being released. (I, for one, am quivering with anticipation.)

Creating Controls in Visual Basic is So Great I Could Just Explode

One of the great unsung promises of ActiveX is that–unlike other cross-platform component technologies, such as Java–you can theoretically build an ActiveX component in any programming language and use it with any programming language.

No longer do VB programmers need to rely on the third-party control market for controls written in C++. In fact, the advent of VB as a control-development environment means that a Visual Basic developer can now turn the tables, providing ActiveX components for developers who create applications in Visual C++. What a concept.

It's likely that more languages and development environments will support the creation of ActiveX controls as time goes by. In fact, as this book was being written, a beta version of a new tool for creating ActiveX controls called VisualX from InterGroup Technologies was released. It's not quite as good as Visual Basic's Control Creation Edition (for reasons I'll let you discover on your own), but it is worth checking out. You can download it for free from http://www.intergrouptech.com/form.html.

Why Johnny Can't Create Controls

Visual Basic programmers have been whining for years about their inability to create ActiveX controls in Visual Basic. "How hard could it be to include this ability in VB?" they ask. Well, the Visual Basic gnomes at Microsoft listened. And they came up with a bonus: In addition to giving you a way to create ActiveX controls in Visual Basic, they made it a free download from the Microsoft Web site.

Because it's so easy to create controls using Visual Basic (easy, that is, once you've purchased and read the informative tome you now hold in your hands), it's likely that we'll begin to see a number of new, interesting, fascinating, and perhaps disgusting contributions to the world of ActiveX controls in coming years.

So, there it is. You have before you the Visual Basic Control Creation Edition. Please use its powers only for good, never for evil.

This Is Not What This Book Is About

Now that you have an idea about what this book is about, I'll go into some of the things it isn't about. (By the way, I always hate it when authors say "er, um, this topic is beyond the scope of this book." It seems like such a cop-out. So when a topic *is* beyond the scope of this book, I try to give you a reference to a book where the topic is covered in more depth.)

This book does not delve into the technology initiatives behind ActiveX controls such as COM, DCOM, and OLE, except where they are necessary to convey points directly related to building controls in Visual Basic. I did this by design; you don't need to be steeped in these initiatives in order to create good controls any more than you need to know everything about the Windows API to create good Visual Basic applications. If you want information on the forest rather than the trees, I'll refer to you the documentation and tools available in the ActiveX Software Development Kit, downloadable from http://www.microsoft.com/activex.

You'll also notice that I conspicuously avoid referring to Java in this book. This isn't because I don't have anything to say about ActiveX versus Java; it's more a function of the fact that I didn't want to muddle the instructional material in this book with pointless factoids on this alleged clash of the technology titans. My opinion on the whole ActiveX versus Java hubbub, for what it's worth, is this: Viewing ActiveX and Java as a winner-take-all competition for domination of the Internet is like viewing lowfat milk versus skimmed milk as a competition for domination of your refrigerator.

To get your very own copy of Visual Basic 5.0 Control Creation Edition for free, go to the Microsoft site at http://www.microsoft.com/vbasic/controls/.

Who Should Use This Book

This book is designed for intermediate to advanced Visual Basic programmers who are interested in creating ActiveX controls in Visual Basic. You may be interested in creating controls that will reside in Web pages, or you may want to create controls that will reside in compiled Visual Basic applications. Either way, this book addresses all of the steps you'll need to take to create a control in VB.

Although this book uses the Control Creation Edition for its examples, you can use any version of Visual Basic 5.0 to create controls. The concepts are the same from one edition of Visual Basic to the next.

You should be aware that this book is not a comprehensive reference to programming in VB. It would, however, serve as an excellent companion to a more general book on VB. If you're a beginner and you want to learn how to create ActiveX controls, it might behoove you to learn how VB works in general before jumping into control creation. You'll save yourself some time and some grief.

Finally, enjoy the book. And don't forget to check out the Web page at http://www.well .com/user/jeffreyp/activex/. I'll try to keep it updated with as much control-creation information and links to VB resources as I have time for.

What's New in the Integrated Development Environment

New Language Features

Chapter 1
What's New In Visual Basic 5.0

This chapter describes important new features in Visual Basic 5.0, including changes to the interface and changes in the Visual Basic (VB) programming language.

At first glance, the changes in the interface might look daunting. Fortunately, though, the designers of Visual Basic 5.0 have given you an unprecedented number of customizable features. You can make the interface look just like the one for Visual Basic 4.0 and then add new features as you need them until the interface is well nigh unrecognizable. It's up to you.

What's New in the Integrated Development Environment

The IDE is where you'll spend most of your time when you're developing a Visual Basic project. It's where you write code, add components to your project, and design your application's visual interface.

Visual Basic 5.0 adds a number of new features to the IDE to make it even easier to develop applications quickly with a minimum of mental anguish.

Projects, Files, and the Project Explorer

The *Project Explorer* is the where you manage the files that comprise your Visual Basic 5.0 project; it is analogous to the Project window in previous versions of Visual Basic.

The main reason why the Project Explorer is necessary in Visual Basic 5.0 is that you can now have multiple projects open at once. This might seem excessive to a Visual Basic veteran, but it makes sense once you take a look at how control creation works. Because an EXE project and an ActiveX project are two separate things and you need an EXE project to test the ActiveX controls you create, you'll likely use multiple projects quite often.

With all these new files and multiple projects, it can be hard to keep track of what's what. Figure 1.1 displays the hierarchy of files and filename extensions.

Note that both ActiveX project files and EXE project files end in .VBP. This means you'll probably want to add some other identifying characteristic to your project files to differentiate them from each other. You may want to denote project files that contain ActiveX controls by including the word "Control" in their filenames, for example.

For example, say you have a project called **StickShift**. This project is an ActiveX control for a graphical push button shaped like the stickshift for a 1989 five-speed Jeep Wrangler. For this project, at a minimum, you need a file for the StickShift control itself (StickShift.ctl) and a project file (StickShiftControl.vbp). If StickShift has a custom property sheet, you'd call that file StickShift.pag.

You will almost always use an EXE project in order to test your ActiveX control project. For the StickShift project, that means you'll add a project file (TestStickShift.vbp) and a form (TestStickShift.frm). Finally, your project would require a Project group file, StickShift.vpg, to house the EXE project and the ActiveX project.

> **Tip** *It is not a bad idea to put each project you create into its own folder, in order to keep all the files you need in one place. The projects on the CD-ROM that accompanies this book are organized in this way.*

Single Document/Multiple Document Interface Options

When you launch Visual Basic 5.0 for the first time, the first thing you'll probably notice is that the layout of the windows and menus has changed somewhat. The Visual Basic Integrated Development Environment (IDE) now has a Multiple Document Interface (MDI). The advantage of MDI is that all the subwindows (of which there are many) stay in one big window that stays in the background (called a *parent window*).

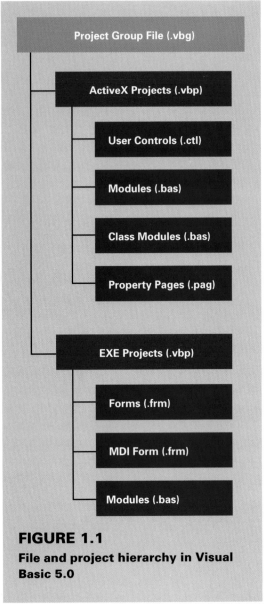

FIGURE 1.1
File and project hierarchy in Visual Basic 5.0

The disadvantage of MDI is that you don't have quite as much flexibility in moving and re-sizing windows. Also, the new interface can be a little jarring when you've been working with Visual Basic for years. Fortunately, there is a way to get the Visual Basic IDE to look like it did in previous versions: with a style known as Single Document Interface (SDI). To change Visual Basic to an SDI interface:

1 From the menu, select Tools, then Options.

2 The Options dialog box appears. Select the Advanced tab.

3 Check the box labeled SDI Development Environment.

4 Click on OK.

You will have to re-start Visual Basic after doing this, but that's a small price to pay to return to the decent, red-blooded, God-fearing Visual Basic interface we've come to know and love for all these years.

> **Note** *The examples in this book assume that you're using the SDI inter-face. The instructions for procedures differ only slightly between the two in-terfaces. You'll be able to figure out what to do if you insist on using the new MDI interface, but for certain things like closing and resizing windows, the SDI interface is easier to use. If you're getting the impression that I have a personal vendetta against the MDI interface, you're right. This is because an MDI interface killed my brother.*

Form Layout Window

The Form Layout window is just below the Properties window on the right side of the screen. It enables you to see just where a form will appear on the screen at runtime by visually positioning forms on the screen. Now instead of having to write the tedious few lines of code to center each form with respect to the screen, you can use the Form Layout window.

By right-clicking on the Form Layout window, you can display resolution guides. These guides show you what your form layout will look like on a standard VGA screen at 640 by 480 resolution. This can be helpful, since many developers have higher-resolution screens, although some users are still trapped in the low-res world. Figure 1.2 shows the location of the Form Layout window on the screen.

By right-clicking on the Form Layout window and selecting Startup Position, you can denote where a form should be located when your application starts. (You need to have a form in the foreground of your project to see this feature in action.)

You can also specify that a form should be centered with respect to the screen at startup time by setting the form's Startup Position property to 2—Center Screen (this is a new property for forms in Visual Basic 5.0).

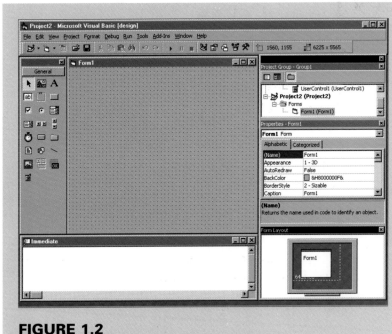

FIGURE 1.2
The Form Layout window

You probably won't use the Form Layout window much when creating controls using Visual Basic 5.0, unless your control displays forms that act as custom dialog boxes. In that case, you should use the Form Layout window to ensure that your custom dialog box is displayed correctly.

Indent/Outdent

Visual Basic 5.0 gives you the ability to automatically indent or outdent one or more lines of code. This can go a long way toward making your code more readable. And the fact that it's automatic means that you won't have to change the individual indents for 30 lines of code every time you decide to enclose that big code chunk in an If…Then statement. To see how automatic indent/outdent works:

1 Start Visual Basic. When the Startup screen appears, create a new standard EXE project.

2 When the project is created, open Form1's code window by double-clicking on it.

3 Type in a few lines of code. Comments (starting with single apostrophe or the Rem statement) are okay, just as long as you have multiple lines.

4 Select two or three lines of code.

5 Press Tab once or twice. The code indents.

6 Press Shift+Tab. The code outdents.

Customizable Toolbars

You have the ability to move, resize, and customize Visual Basic's toolbars. This feature is not unlike the dockable and customizable toolbars that have existed in Microsoft Office applications for years.

There are four toolbars in Visual Basic: Standard, Edit, Form Editor, and Debug. Visual Basic will generally display whatever toolbar is appropriate for what you're doing. But there are situations where you might want to add a frequently used command to an existing VB toolbar. For example, say you use the Toggle Bookmark command frequently and you'd like the command to appear on the toolbar instead of in the Edit menu. To add a Bookmark button to the Visual Basic toolbar:

1 Using the mouse, right-click on an existing toolbar (or use the menu commands View, Toolbars, Customize).

2 The Customize dialog box will appear.

3 Click on the Commands tab.

4 Under Categories, click on Edit.

5 A list of edit commands will appear in the list box under Commands. Scroll down and locate Toggle Bookmark. Figure 1.3 shows the dialog box with this command highlighted.

6 Click and drag the Toggle Bookmark command from the Commands list to the toolbar. The Toggle Bookmark command now resides on the toolbar.

If you like, at this point you can modify the Toggle Bookmark toolbar button you just created. To do this:

1 In the Customize dialog box, click on the Modify Selection button.

2 The Modify Selection menu will appear, as shown in Figure 1.4.

3 Select Change Button Image, then click on the image of your choice. (I'm partial to the eight ball, but that's just me.)

4 Go back to the Modify Selection menu and choose Image and Text. This is a good selection to make when you're not familiar with the command or when the button's icon alone doesn't jog your memory as to what the button is supposed to do.

5 If you want to remove the new button from your customized toolbar, simply click and drag it off the toolbar. (This only works if the Customize dialog box is open.)

6 When you're done with the Customize dialog box, click on Close.

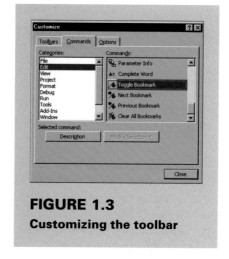

FIGURE 1.3
Customizing the toolbar

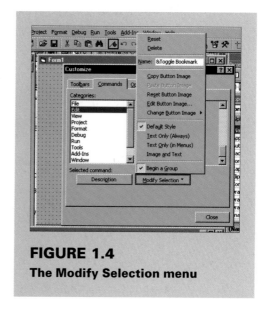

FIGURE 1.4
The Modify Selection menu

Wizards

Visual Basic 5.0 comes with two new wizards that automate the process of developing controls.

The ActiveX Control Interface Wizard is a tool that automatically inserts property and event code in controls you write. You can use it to add the properties of existing controls to your control (a process known as *delegation*) or create entirely new properties and methods. Since controls have lots of properties, but the code to implement them is exactly the same, this wizard can take the drudgery out of creating a programmable interface.

The Property Page Wizard is a tool that helps you create property pages for your controls. A *property page* is a customized version of the Visual Basic property window. Property pages are good ways to give access to a control's properties to its users, particularly if your control has many properties or if it has a few complicated properties.

The ActiveX Control Interface Wizard and the Property Page Wizard are both discussed in more detail in Chapter 4, "Control Properties."

Procedure View/Full Module View

Visual Basic 5.0 gives you the ability to switch between two views of your code. Procedure View displays one procedure at a time, while Full Module View shows all the procedures in a module, one after the other. Procedure View was the default in versions of Visual Basic prior to 5.0; Full Module View is the default in Visual Basic 5.0.

Many programmers who are new to Visual Basic get annoyed because they can't see all their code at once—they're afraid they're going to write code that will later "get lost" in the interface. Full Module View is handy because it lets you compare several adjacent procedures in your code. This is particularly useful when you're defining a new property for a control, since implementing a property always requires at least two procedures (and usually more). To demonstrate the difference between Procedure View and Full Module View:

1 Double-click on a standard EXE project form to open its code window.

2 Type some code. A few lines worth of comments are fine here.

3 Using the Procedure combo box on the upper-right side of the code window, switch to a different procedure.

4 You should be able to see both procedures in the code window. Click on the Procedure View button in the lower-left corner of the code window. You should now be able to see only the current procedure in the code window.

You'll probably switch between Procedure View and Full Module View frequently as you work with Visual Basic 5.0, depending on what kind of code you're working on. If you're working with a set of small property procedures, you're likely to want to use Full Module View. But if you're slogging through a giant global procedure with lots of lines of code, it might make sense to switch to Procedure View in order to reduce the amount of clutter on your screen.

If you always want code to start in Procedure View (that is, you want Visual Basic 5.0 to work the way previous versions of Visual Basic did), do the following:

1 Choose the menu commands Tools, Options.

2 Make sure the Editor tab is selected.

3 Clear the box labeled Default To Full Module View.

4 Click OK.

Bookmarks

In Visual Basic 5.0 you can set bookmarks in code to make it easier to return to a piece of code you're working on or to flip between two pieces of code quickly. You have the ability to move to the next or previous bookmark and to clear all the bookmarks in your project. In this respect, bookmarks work a lot like breakpoints, except they don't cause your code to pause.

To see how bookmarks work:

1 Open any code window.

2 Click on the Procedure View button in the lower left corner of the code window to switch to Procedure View.

3 Type some code. These can be comments if you wish.

4 Move the insertion point to the middle of the code you typed.

5 Choose the menu commands Edit, Bookmarks, Toggle Bookmark.

6 A light blue lozenge-shaped bookmark will appear to the left of the line you bookmarked.

7 Using the Procedure combo box in the upper right corner, switch to another procedure in the module.

8 Choose the menu commands Edit, Bookmarks, Next Bookmark. You'll be speedily returned to the position of your original bookmark.

9 Select the menu commands Edit, Bookmarks, Clear All Bookmarks to clear your bookmark.

Automatic Code Completion

As you write code in Visual Basic 5.0, you'll notice that helpful hints will appear on your screen as you type. These hints are comprised of several features of the Visual Basic 5.0 editor, collectively known as Automatic Code Completion. Table 1.1 lists code completion features in Visual Basic 5.0.

All three elements of automatic code completion are available by default. You can also shut off these features if you wish. To demonstrate how Auto List Members works, open any code window. Type **Debug.P**. An Auto List Members window will pop up at the point where you were typing, displaying the two members of the Debug object, Assert and Print. (Assert is new to Visual Basic 5.0 and is discussed later in this chapter.) Figure 1.5 shows what an Auto List Members window looks like. Type a Tab to accept Print as the completed statement.

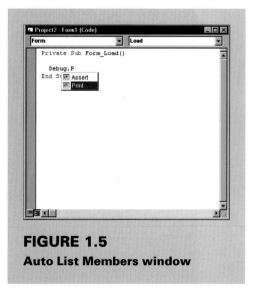

FIGURE 1.5
Auto List Members window

TABLE 1.1   CODE COMPLETION FEATURES IN VISUAL BASIC 5.0

Feature	Displays
Auto List Members	Members of object classes
Auto Quick Info	Syntax of Visual Basic functions
Auto Data Tips	Displays the value of the variable under your cursor

To demonstrate how Auto Quick Info works:

1 In any code window, type the following code:

```
MsgBox
```

2 Type a space, as if you're now going to complete the statement by typing a parameter for the MsgBox statement.

3 An Auto Quick Info window will appear, providing the syntax of the MsgBox statement. Figure 1.6 shows what an Auto Quick Info window looks like.

4 Finish typing the MsgBox statement, or press Esc to dismiss the Auto Quick Info window.

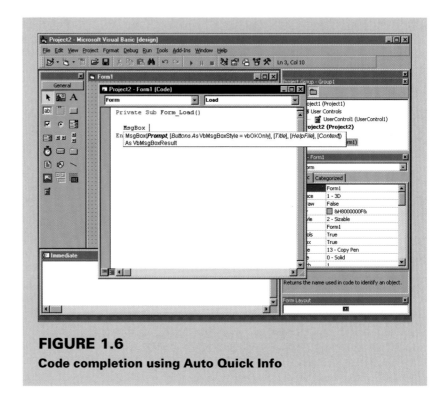

FIGURE 1.6
Code completion using Auto Quick Info

Auto Data Tips are like the ToolTips you might be familiar with if you're a user of any of the Microsoft Office products. In Microsoft Word, for example, when you position your mouse pointer above a toolbar button and wait a second, a ToolTip appears telling you what the button does. The difference is that Visual Basic's Auto Data Tips work only on running code. So to demonstrate how they work, you'll have to create some running code.

1 Add a form to your project using the menu commands File, Add Project.

2 Select EXE Project from the Add Project dialog box, then click on OK.

3 A new form, Form1, will appear in the Project Explorer. Double-click on it to open it.

4 Double-click on Form1 to expose its code window. You should be in its Load event procedure.

5 Type the code in Listing 1.1.

6 Run the code by pressing the function key F5 or by using the menu commands Run, Start.

7 Position your mouse on top of ImportantVariable. The value of ImportantVariable will pop up. Figure 1.7 shows what an AutoDataTips window looks like.

I think these features are extremely cool additions to the Visual Basic IDE, but if they bug you, you can turn them off. To turn off these editing features:

1 Choose the menu commands Tools, Options.

2 The Options dialog box appears. Make sure the Editor tab is selected.

3 Clear Auto List Members, Auto Quick Info, and/or Auto Data Tips.

4 Click on OK.

Drag-and-Drop Editing

In Visual Basic 5.0 you can now use drag-and-drop editing, just as in any Microsoft Office application. Drag-and-drop editing lets you move code quickly and easily. For example, take the code of Listing 1.2.

Say that the Stop statement needs to be moved down a line. You could select it, copy it, reposition the insertion point, and paste it, but that's the old-fashioned, backward-thinking way. Instead, try this:

1 In any Visual Basic form, open a code window.

2 Type the code in Listing 1.2. (You'll note that, for your convenience, this code is astoundingly similar to Listing 1.1.)

LISTING 1.1   Code to demonstrate Auto Data Tips

```
Private Sub Form_Load()

    Dim ImportantVariable As Integer
    ImportantVariable = 45
    Stop
    Debug.Print ImportantVariable

End Sub
```

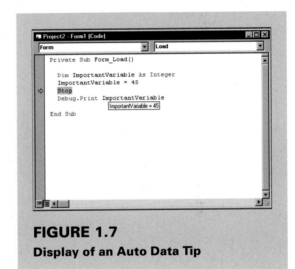

FIGURE 1.7
Display of an Auto Data Tip

LISTING 1.2   Code to demonstrate drag-and-drop editing

```
Private Sub Form_Load()

    Dim ImportantVariable As Integer
    ImportantVariable = 45
    Stop
    Debug.Print ImportantVariable

End Sub
```

3 Select the Stop statement by clicking and dragging across it with the mouse.

4 Release the mouse button.

5 Click on the center of the selected text and drag it to the blank line under the Debug.Print statement.

6 The Stop statement should now appear in the code after the Debug.Print statement.

You can use a little-known additional feature of drag and drop, *drag-and-copy*, to duplicate text. For example, say you need two Stop statements in your code. To do this using drag-and-copy:

1 Select the Stop statement by click-dragging.

2 Release the mouse key.

3 Hold down Ctrl as you click-drag the selected text with the mouse. You should notice the drag icon includes a plus to indicate the item you are copying.

4 Release the mouse key on the blank line between the Debug.Print and End Sub statement. The Stop statement will be copied to the blank line.

If drag-and-drop editing bugs you, you can turn it off. To do this:

1 From the Tools menu, select Options.

2 Make sure the Editor tab is selected.

3 In the Window Settings panel, clear the box labeled Drag-and-Drop Text Editing.

4 Click on OK.

New Language Features

The Visual Basic 5.0 programming language contains a number of new keywords, program objects, and concepts. The new language features that apply to control creation are discussed in detail throughout this book and are summarized in a table at the end of this chapter. In addition, here's a quick summary of the features that are not directly pertinent to control creation.

Assertions

An *assertion* is a debugging tool designed to conditionally pause your code if a fatal error is raised. Essentially, an assertion tests a condition. The condition can be a variable, a function call, or what have you. If the assertion is True, code continues executing. If the assertion is False, code pauses so you can diagnose the problem.

It's possible to have assertions in virtually any language using a function call, but now Visual Basic supports assertions as a method of the Debug object.

For example, say you have a function called OpenMyFile() that opens a file. The function returns True if it succeeds and False if it fails. You can incorporate the return value of this function in an assertion like this:

```
Sub AssertOpen()
    Debug.Assert OpenMyFile("c:\windows\myfile.txt")
End Sub
```

In this code, if the OpenMyFile function failed, the Assert method would pause the code, enabling you to see exactly where the problem took place.

Because your code can only be paused in the development environment, using the Assert method only makes sense in that context. When your code is compiled, any Assert methods remaining in your code are ignored.

Enumerated Constants

An *enumerated constant* is a concept that programmers from other languages such as C will be familiar with. The idea behind an enumeration is that constants can often be grouped together in categories. Since people have an easier time remembering words than numbers, it makes sense to name, or enumerate, these constants.

An Enum declaration goes in the declarations section of a code module. A typical Enum declaration looks like this:

```
Public Enum Shoes
    TennisShoes = 0
    HikingBoots = 1
    HipWaders = 2
    StilletoHeels = 3
End Enum
```

You can make reference to the values in an enumeration using code that looks like this:

```
Sub SetShoes()
    Dim MyShoes As Shoes
    MyShoes = HipWaders
End Sub
```

You may be thinking that this feature is suspiciously similar to the Type declaration, which has existed in VB forever. Types and Enums are similar, although Enums are used to declare related constants, while Types are used to create a custom variable type. But the place where Enums come in handy is in the area of defining properties for controls.

If you've used Visual Basic in the past, you've probably run across enumerated properties without realizing it. For example, consider the Align property of the Picture Box control. The legal values for an Align property are the numbers 0 through 4. But when you set the Align property control in the Properties window, you're shown these choices:

```
0 - None
1 - Align Top
2 - Align Bottom
3 - Align Left
4 - Align Right
```

The values stored by the Align property are the numbers 0 through 4, but the choices displayed by the combo box include enumerated names for each value. You do the same thing for properties in controls you create by using Enums. See Chapter 4, "Control Properties," for information on how to do this.

AddressOf

The AddressOf operator permits the use of callbacks in Windows API and DLL calls. This is a pretty advanced topic that is way beyond the scope of this book, but it's the kind of thing that causes C programmers to either jump up and click their heels or moan in grief. Go figure.

The AddressOf operator was added to Visual Basic 5.0 so VB programmers can place calls to Windows API functions that take function pointers as arguments. There are a few cases in the dark, foreboding world of the Windows API where you'd need to do this; the VB5 Help file demonstrates how you can use the AddressOf operator to generate a list of all the fonts installed on your system.

I was thinking about providing my own code example using AddressOf but realized that I'd approach mandatory retirement age before I was able to come up with a good example of my own; second, it wouldn't be as good as the example in the VB Help file; and third, it wouldn't be pertinent to control creation anyway. So I'll leave it to some other enterprising author to cover Windows API calls using AddressOf.

Language Features Pertaining to Control Creation

Table 1.2 summarizes new features of the Visual Basic language that have specific implications for control creation. All of these features are discussed in depth elsewhere in this book.

TABLE 1.2   LANGUAGE FEATURES PERTAINING TO CONTROL CREATION

Language Feature	Description	Discussed in
AmbientProperties Object	Holds properties of a control container to enable a user control to initialize itself	Chapter 4, "Control Properties"
AsyncRead method, AsyncProperty object, AsyncReadComplete event	Enables a control to read a property from a source located on the Internet	Chapter 14, "Controls That Interact with the Internet"
DataBindings collection, DataBinding object, IsBindable property	Enables you to bind your control to databases	Chapter 17, "Database Access"
Extender object	Holds properties of a control provided by its container	Chapter 4, "Control Properties"
Hyperlink object, GoBack method, GoForward method, NavigateTo method	Enables you to tell a Web browser object to jump to a particular URL	Chapter 14, "Controls That Interact with the Internet"
PropertyBag object, ReadProperty method, WriteProperty method	Stores design-time properties of a user-defined control	Chapter 4, "Control Properties"
PropertyPage object	Provides a custom property page for your control	Chapter 4, "Control Properties"
UserControl object	The object used to create your own ActiveX control	Hither and yon throughout the whole book
Event statement	Defines a custom event	Chapter 5, "Control Events"
RaiseEvent statement	Fires a user-defined event	Chapter 5, "Control Events"
Implements statement	Specifies a interface or class that will be a class module	Chapter 16, "Object-Oriented used in Programming"

Summary

This chapter introduced a number of new features of Visual Basic 5.0. In addition to changes in the integrated development environment, a number of new language features were discussed.

Chapter 2 is a brief walk-through demonstrating how to set up a very simple control project. In this chapter, you'll learn a number of basic concepts pertaining to control creation while putting the new features of Visual Basic 5.0 into action.

What Is an ActiveX Control?

Your Control's Interface

Chapter 2
Control Basics

This chapter covers the basic concepts of controls: events, properties, and methods.

If you're an intermediate to advanced Visual Basic programmer, you might be able to get away with just skimming this chapter, since you already have a handle on how VB works. However, this chapter will cover a few new topics, such as the difference between OCX and ActiveX components and the various contexts in which you can use ActiveX controls. In addition, this chapter outlines how the old, familiar topics pertain to control creation. This chapter is also something you can show your boss when she asks you what this kooky ActiveX thing is all about.

What Is an ActiveX Control?

In the beginning, there were VBXes. And Visual Basic programmers saw them, and said, "Yea, verily, we can use these to provide plug-in programmable objects for our Visual Basic applications. Yah-hoo."

The VBX, or Visual Basic Extension, was the first type of programmable component used in Visual Basic. An entire industry of small software development companies sprung up around this specification. Visual Basic programmers were overjoyed because they could beg, borrow, steal, or (in most cases) buy custom controls that they could then drop into their projects.

But, as always happens, things started changing. Visual Basic 4.0 came out, the 32-bit world began to take over, and Microsoft re-architected VBXes for the 32-bit world, renaming them OCXes. Later, when the Internet came along, they repositioned them again, renamed them ActiveX controls, and gave developers the ability to embed them in Web pages.

VBX, OCX, ActiveX—it's all essentially the same alphabet soup. However, there are a few subtle differences. Briefly, the differences are:

▶ VBX is a 16-bit software component generally usable under 16-bit versions of Visual Basic.

▶ OCX is a 32-bit software component usable under Visual Basic 4.0 and later, as well as some other development environments, such as Visual C++, Microsoft Access, and Borland Delphi.

▶ An ActiveX component is also a 32-bit software component usable under in the same contexts as an OCX control, but also usable in Microsoft Internet

Explorer 3.0. (As well as any other Web browser that might hypothetically support ActiveX, such as Netscape Navigator—more on that later.)

There's more to it than that, but these are good working definitions if you're just trying to get a handle on the evolution of custom controls. In the next few sections of this chapter we'll go a little bit more into the details of what an ActiveX control is and how ActiveX controls relate to other component technologies, past and present.

Differences between OCX Controls and ActiveX Controls

Although there are enough OCX and ActiveX to make some people think that an ActiveX control is just an OCX with a name that can be trademarked, there are actually some important differences. Every ActiveX control is also an OCX, although not every OCX is an ActiveX control.

> **Note** *Many of the enhancements in the ActiveX architecture are under the hood, shielded, like so much basic Windows API technology, from the Visual Basic developer. For this reason, it's easy for a VB programmer to think of an ActiveX control as nothing more than an OCX with a fancy name. If you want the complete story—perhaps more complete than you'd ever want—on the basic technology behind ActiveX, check out the ActiveX Software Development Kit (SDK). This is a very detailed, very technical set of specifications, descriptive documents and code examples, mostly aimed at C++ programmers. The PC version of the ActiveX SDK is on the Microsoft Web site at http://www.microsoft .com/intdev/sdk/. The Macintosh version of the ActiveX SDK is located at http://www.microsoft.com/intdev/sdk/mac/.*

ActiveX Controls Are Light

ActiveX controls are supposed to be lighter (smaller, faster, less greasy) than OCX controls. This is to facilitate downloading them over networks and the Internet. But there's no hard-and-fast rule that says that ActiveX controls *have* to be lighter than their OCX progenitors. In fact, creating an ActiveX control using Visual Basic forces you to distribute a fairly large file: the Visual Basic virtual machine.

Fortunately, users only need to get this file the first time they install or download a file using Visual Basic. For more information on this, see Chapter 12, "Distributing Your Control."

ActiveX Works with the Internet

ActiveX controls designed to be used on the Internet in the context of a Web browser are not supposed to have unrestricted access to things like the user's file system or system registry. You have the ability to designate whether an ActiveX control you create meets this requirement. If you don't do this, users will receive a warning message from the browser when encountering your control on a Web page.

This is not to say that ActiveX controls can't perform file input/output. It doesn't even mean that ActiveX controls destined for use on the Internet can't perform file input/output. It just means that in order to deploy your controls on the Net, you need to spend a little more time considering all the things a malicious or incompetent Web page designer might do with your control.

To denote that a control is permissible for use on the Net, you can mark the control you develop as *script safe* (meaning there's nothing anyone can do with the control in a script that will make it do bad things to a person's computer) and/or *initialization safe* (which means there are no parameters you can pass to the control that will cause it to do bad things to a person's computer).

For more information on script safety and initialization safety, see Chapter 13, "Using Your Control on the Web."

ActiveX Is Multiplatform, Sorta

As of this writing, the ActiveX SDK (the collection of documents and code that enables C programmers to develop ActiveX components) is available for Windows and the Macintosh. Microsoft has also announced UNIX support for ActiveX, slated to arrive in 1997.

As of this writing, Microsoft had just released a beta of Internet Explorer 3.0 for the Macintosh. This version of Internet Explorer is supposed to support ActiveX controls—eventually. It may very well support ActiveX by the time you read this.

There is also a beta of Microsoft Internet Explorer 3.0 out for 16-bit Windows (i.e., Windows 3.1). This version does not support ActiveX controls, which would make sense, since ActiveX is a 32-bit thing.

Contexts in Which You Can Use ActiveX Controls

It's important to understand all the contexts in which your control might be used, for testing as well as marketing purposes. From the testing perspective, if your ActiveX control works fine in Visual Basic 4.0 but blows up in Microsoft Access 95, you obviously have a problem. From the marketing perspective, if you're creating a commercial control, your market increases if you can state confidently that your control will work in all of the applications and development environments that support ActiveX.

As of this writing, you can use ActiveX controls in these contexts:

▶ Microsoft Visual Basic 4.0

▶ Microsoft Visual C++

▶ Microsoft Visual Basic 5.0

▶ You can use ActiveX controls in all editions of Visual Basic 5.0, including the Control Creation Edition (see Chapter 8, "Constituent Controls," for more on this).

▶ Microsoft Access 2.0 supports 16- and 32-bit OCX controls, although with less robustness than you'd probably like. (I consider myself to be pretty handy with Access, yet I was never able to get Access 2.0 to do anything meaningful with OCXes, and it wasn't for lack of trying.) The 16-bit OCX is pretty much an orphan technology at this point.

▶ Microsoft Access 95. You can embed ActiveX controls on forms and program them using Access's programming language, Access Visual Basic for Applications. Support for custom controls is much more robust than under Access 2.0.

For Access power-users, there are several good books with material on using OCXes and ActiveX controls. There's *Access 97 Power Programming*, by F. Scott Barker, Que, 1996. There's also *Access 97 Unleashed*, by Dwayne Gifford et al., Sams, 1996. The previous editions of both of these books talk about OCX (or OLE). Finally, there's *Mastering Access 97 Development*, by Alison Balter, from Sams, 1997.

▶ Microsoft Internet Explorer 3.0 for Windows 95 and Windows NT 4.0. You can use the VBScript or JavaScript languages to manipulate ActiveX controls in an HTML Web page. See Chapter 13, "Deploying Your Control On The Web," for more information on how to do this.

▶ Microsoft Visual FoxPro 3.0

▶ Microsoft Visual FoxPro 5.0. A good reference is *Special Edition Using Visual FoxPro*, by Michael Antonovich, from Que, 1996.

In the future, you will be able to use ActiveX controls in these contexts:

▶ Microsoft Office 97. Microsoft has incorporated the Visual Basic for Applications (VBA) 5.0 engine in Microsoft Office applications such as Access, Powerpoint, and Excel.

▶ Third-party products containing VBA 5.0. Because Microsoft is licensing VBA 5.0 to other software development companies, it's likely that you'll be able to use ActiveX controls in their products, too. For example, the graphics application, Visio, which has traditionally been very close in following Microsoft's OLE initiatives, is one of the products slated to support VBA 5.0. (The version of Visio containing VBA 5.0 may have been released by the time you read this.)

▶ Microsoft Internet Explorer 3.0 for Windows 3.1. Microsoft has stated that the 16-bit version of Microsoft Internet Explorer will support ActiveX in some form, possibly by the time you read this.

▶ Microsoft Internet Explorer 3.0 for the Macintosh. This product is in beta as of this writing; it is scheduled to be completed in 1997.

▶ Microsoft Internet Explorer 3.0 for UNIX. This product is supposed to be released in mid-1997.

▶ Netscape Navigator. Netscape has announced that they will include support for ActiveX controls in a future product, although when this product will appear and what form it will take is anybody's guess. You are supposed to be able to use ActiveX controls with a Netscape browser using a plug-in called ScriptActive, produced by NCompass Laboratories (http://www.ncompasslabs.com).

Note *It seems to me that using a Netscape plug-in to view ActiveX content is a little like standing in line to breathe air. Just download MS Internet Explorer, for Pete's sake! NCompass does have a cool line of ActiveX controls, though, so their site is worth checking out.*

What Is a User?

In traditional software development, the person writing the code is the developer and the person using the software is the user. But in the world of component development, while you're still the developer, your user is actually another developer. Say you use Visual Basic Control Creation Edition to create WhizzyWidgets, an add-in ActiveX control. Later, Jill Programmer incorporates WhizzyWidgets into her magnum opus, CowWare 1.0, an automated dairy farm management system, written in Visual Basic. Jill then sells a copy of CowWare 1.0 to Farmer Brown.

Now then. You are the ActiveX control developer. Jill is the EXE developer. However, because she uses the ActiveX component you developed, from your perspective, Jill is also a user. Farmer Brown is nothing to you, but to Jill, he's a user.

To avoid this confusion, this book will use the term user as shorthand to mean "the user of the ActiveX control you develop." When and if I talk about Farmer Brown and it's not obvious what I'm talking about, I'll refer to him as the end user. And if I need to refer to Jill Programmer as distinct from Farmer Brown, end user, I'll use the term "programmer."

A similar terminology problem arises when you talk about an ActiveX control's interface. To most people, an interface is the same as a graphical user interface—that is, the part of your application the user sees. But from a programming perspective, the interface of your control is the set of properties, events, and methods that can be accessed. In this book, when I refer to your control's interface, I'm talking about its properties and methods. When I specifically mean graphical user interface, I'll use that term unless I'm obviously talking about a control interface.

Your Control's Interface

The interface of a control isn't just the graphical user interface. To a developer, the word interface means *programming interface*. A programming interface is the set of programming procedures used to gain access to an object's features. In the ActiveX world, a control's programming interface is comprised of properties, methods, and events.

Properties

A *property* can be defined as any element of an object that can be altered, either directly (through code) or indirectly (through the actions of an end user). Properties of controls tend to be persistent throughout the lifetime of an application. Unlike variables, which persist only for the lifetime of the procedure or module in which they are declared, properties don't change unless they're explicitly altered.

Consider a command button. A command button is a control. Because it is a Visual Basic control, it is also a type of object. This object has such properties as Width, Height, and Caption.

Every control in Visual Basic belongs to a *class*, a basic template from which the control is derived. The class of a command button is called CommandButton; the class of picture is the PictureBox class, and the class of a form is called Form.. A class, then, is like a cake mold, and the individual controls you create in your Visual Basic projects are like individual servings of cake created with the same mold.

They may not have the exact same properties, but they were all created from the same mold.

You use Visual Basic 5.0 to create your own custom classes of controls, which users can then *instantiate* in their projects. Instantiating a control means that you've taken a control class (such as CommandButton) and created an instance of a control from it. So when you get right down to it, you're not creating controls, but rather, you're developing control classes. These distinctions may seem nit-picky now, but it helps to get them straight early on because they can get a bit tricky later.

Programming Properties

Once a control is instantiated in a project, you can alter its properties using code that looks like this:

```
Command1.Caption = "Click Me!"
```

If you are developing a new type of command button that plays a sound every time an end user clicks it (as we'll do in Chapter 11, "Making Windows API and DLL Calls"), you can add a few new properties pertaining to the sound. These could include a Sound or SoundFile property, to denote the name of the sound file to play when the user clicks the button. You might even add a few more properties to govern the manner in which the sound should be played.

Implementing Property Set, Property Let, and Property Get

Control creation in Visual Basic gives you the freedom to implement any Visual Basic code as a property in your control. You can implement properties in your control by using the *Property Set*, *Property Let*, and *Property Get* statements.

A Property Set statement is run when a user assigns an object to a property of your control. The Picture property of a PictureBox control, for example, is assigned using a Property Set.

A Property Let statement is executed when a user assigns a value to a property of your control.

A Property Get statement is run when a user reads a property of your control. For example, consider the code:

```
Sub StoreStatus()
  Dim strStatus As String
  strStatus = ctlYourFunControl.Text
End Sub
```

Whenever the user assigns the variable strStatus to the Text property of ctlYourFunControl, the Property Get procedure of YourFunControl is executed. The user doesn't have access to this function, of course—it's compiled into the ActiveX control.

Now consider what happens when a value is assigned to a property, as in the following code:

```
Sub GetCaption()
  ctlYourFunControl.Text = "3.14159"
End Sub
```

The Property Let procedure of YourFunControl is executed when the control's Text value is assigned. The Property Let would then ensure that the value you assigned was stored in a variable. At this time, the Property Let could also validate or otherwise manipulate the value the user assigned to it.

For more information on how these statements work, see Chapter 4, "Control Properties."

Events

An *event* can be defined as something that happens during the lifetime of your application. A user clicking a command button is an example of an event. Examples of other events include a database validation, the application loading or shutting down, and a text box receiving input from a user.

Every event can be associated with an piece of code, called an *event procedure.* Visual Basic programs are said to be *event-driven,* because the code that drives their functionality, particularly those functions that are bound to the graphical user interface, tend to be triggered by events. Accordingly, one measure of the robustness of your control is the number of events that can be triggered.

You implement events in your control by using the Event statement. When a procedure needs to trigger an event, it does so by executing the RaiseEvent statement.

For more information on how to implement events in your control, see Chapter 5, "Handling and Raising Events."

Methods

Methods are the way a programmer causes your control to take an action or perform work. There is a thin syntactical line between properties and methods. If you think of a property as an adjective, think of a method as a verb.

Consider the Visible property, a standard property of most controls. This property could be implemented as a Hide method. But you wouldn't want to do this, because Visual Basic programmers expect controls to have a Visible property rather than a Hide method.

Other issues to consider are conciseness (that is, how difficult is it for a user to call your function) and maintainability (how difficult is it for you to understand and manage what's going on with your control). For example, it might seem more concise to write:

```
MyCommandButton.Visible = False
```

rather than:

```
MyCommandButton.Hide
```

At least, you'd think this would be more concise. But if you implement the Visible property of a control as a Hide method, you'd then have to implement a Show method as well. So perhaps it's not so concise after all.

In many cases it's a judgment call as to whether you implement a feature of your control as a property or a method. The rule I use goes along with the "property as noun, method as verb" analogy. If the feature I'm working on seems more verb-ish, I'll implement it as a method. If it seems more like a adjective, it goes in as a property.

I also pay attention to how other controls implement properties and methods, particularly inherent Windows controls. If every single Windows control implements a Visible property rather than a Hide method, then you probably want your control to have a Visible property too.

You implement methods in your control by using the Event statement. For more information on how methods work, see Chapter 6, "Control Methods."

Summary

This chapter discussed the history of the ActiveX control technology and how it fits into Visual Basic and other development environments, past, present, and future. We also reviewed the basic concepts behind controls, and how those concepts change when your perspective goes from control user to control developer.

In Chapter 3, we'll put these concepts to work, building a basic control step by step.

Chapter 3
Developing Your First Control

This chapter steps you through a basic control project without going into too much detail about why things are the way they are. (We'll go back and cover each topic in detail later.) The objective is to familiarize you with how control development works in Visual Basic and to get you comfortable with the various terms and techniques you'll use on a regular basis.

The control you'll build in this chapter is designed to notify a company's employees of special events. The control could be deployed in either an executable application or a Web page. It is comprised of a graphical component and a textual component, combining the functionality of the standard Windows PictureBox and Label controls.

Getting Started

Start by creating a control project. To do this:

1 Start Visual Basic Control Creation Edition.

2 The New Project dialog box will appear (see Figure 3.1). Select ActiveX control.

You're now in the Visual Basic IDE window (see Figure 3.2). On the right side is the Project Explorer, an outline list of all the files in your project. (If you can't see the Project Explorer, choose the menu command View, Project Explorer or use the keystroke shortcut Ctrl+R.)

Setting Up the IDE

You'll want to make sure that a few other Visual Basic windows are open before you start working. The Toolbox enables you to manipulate existing controls, as well as the control you're working on. To make the Toolbox visible, use the menu command View, Toolbox.

The Immediate window enables you to type in Visual Basic code while your project is running. This can be a great help when you're testing and debugging your code. To display the Immediate window, use the menu command View, Immediate Window or use the keystroke shortcut Ctrl+G.

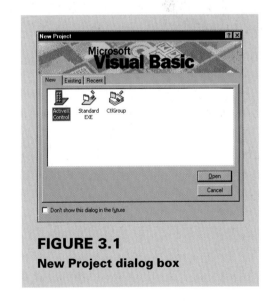

FIGURE 3.1
New Project dialog box

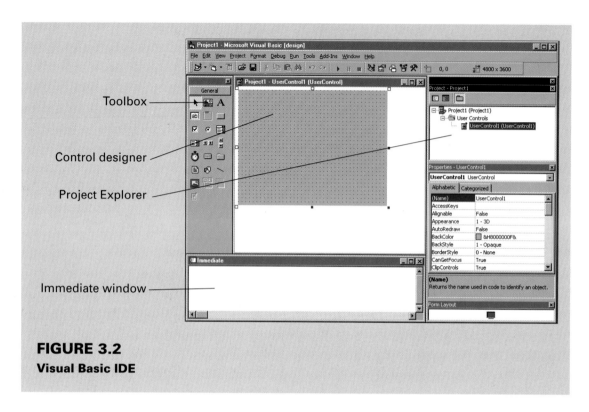

FIGURE 3.2
Visual Basic IDE

Finally, for the purposes of this walk-through, you'll want to change the Visual Basic development environment from the default MDI to SDI. To do this (if you haven't done it already):

1 Choose the menu command **Tools, Options**.

2 Select the Advanced tab.

3 Activate the SDI Development Environment checkbox (see Figure 3.3).

4 Click on **OK**.

5 Restart Visual Basic. VB's interface will have changed; it's now equipped with close buttons for individual windows that you can drag around the screen.

Managing the Project

The Project Explorer currently contains two files: the project file, called Project1, and a new control, currently called

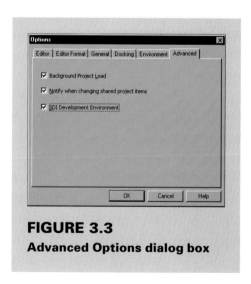

FIGURE 3.3
Advanced Options dialog box

UserControl1. Start by changing the names of these objects to something more meaningful. To change the name of the project:

1 In Project Explorer, click on Project1. The Properties window changes, displaying properties for Project1. At the top of the list is the Name property.

2 Double-click on the name UserControl1 to select it. Type the new name of this project, HappyHourProject. Figure 3.4 shows all the changes that will occur to reflect the new name.

Now give the control a more meaningful (and festive) name. To do this:

1 In the Project Explorer window, double-click on the control UserControl1.

2 The Properties window will change to display properties for the control. In the control's Name property, change UserControl1 to HappyHour.

When you're done, the Project Explorer will look as in Figure 3.5.

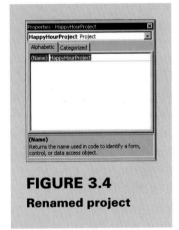

FIGURE 3.4
Renamed project

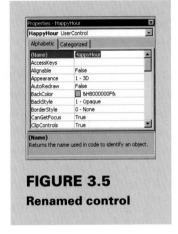

FIGURE 3.5
Renamed control

Designing Your Control

On the screen you'll see a window containing a nondescript gray rectangle. This is known as the *control designer*. The control designer is the visual representation of the control, analogous to a form in a Visual Basic EXE project.

Every control you create using Visual Basic has a designer–even controls designed to be invisible at runtime have them.

The HappyHour control you'll create will be comprised of two standard Windows controls: a PictureBox control and a Label control. The Label control will act as a caption for the graphic that appears in the PictureBox control. To add these controls to the form designer:

1 In the Toolbox, double-click on the PictureBox control, shown in Figure 3.6.

2 A PictureBox control will appear in the middle of the control designer.

3 Set the PictureBox's properties as shown in Table 3.1.

4 Double-click on the Label control icon in the Toolbox to create a Label control on the control designer. Move the Label below the PictureBox and resize it so it takes up the bottom third of the designer.

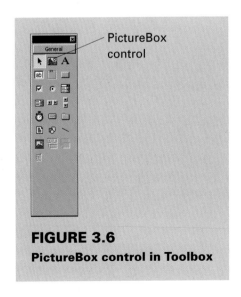

PictureBox control

FIGURE 3.6
PictureBox control in Toolbox

5 In the Properties window, change the properties of the Label as shown in Table 3.2.

6 Before you go any further, save the project. To do this, use the menu command **File, Save Project**. You'll be prompted to save the files (use the file names shown in Table 3.3).

Later you'll add more files to the project and re-save them. The project file keeps references to all the files in your projects, so when you quit and restart Visual Basic, you won't have to re-load all the files in your project one at a time.

The visual design of this control is done for now. Close the HappyHour designer by clicking on its close button. The close buttons for the control designers–in both the MDI and SDI interfaces–are shown in Figures 3.7 and 3.8.

Testing the Control

Even though your control technically doesn't do anything at this point, you can still instantiate it on a form and view its visual interface.

TABLE 3.1 PICTUREBOX PROPERTIES FOR CONTROLS

Property	Value
Left	0
Top	0
Height	1500
Width	4000

TABLE 3.2 LABEL PROPERTIES

Property	Value
Name	lblCaption
Caption	(nothing)
WordWrap	True
Top	1500
Height	1000
Left	0
Width	4000

TABLE 3.3 CONTROL FILENAMES

File	Description
HappyHour.ctl	The control designer
HappyHourProject.vbp	The project file

The problem, though, is that ActiveX control projects can't be run like conventional Visual Basic programs can; they can only be run in the context of a *container*. A container can be a form in a Visual Basic executable, an HTML Web page displayed in Microsoft Internet Explorer, or another application that supports ActiveX controls.

In order to test your controls without having to mess around with a completely different development environment, Visual Basic gives you the ability to insert an *EXE project* into your control project. Forms in an EXE project are identical to Visual Basic forms; they just can't be compiled into an actual EXE file under VB. To insert an EXE project into your current project:

1 Make sure that the control designer for the HappyHour control is closed. You won't be able to test the control unless it is closed.

2 Select the menu command **File, Add Project**.

3 The Add Project dialog box will appear. (This window appears startlingly similar to the New Project dialog box, so be sure you pull up the one that lets you add a project rather than create a new one.)

4 Choose **Standard EXE**, then click on **Open**. In the Project Explorer, two new files are added to your project: Project1, a Visual Basic EXE project file, and Form1, a standard Visual Basic form. Form1 appears in the middle of the screen.

> **Note** *You can't insert a control onto a form if that control's designer is open. When a control's designer is open, the control's icon in the Toolbox will appear disabled. To close the control designer, click on its close button.*

5 Insert a HappyHour control on the form by double-clicking on its icon in the Toolbox (illustrated in Figure 3.9). An instance of your control, called HappyHour1, is created.

Even though you haven't written any code yet, the HappyHour1 control already has a rudimentary set of properties and events. By looking at the Properties window, you can see that HappyHour1 has Height, Width, and Visible properties, as well as GotFocus and LostFocus events, among others. These properties and

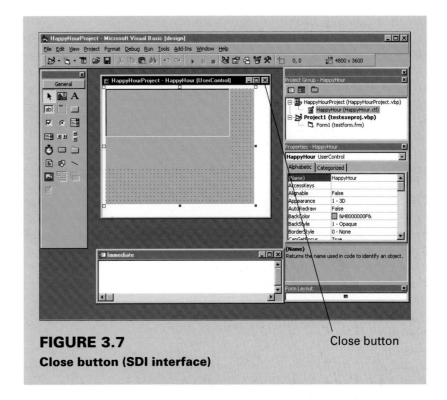

FIGURE 3.7
Close button (SDI interface)

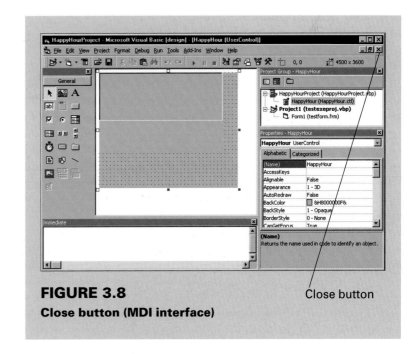

FIGURE 3.8
Close button (MDI interface)

events are not really a part of your control, but rather passed through from the container in which your control resides. You can see these properties by looking in the Properties window, as illustrated in Figure 3.10.

I'll discuss more about the relationship between controls and containers in Chapter 7.

Although you now have a basic control with a few properties and events, this isn't nearly enough. For one thing, if you resize HappyHour1 and make it smaller, the Label and PictureBox controls inside can easily get lost. And nothing makes a constituent control more angry, believe me.

For another thing, the important properties of the controls within HappyHour1 (such as the Caption property of the Label and the Picture property of the PictureBox control) can't be accessed.

We'll spend the rest of this chapter rectifying this situation. Start by closing Form1 by clicking on its close button, then returning to the control designer for HappyHour through the Project Explorer.

Exposing the HappyHour Control's Caption Property

The easiest way to implement a property in a control you create is to use an existing property of another control. Controls included in your controls are called *constituent controls*; the process of hijacking their properties and events is referred to as *delegation*. In this case you'll delegate the Caption property of the constituent Label control to provide a Caption property for the HappyHour control.

To give the HappyHour control a Caption property, do the following:

1 In the Project Explorer, double-click on HappyHour.ctl to open it.

2 Double-click on the HappyHour control's designer to bring up its code window.

3 Choose the menu command **Tools, Add Procedure**. The Add Procedure dialog box will appear.

4 In the Name box, type **Caption**.

5 In the Type panel, select the Property option. The Add Procedure dialog box should look like Figure 3.11.

FIGURE 3.9
HappyHour control in the Toolbox

HappyHour control icon

FIGURE 3.10
Properties window of the HappyHour control

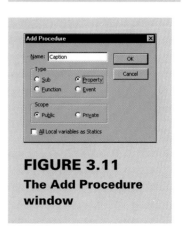

FIGURE 3.11
The Add Procedure window

6 Click on **OK**. The code window will create two new procedures, a Property Get and a Property Let, as illustrated in Figure 3.12.

Coding the Property Get

To cause the label's Caption property to be read whenever the HappyHour control's Caption property is accessed, modify the Property Get procedure like this:

```
Public Property Get Caption() As String
    Caption = lblCaption.Caption
End Property
```

Note that you must change the first line of the procedure to be defined As String instead of As Variant, since captions should be treated as strings.

> **Tip** *Remember, you can toggle between Full Module view and Procedure view by using the buttons in the lower left corner of the code window.*

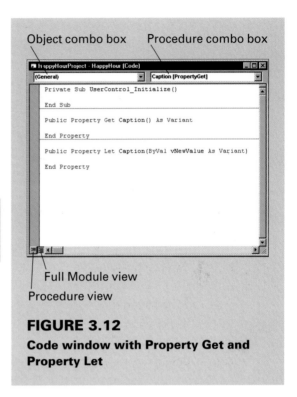

Object combo box   Procedure combo box

Full Module view

Procedure view

FIGURE 3.12
Code window with Property Get and Property Let

Property Get versus Property Let

The concepts of Property Get and Property Let were first introduced in Visual Basic 4.0. For some reason, when this feature was first introduced, I had trouble remembering that Property Get was the code that was run when the property was read, and Property Let was the code that was run when the property was altered. If you have this problem, too, and you're an old hand with Basic, it might help you to remember that Let is a Basic keyword from the old days of Basic programming. The code

```
Let x = 5
```

was the way you set the variable x to the value 5. So it is with properties, thereby proving that everything old is new again.

To know when to use Property Let vs Property Set, it helps to remember that assigning a value to an object variable always requires a Set statement; similarly, properties that represent objects (such as the Picture property of a PictureBox control) require a Property Set instead of a Property Let.

Coding the Property Let

Property Let is the procedure that runs when the value of a property is set or changed. To cause the label's Caption property to pass through to the HappyHour control's Caption property, alter the Property Let procedure so it looks like this:

```
Public Property Let Caption(ByVal NewCaption As String)
    lblCaption.Caption = NewCaption
    PropertyChanged "Caption"
End Property
```

Note that the data type of the Property Let procedure was changed from Variant to String, to reflect the fact that captions are strings.

PropertyChanged looks like a statement, but it's actually a method of your control's container. The method sends a message to the container, informing it that a property of your control has been changed. This flags the container to trigger a WriteProperties event, which saves any design-time changes to this property that you make. (We'll deal with the WriteProperties event again later on.)

Testing the New Caption Property

To test that the HappyHour control's new Caption property works properly, you can go back to the instance of your HappyHour control that exists on Form1. To do this:

1 Close the code window by clicking on its close button.

2 Close HappyHour's designer by clicking on its close button.

3 Using the Project Explorer, open Form1 by double-clicking on it.

4 There should still be an instance of your HappyHour control on Form1. Click on it to select it, if it isn't selected already.

Look in the Properties window. You should be able to see that there is now a Caption property available for HappyHour1. Try changing the property by typing something else in the Caption property. Your control should look something like Figure 3.13.

We're finished exposing the HappyHour control's Caption property. We'll expose the Picture property of the PictureBox control through the HappyHour control later. For now, there's another problem to solve: resizing.

Resizing the Control

When HappyHour1 is resized, the two controls contained in it aren't resized along with it. This can cause the Label or the PictureBox to become lost if the control is made too small. And we can't have that. To rectify this, we can insert code that will cause the components of the HappyHour control to resize themselves. To do this:

1 Close Form1, if it is open, and reopen the control designer for HappyHour from the Project Explorer.

2 Double-click on the control designer to open a code window.

3 In the Object combo box (at the top left of the code window), select UserControl, if it isn't selected already. This exposes the events for the control itself. The UserControl object is to a control what the Form object is to a conventional Visual Basic application.

4 In the Event combo box(at the top right of the code window), select **Resize**.

5 In the UserControl's Resize event, insert the following code:

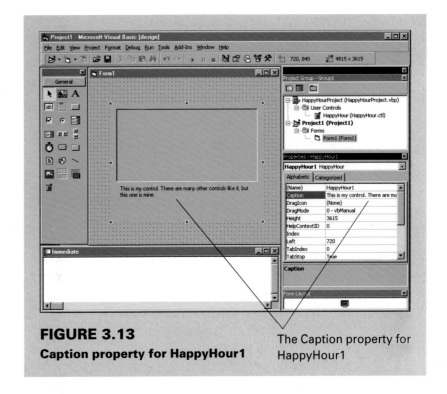

FIGURE 3.13
Caption property for HappyHour1

The Caption property for HappyHour1

```
Private Sub UserControl_Resize()
    'To make this more concise as well as faster executing,
    'You can also use a Move method instead of setting
    'Width and Height separately. I did it this way for clarity.

    Picture1.Width = UserControl.ScaleWidth
    Picture1.Height = (UserControl.ScaleHeight / 3) * 2
    lblCaption.Width = UserControl.ScaleWidth
    lblCaption.Height = UserControl.ScaleHeight / 3
    lblCaption.Top = Picture1.ScaleHeight + 60
End Sub
```

This code will ensure that the width and height of the HappyHour control will always be slightly less than the overall width of the control.

> **Note** *In the preceding code example, you use the ScaleWidth and ScaleHeight properties of the UserControl because you don't know whether the user will reset the ScaleMode property to a measurement value other than the standard Visual Basic unit of measurement (the twip, equal to 1/1440th of an inch). Your control doesn't have a ScaleMode property yet, but writing code like this protects you in case you ever decide to give it one.*

You can see how this code works if you close the control designer, return to Form1, and stretch the control HappyHour1. You should be able to see that the PictureBox and the Label stretch proportionately.

Supplying a Default Caption Using the Extender Object

Controls that have a Caption property should supply a default value for their captions. The default caption for a CommandButton is Command1, the default caption for a Label is Label1, and so forth. You can supply the same functionality in your control by reading a property of the Extender object in your UserControl's InitProperties event.

Extender properties are supplied by the container in which your constituent control resides. So if you set the default Caption property of the HappyHour control to be equal to Extender.Name, you can achieve the effect that users expect. To do this:

1 Close Form1, if it is open, and reopen HappyHour.ctl.

2 Double-click on HappyHour's designer to open its code window.

3 In the Procedures combo box of the UserControl code window, choose InitProperties.

4 Type the following code:

```
Private Sub UserControl_InitProperties()
    Caption = Extender.Name
End Sub
```

5 Close the control designer and return to Form1.

6 Now you'll have to re-create the HappyHour control to see the default you just created. To do this, click on HappyHour1, then press **Delete**.

7 Create another instance of HappyHour1 on your form by double-clicking on its icon in the Toolbox. You should be able to see that the default Caption property for the new instance of HappyHour1 has been set properly, as illustrated in Figure 3.14.

Storing Design-Time Property Changes

You've probably noticed that the changes you've been making to the HappyHour1's Caption property have vanished into the ether each time you flip between the control designer and Form1—specifically, the Caption property has been wiped out each time you make a change to the control designer.

You can make design-time property settings persistent by writing code in the WriteProperties event of the UserControl. The WriteProperties event is triggered each time the user's design-time property settings need to be saved.

Property settings are made persistent by the use of the PropertyBag object. You have the ability to put data into the PropertyBag and take data out of the PropertyBag. The WriteProperty method of the PropertyBag object stores a property in the PropertyBag, while the ReadProperty method does the opposite. Either way, Visual Basic is left holding the PropertyBag, which is a good thing.

To make your control save its design-time Caption property, do the following:

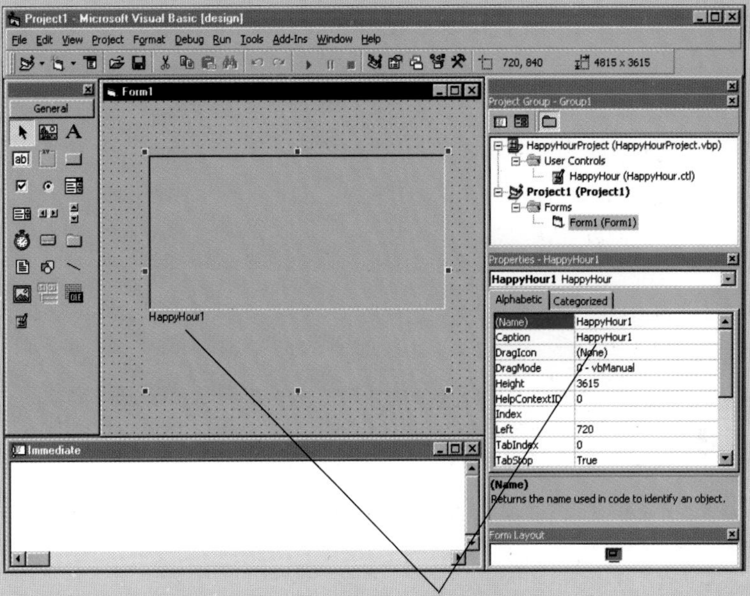

FIGURE 3.14
HappyHour control with default caption set

The proper default caption

1 Close Form1, if it is open, and open the HappyHour control designer.

2 Double-click on the control designer to expose its code window.

3 In the Procedure combo box at the upper right side of the code window, select WriteProperties.

4 Into the code window, insert the following code:

```
Private Sub UserControl_WriteProperties(PropBag As PropertyBag)
    PropBag.WriteProperty "Caption", Caption, Extender.Name
End Sub
```

This code uses the WriteProperty method of the PropertyBag object to save the value of the Caption property of your control. There's more information on how the PropertyBag works in Chapter 4, "Control Properties."

Conversely, just as you must write code to save a design-time property change to the PropertyBag, you must also write code to retrieve previously set properties from the PropertyBag in your control's ReadProperties event. To do this, add the following code to your code window:

```
Private Sub UserControl_ReadProperties(PropBag As PropertyBag)
    Caption = PropBag.ReadProperty("Caption", Extender.Name)
End Sub
```

> **Note** *The value for Extender.Name is a parameter to the WriteProperty and ReadProperty methods so those methods can know whether the design-time properties have been changed by the user. If the properties haven't been changed (that is, they're equal to Extender.Name) then there's no need to write a specific entry to the PropertyBag. This makes the process of managing saved property settings more efficient.*

Your control should now have the ability to retain the properties set for it at design time. To test this:

1 Close the code window and the form designer.

2 Open Form1.

3 Set the Caption property of the HappyHour control to the text of your choice.

4 Close Form1.

5 Re-open Form1. You should be able to see that the change you made in the Caption property has been retained.

Exposing Properties Using the ActiveX Control Interface Wizard

Now that you know how things work under the hood, try exposing a property of a constituent control the easy way, using the ActiveX Control Interface Wizard. This tool takes care of much of the busywork involved in control creation, particularly when your control is primarily comprised of one or more constituent controls.

You can use the ActiveX Control Interface Wizard to delegate a Picture property for your control to the constituent PictureBox control. To do this:

1 From the Add-Ins menu, select ActiveX Control Interface Wizard. The Wizard launches, as shown in Figure 3.15.

2 Click on **Next**.

3 The Select Interface Members screen appears. In this panel, you choose the interface elements (properties, methods, and events) you want your control to have.

4 On the left side of this screen is a list, labeled Available names, of interface elements that can

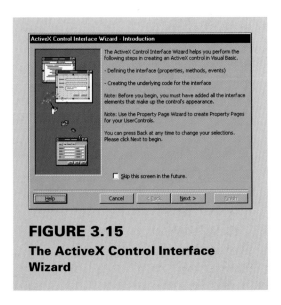

FIGURE 3.15
The ActiveX Control Interface Wizard

be delegated to constituent controls. Scroll down the list until you find the Picture property.

5 Double-click on the Picture property to add it to the Selected names list, as shown in Figure 3.16.

6 Click on **Next**.

7 The Create Custom Interface Members window appears (see Figure 3.17).

8 You won't be adding any custom elements to the interface for now, so click on **Next** once again.

9 The Set Mapping screen appears.

10 Here you will delegate the Picture property of your control to the Picture property of the constituent PictureBox control. To begin, click on Picture property in the Public Name list.

11 In the Control combo box in the Maps To panel, select Picture1. The Member combo understands that you're trying to map your control to the Picture property of Picture1, so it displays the Picture property.

12 The Set Mapping screen should look like Figure 3.18.

13 Click on **Next**.

14 The Set Attributes window appears, as shown in Figure 3.19.

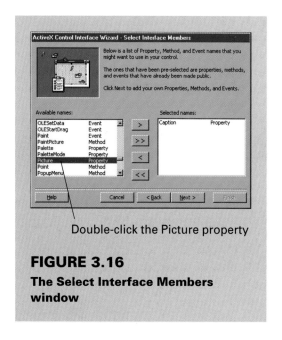

Double-click the Picture property

FIGURE 3.16
The Select Interface Members window

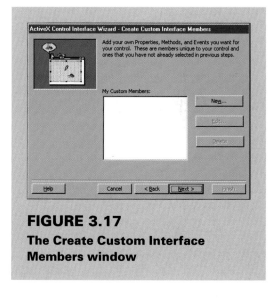

FIGURE 3.17
The Create Custom Interface Members window

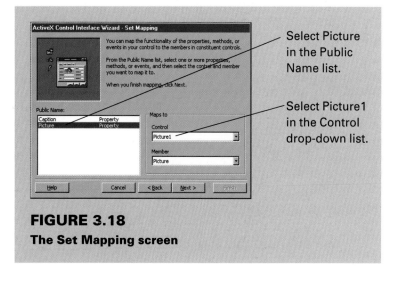

Select Picture in the Public Name list.

Select Picture1 in the Control drop-down list.

FIGURE 3.18
The Set Mapping screen

15 Your control doesn't have any unmapped members, so click on **Next**.

16 The Finished! window appears. Make sure the View Summary Report checkbox is selected, as shown in Figure 3.20. Then click on **Finish**.

The wizard now goes to work, writing the code that will support the property mapping you asked for. When it is done writing code, the wizard displays a summary reminding you of what you need to do to complete your control project (see Figure 3.21). Note this information, then click on Close.

Open the HappyHour control and double-click on its designer to view its code. You should be able to see that the following code has been added to your project:

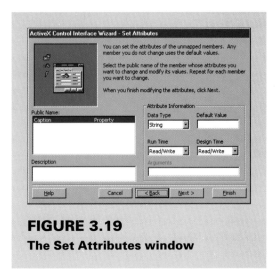

FIGURE 3.19
The Set Attributes window

```
Private Sub UserControl_WriteProperties(PropBag As PropertyBag)
    PropBag.WriteProperty "Caption", Caption, Extender.Name
    Call PropBag.WriteProperty("Picture", Picture, Nothing)
End Sub


Private Sub UserControl_ReadProperties(PropBag As PropertyBag)
    Caption = PropBag.ReadProperty("Caption", Extender.Name)
    Set Picture = PropBag.ReadProperty("Picture", Nothing)
End Sub
```

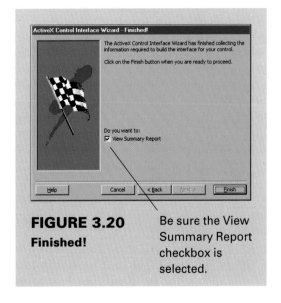

FIGURE 3.20
Finished!

Be sure the View Summary Report checkbox is selected.

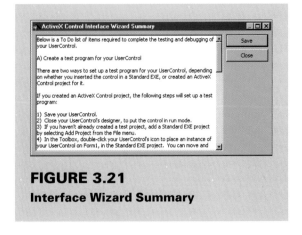

FIGURE 3.21
Interface Wizard Summary

The WriteProperty and ReadProperty methods inserted by the wizard are essentially identical to the code you wrote for the Caption property; the wizard just uses an alternate syntax.

```
'WARNING! DO NOT REMOVE OR MODIFY THE FOLLOWING COMMENTED LINES!
'MappingInfo=Picture1,Picture1,-1,Picture
Public Property Get Picture() As Picture
    Set Picture = Picture1.Picture
End Property


Public Property Set Picture(ByVal New_Picture As Picture)
    Set Picture1.Picture = New_Picture
    PropertyChanged "Picture"
End Property
```

The only really new thing here is the Property Set procedure. Property Set (rather than Property Let) is required here because the Picture property is an object, rather than a conventional value.

Testing the New Code

This code enables you to include a picture in your control at design time. To test this, you'll need some graphics file on your hard disk.

1 Close the code window and the designer for the HappyHour control.

2 Open Form1.

3 Select the control HappyHour1, then look at the Properties window. You should be able to see that HappyHour1 now has a Picture property.

4 Click on **None** next to the Picture property, then click on **Browse**.

5 A file open dialog box appears. Locate any graphic file (such as Windows Bitmap, .GIF, .JPG) on your disk. If you're stuck, try my personal favorite, the file cars.bmp in your Windows folder.

   Note *Support for GIF and JPEG images is a new feature in Visual Basic 5.0.*

6 Click on the file, then click on **Open**. The graphic is assigned to your control's Picture property. See Figure 3.22 for the result.

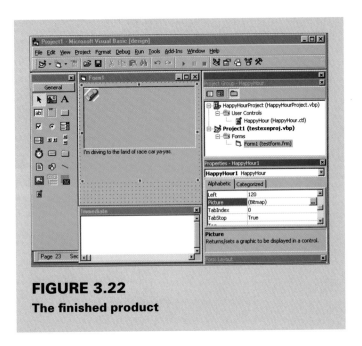

FIGURE 3.22
The finished product

Summary

In this chapter you stepped through the creation of a very simple control. You added properties using two methods: manually, by writing code, and automatically, using the ActiveX Control Interface Wizard.

The next few chapters will discuss control properties, events, and methods in more detail. This discussion will enable you to create a richer, more full-featured control.

Creating Property Procedures

Creating Custom Property Pages

Chapter 4
Control Properties

Properties are the most commonly used elements of an ActiveX control's interface. They're also fairly easy to implement in Visual Basic.

Much of the behavior of Visual Basic 5.0 properties is not new; the concept of properties existed in Visual Basic 4.0 as an element of classes. However, there are a number of new considerations, new language features, and additional tricks and traps to watch out for as you write properties for your ActiveX control.

Creating Property Procedures

You create a property in your control by following these steps:

1 Declare a module-level variable in the Declarations section of your control designer.

2 Write a Property Let procedure (or, for object variables, a Property Set procedure) to enable the user to change the property.

3 Write a Property Get to enable the user to read the variable.

4 Set the procedure attributes for your property (optional). These attributes determine whether the property is the control's default property and whether the property is database-aware, as well as provide the help text that appears in the Properties window when the property is selected.

After you've written Property Let and Property Get procedures, you'll take care of these additional tasks:

▶ Write the necessary code to save the control's design-time properties using the PropertyBag object.

▶ Create a custom property page for your control (recommended, but optional).

▶ Determine which property will be the control's default object (also optional).

Using the Example Files on the CD-ROM

The example you'll use in this chapter is the LightBulb control, which you'll find on the CD-ROM accompanying this book. The group file this project is based on is called LightBulbGroup.vbg. The version of LightBulbGroup.vbg in the \Before folder contains

43

a minimal version of the LightBulb control, with a visual design only and no code. The version of LightBulbGroup.vbg in the \After folder contains a version of the LightBulb control that includes all the code examples in this chapter. If you want to step through the examples in this chapter one at a time as a tutorial, start by opening the version of LightBulbGroup.vbg in the \Before folder.

Declaring Properties

Creating a property generally involves declaring a variable and creating Property Get and Property Let procedures to read from and write to the variable.

> **Note** *Properties that are delegated to constituent controls don't require a variable declaration; the state of their properties is stored in the constituent control's property. This concept was introduced in Chapter 2 and is covered in more detail later in this chapter.*

This example shows you how to create an Illuminated property for the LightBulb control. The Illuminated property is stored in a Boolean variable, mIlluminated. When the user sets the Illuminated property to True, the LightBulb control displays the illuminated light bulb graphic. When the Illuminated property is set to False, the LightBulb displays the dimmed light bulb graphic.

To implement the Illuminated property, begin by declaring a variable to store the state of the property in the Declarations section of the LightBulb code designer:

```
Private mIlluminated As Boolean
```

Declare property variables as Private. This is because you don't want external procedures to get access to the value in the property. Rather than giving external procedures access to the variable directly, you give them access through Property Get and Property Let procedures. This lets you perform validation and other actions (such as changing in the graphical portion of the control) when the variable is accessed or changed.

> **Tip** *If you're coming to Visual Basic from another programming language, you might be familiar with the terms "reader function" and "writer function." You can think of Property Get as a way to declare a reader function and Property Let and Property Set as ways to declare writer functions.*

Using Property Let and Property Get

After you've declared a variable to store your property, you next need to write Property Let and Property Get procedures. (Properties that can be set to object variables require a Property Set instead of a Property Let, but the syntax is essentially the same.)

Here is the skeletal syntax of a Property Let declaration:

```
Property Let propertyname ([argument_list,] value)
```

```
             .
             .
      Exit Property
             .
             .
             .
End Property
```

Property Let and Property Get statements can be declared as Public, Private, Friend, or Static. For more information on declaring procedures as Friend, see Chapter 16, "Object-Oriented Programming."

Here is the syntax of the Property Get declaration:

```
Property Get propertyname [(argument_list)] [As data_type]
             .
             .
             .      [propertyname = expression]
[Exit Property]
             .
             .
             .      [propertyname = expression]
End Property
```

Note that properties can be declared as any Visual Basic data type, including object variable types and user-defined types. But remember that if your property type is an object variable, you need to use Property Set instead of Property Let to set the value of the property.

Additionally, if you declare a property to be of a particular data type in its Property Let declaration, make sure that its Property Get is of the same type. Don't mix types, as you see here:

```
Public Property Let Wattage(ByVal NewValue As Wattage) ' Wattage is an
    mWattage = NewValue                                ' enumerated
    PropertyChanged "Wattage"                          ' data type.
End Property

Public Property Get Wattage() As Integer  ' Integers are not good for
    Wattage = mWattage                    ' children and other living
End Property                              ' things
```

This code will produce a compile error when you attempt to instantiate the control. To fix the problem, change the type declaration of the Property Get from Integer to Wattage.

The concept of enumerated properties, such as Wattage, is introduced later in this chapter. For now, you can write the code now and make the declaration it depends on later: .

```vb
' Declarations - We'll define the Wattage
' type later

Dim mWattage As Wattage

Public Property Let Wattage(ByVal NewValue As Wattage)
    mWattage = NewValue
    PropertyChanged "Wattage"
End Property


Public Property Get Wattage() As Wattage
    Wattage = mWattage
End Property


Public Property Get Illuminated() As Boolean
    Illuminated = mIlluminated
End Property


Public Property Let Illuminated(ByVal bNewValue As Boolean)

    If IsNumeric(bNewValue) Then
        If bNewValue = True Then
            picMain.Picture = picOn.Picture
            mIlluminated = bNewValue
        Else    ' false
            picMain.Picture = picOff.Picture
        End If
        PropertyChanged "Illuminated"
    End If


End Property
```

Don't test this code yet, because the Wattage property won't work until you declare the Wattage enumeration. You'll do that in the next section.

Enumerated Properties

You know from working with controls in Visual Basic in the past that some properties have the ability to limit the user to a specific range of settings. For example, consider the Alignment property of a TextBox control. This property can be set to one of three numbers: zero, 1, or 2. You can't choose another value in the Property window at runtime, because Visual Basic provides a combo box for the Alignment property that limits you to these three choices.

Fortunately, you don't have to memorize what the values zero, 1, or 2 mean in order to set this property, because the numeric values are associated with textual values in the design-time environment, as illustrated in Figure 4.1. A property that provides a list of choices for the user at design time is called an *enumerated property*.

You can provide a pre-defined list of legal property values for your user by using an *enumeration*. An enumeration is a new programming feature in Visual Basic 5.0 that enables you to define a related set of constant values.

You define an enumeration in a block of code inserted at the Declarations section of a module using the Enum statement. A typical enumeration looks like this:

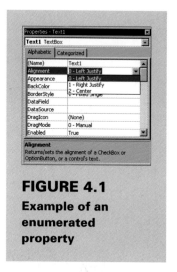

FIGURE 4.1

Example of an enumerated property

```
Public Enum HappyHourStatus
    WorkTime = 0
    HappyHour = 1
    NightTime = 2
    Holiday = 3
    Weekend = 4
End Enum
```

Note *Remember, an enumeration is a type of constant, so the values you declare in an Enum statement can't be altered at runtime. Also, remember that you can use Enums for purposes other than supplying a list of valid properties; you can use an enumerated variable anywhere you'd use a normal constant.*

A cool thing about enumerated constants is that you don't have to declare their values explicitly. If you don't set them to a value, then their values are set automatically, starting at zero.

For example, the following code is functionally identical to the preceding example:

```
Public Enum HappyHourStatus
    WorkTime
    HappyHour
```

```
        NightTime
        Holiday
        Weekend
    End Enum
```

Handling Similarly Named Enumerated Constants

You can have two enumerated values with the same name defined in different enumerations. When you do this, you must refer to the variables by a fully qualified name of the form

```
EnumName.ConstantName
```

For example, say you have an application that contains enumerations for both HappyHourStatus and CalendarDay. The CalendarDay enumeration looks like this:

```
Public Enum CalendarDay
    WorkDay
    Weekend
    Holiday
    Vacation
    SickDay
End Enum
```

There's a big problem here–the Holiday and Weekend constants exist in both the HappyHour and CalendarDay enumerations. What's more, they are equal to different values. Holiday is equal to 3 in the HappyHour enumeration, while it's equal to 2 in the CalendarDay enumeration.

You can refer to the identically named constants in different enumerations by using code like this:

```
iToday = HappyHour.Holiday        ' iToday = 2
iTomorrow = CalendarDay.Holiday   ' iTomorrow = 3
```

You may be shrieking with horror at the prospect of collisions between different enumerated constants, and rightly so. Failing to plan ahead to avoid conflicting enumerations will make your code as confusing as heck. How confusing is heck? That's the point. Try to avoid such conflicts in the first place so you won't have to jump through hoops to deal with them.

One alternative is to provide a unique prefix for each enumerated constant, like this:

```
Public Enum CalendarDay
    cdWorkDay
    cdWeekend
```

```
        cdHoliday
        cdVacation
        cdSickDay
    End Enum


    Public Enum HappyHourStatus
        hhWorkTime
        hhHappyHour
        hhNightTime
        hhHoliday
        hhWeekend
    End Enum
```

Declaring enumerations this way almost ensures you won't run into problems with two enumerated constants crashing into each other, bursting into flames, and making a mess on your carpet.

One small drawback is that your user will see the prefix when selecting the value in the combo box dropdown Property window, but that seems like a small price to pay. Function over form, and all that.

Here's the code that establishes the Wattage enumeration in the HappyHour example project:

```
    Public Enum Wattage
        VeryDim
        FairlyDim
        Bright
        VeryBright
    End Enum
```

Obviously, the values in the Wattage enumeration are oversimplified to make the example clearer. You can still test these enumerations by doing the following:

1 Close LightBulb's form designer, if it is open.

2 Open frmLBTestForm. There is an instance of the LightBulb control on the form called LightBulb1.

3 Click on LightBulb1 to select it.

4 In the Properties window, scroll down to the Wattage property. You should be able to change the property to any of the enumerated values, such as FairlyDim, Bright, or VeryBright (see Figure 4.2).

FIGURE 4.2

Wattage property enumeration

Boolean Properties

You can implement a Boolean property by declaring the control's Property Let procedure As Boolean. When you declare a Property Let in this way, the user is presented with two choices: True and False. You don't have to do anything special to make it happen this way; the Visual Basic IDE realizes that a particular property is Boolean and at design time provides a place in the Properties window to select the values True and False.

The Illuminated property of the LightBulb control is an example of this kind of property. To see how it works, try changing the Illuminated property of a LightBulb control on an EXE project form in the Properties window. You should be able to see that only two options are available, True and False.

Using Standard Property Pages

There are a few properties for which there are standard property sheets. When you specify that a property, such as a font or color property, is of a predefined enumeration, Visual Basic displays a predefined Property window for you.

This is similar to the way the Picture property, introduced in Chapter 3, displays a common Windows File Open dialog box when the user attempts to change the control. You don't need to do anything special to get Visual Basic to display a file dialog box for the Picture property; it is enough to declare your Property Set procedure As Picture.

You can provide this functionality in your control's properties by using predefined enumerations. Table 4.1 lists some of these system-supplied enumerations.

TABLE 4.1   SELECTED STANDARD CONTROL PROPERTY TYPES

Property Type	Declaration	Description
Checked	OLE_TRISTATE	The state of a check box (can be either checked, unchecked, or gray)
Color (BackColor, ForeColor, etc.)	OLE_COLOR	A standard color (stored as a Long)
MousePointer	MousePointerConstants	The icon associated with the mouse pointer (arrow, cross, I-beam, custom icon, etc.).
Value	OLE_OPTEXCLUSIVE	Used by controls that act as grouped option buttons. When the Value property is declared as OLE_OPTEXCLUSIVE, only one such control in a group can have the value of True.
Align	AlignConstants	Used for controls (such as the PictureBox) that can align themselves to the top, bottom, left to right sides of their containers
Alignment	AlignmentConstants	The alignment of text left, right, or center, such as that found in a TextBox control
BorderStyle	BorderStyleConstants	The graphical border around a control; it is either None or Fixed Single.
FillStyle	FillStyleConstants	The graphical fill of a control; it is either solid, transparent, or one of a number of shades, such as horizontal line.

Using the Object Browser to Display Enumerations

Table 4.1 is only a partial list of enumerated properties available to you when you're developing properties in your controls. For information on all the enumerations that are available, open the Object Browser (using the menu command View, Object Browser or the function key F2) and browse the list of enumerated properties displayed there, as in Figure 4.3.

You'll notice that the Object Browser also displays the name and values of the enumerations you've created yourself. To see this:

1 In the Object Browser, scroll through the list of enumerations until you find the Wattage enumeration.

2 Click on the Wattage enumeration. You should be able to see its members: Bright, FairlyDim, VeryBright, and VeryDim.

3 Click on FairlyDim, then look at the bottom of the Object Browser. The status bar tells you that FairlyDim is a constant equal to 1. Your screen should look like Figure 4.4.

Tip *Using Object Browser to keep track of the enumerations you've written can be a great help, because it keeps you from having to hunt through your code when you're trying to remember whether you called something xyzFlag or pdqFlag. It also helps you quickly look up the values of enumerated constants.*

You can tell at a glance that a particular constant is an element of your project (as opposed to an element of a standard VB type library) by looking at the bottom of the Object Browser; this area is called the Details Pane.

Example of Standard Control Property Types

To give an example of a system-provided enumerated constant, you'll add a BorderColor property to the LightBulb control. For simplicity's sake, the BorderColor property of the LightBulb will delegate to the BackColor property of the UserControl. To do this:

1 Open the LightBulb control designer.

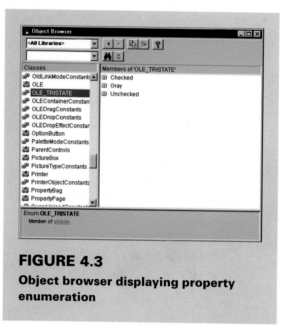

FIGURE 4.3
Object browser displaying property enumeration

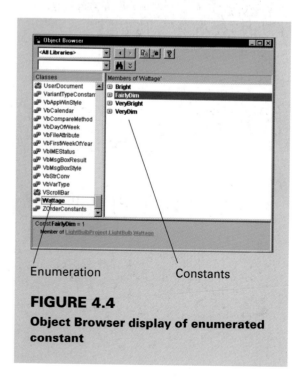

Enumeration   Constants

FIGURE 4.4
Object Browser display of enumerated constant

2 Open the control designer's code window and enter the following code:

```
Public Property Let BorderColor(ByVal NewColor As OLE_COLOR)
    UserControl.BackColor = NewColor
    PropertyChanged "BorderColor"
End Property


Public Property Get BorderColor() As OLE_COLOR
    BorderColor = UserControl.BackColor
End Property
```

3 Close the code window, close the form designer, and switch back to frmLBTestForm.

4 Click on LightBulb1. In the Properties windows, you should be able to see that the control now has a BorderColor property.

5 In the Properties window, click on the BorderColor property. A standard color selection drop-down box appears, as you can see in Figure 4.5.

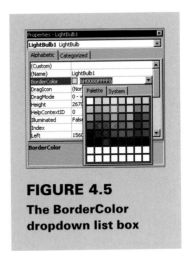

FIGURE 4.5

The BorderColor dropdown list box

Validating Property Procedures

Property Let and Property Set procedures are the place where you'll write validation procedures. Such procedures should reject all invalid property values, either by raising some kind of error or by ignoring the attempt to change the property value.

From an error-trapping perspective, Boolean properties are nice, because you don't have to do numeric boundary checking. For example, consider the Illuminated property of a LightBulb control.

LightBulbs are either Illuminated or not; that is, their Illuminated properties are either True or False. But because Visual Basic defines False as zero and True as any nonzero value, the code

```
Lightbulb1.Illuminated = 3.14159
```

will work fine, triggering no error (LightBulb1's Illuminated property will be set to True). However, the code

```
Lightbulb1.Illuminated = "ringbo"
```

generates an error (13-Type Mismatch). You can avoid error in this case by testing the value supplied by the user with an IsNumeric function, like this:

```
If IsNumeric (NewValue) Then
```

```
        ' perform the property change
            .
            .
            .
    Else
        ' raise an error
            .
            .
            .
    End If
```

This technique is known as validation, and it's important to do. If a run-time error occurs in your control, there's no way for your user to trap it.

You have the option of exiting a Property Let in situations where the input is just too weird to deal with. For example, say you provide a BorderColor property for your control. Windows colors are expressed as long integers. But if your control encounters the code:

```
LightBulb1.BorderColor = "václav"
```

the user gets a Type Mismatch error, because the BorderColor property expects a long integer.

Let's say that instead of raising an error, you want the BorderColor property to ignore, or "eat" the error. To make this happen, you can change your code to look like the following:

```
Public Property Let BorderColor(ByVal NewColor As OLE_COLOR)
    If IsNumeric(NewColor) Then
        UserControl.BackColor = NewColor
        PropertyChanged "BorderColor"
    Else
        Exit Property
    End If
End Property
```

The preceding code was just to introduce the Exit property statement to you; in general, your procedures should eat errors as seldom as possible. The preferred option for validation is to raise an error in your Property Let procedure. For more information on raising errors in your control, see Chapter 15, "Debugging and Error Trapping."

Using the PropertyBag Object

You use the PropertyBag object to store the properties set for your control by a programmer at design time. The PropertyBag object has only two methods: ReadProperty and WriteProperty.

You read from the PropertyBag in the ReadProperties event and write to the PropertyBag in the WriteProperties event. The syntax of the WriteProperty method is:

```
PropertyBag.WriteProperty "property_name", value [, default_value]
```

The parameter property_name is a string that denotes which property you're saving to the property bag. Value is the value of the property you're saving. The parameter *default_value* is optional; it exists only to tell Visual Basic not to save the property unless the user has changed the property from its default. This makes for clearer and faster loading .CTL files.

Here is an example of the WriteProperty method used in the WriteProperties event of a UserControl:

```
Private Sub UserControl_WriteProperties(PropBag As PropertyBag)
    PropBag.WriteProperty "Wattage", mWattage, 0
    PropBag.WriteProperty "Illuminated", mIlluminated, False
End Sub
```

The syntax of the ReadProperty method is:

```
PropertyBag.ReadProperty "property_name" [, default_value]
```

Just as with WriteProperty, the ReadProperty method has an optional *default_value* parameter that tells Visual Basic whether the property needs to be read from disk or not. This accelerates loading the control.

Here is an example of the ReadProperty method in the ReadProperties event:

```
Private Sub UserControl_ReadProperties(PropBag As PropertyBag)
    Wattage = PropBag.ReadProperty("Wattage", 0)
    Illuminated = PropBag.ReadProperty("Illuminated", False)
End Sub
```

Where Design-Time Property Data Is Stored

Officially, you aren't supposed to be concerned with what happens to data once it's put in the PropertyBag. This is because the PropertyBag object is an abstraction, standing between the programmer and the property's storage and shielding you from its complexity. But you might need to know what these files are and what they do (especially when you're backing up your project, using version control, or moving your project from one disk to another).

For forms, most design-time property settings are saved to a .FRM file. This is also true for controls, except the settings are saved in the .CTL file. You can inspect the format of these files by opening a .FRM or .CTL in a text editor; just make sure not to make any changes to these files, or Visual Basic won't be able to read them.

Some properties, such as the Picture property of a PictureBox control, can't be stored in standard form or control files, because they are too large and consequently need to be stored in a binary format. When you set a property such as Picture in a form or control designer, Visual Basic creates a binary file that has the same name as your file, but with a different extension. This file is created and updated when the user saves the corresponding form or user control file; under normal circumstances, Visual Basic programmers never work with these files directly. Table 4.2 summarizes the files' extensions.

Properties of Constituent Controls

You learned in Chapter 3 how to pass through, or *delegate*, the property of your UserControl to a constituent control. In general, the code you use to read and write the properties of constituent controls to your UserControl is very simple. Given a UserControl called LightBulb with a constituent PictureBox control called picMain, the code to read and write the control's Picture property looks like this:

```
Public Property Get Picture() As Picture
    Picture = picMain.Picture
End Property


Public Property Set Picture(ByVal NewPic As Picture)
    picMain.Picture = NewPic
    PropertyChanged "Picture"
End Property
```

This is a code cliché—a piece of code you'll write dozens if not hundreds of times in your career as a Visual Basic control developer. (The code is so straightforward, in fact, it makes more sense for you to let the ActiveX Control Interface Wizard write it for you. The ActiveX Control Interface Wizard is introduced in Chapter 2.)

Limitations of Constituent Controls

When using constituent controls, there is a caveat you must bear in mind. When you place a constituent control on your UserControl designer, the constituent control is in run-time mode, even though no code is being executed. That means you will not be able to gain access to runtime-only properties of the constituent control (such as the Sorted property of the ComboBox control).

TABLE 4.2   FILENAME EXTENSIONS OF VISUAL BASIC BINARY FILES

File Type	Filename Extension	Binary Filename Extension
Forms	.FRM	.FRX
Controls	.CTL	.CTX
Property pages	.PAG	.PGX

Fortunately, the number of runtime-only properties of standard Windows control are few, so hopefully this shortcoming won't hinder you too often. But it is something to bear in mind as you build controls comprised of constituent controls.

Properties Your Control Should Provide

There are a number of properties that your control is supposed to always provide. This being a free country and all, you don't *have* to provide any properties you don't want to. If your control is unusual (for example, it's invisible at runtime), then you obviously would.

The properties your control should provide are:

- ▶ Appearance
- ▶ BackColor
- ▶ BackStyle
- ▶ BorderStyle
- ▶ Enabled
- ▶ Font
- ▶ ForeColor

You should also provide properties for controls that are similar to your control. Make sure your control's property interface make sense, and you will avoid legions of users throwing rocks through the windows of your home in the middle of the night.

Creating a Procedure Description

One helpful new feature of the VB5 IDE is the procedure description of properties. When you click on a property in the Properties window, a (hopefully) helpful piece of text appears at the bottom of the Properties window (see Figure 4.6) telling you what the property is used for.

You can implement procedure descriptions in properties you create. To do this:

1 Open the form designer for your control.

2 Double-click on the designer to open a code window.

3 Choose the menu command Tools, Procedure Attributes. The Procedure Attributes dialog appears.

4 Using the Name combo box, choose the property of your control you wish to annotate.

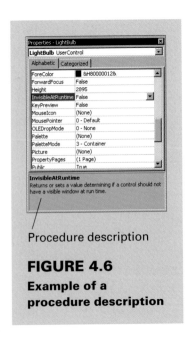

Procedure description

FIGURE 4.6

Example of a procedure description

5 In the Description text box, type the description of your property. The Procedure Attributes dialog box will look like Figure 4.7.

6 Click on OK.

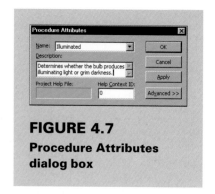

FIGURE 4.7
Procedure Attributes dialog box

To test your property description:

1 Click on the control LightBulb1 on frmLBTestForm.

2 Scroll through the list of properties in the Properties window.

3 Click on the Illuminated property. As shown in Figure 4.8, you should be able to see the description text you entered at the bottom of the Properties window.

Designating a Property as the Default

Most controls have a *default property*. If you choose to designate a default property in your control, the user will not have to explicitly type the name of the property when referring to it in code. Denoting a default property in your control saves the user time at the expense of clarity. For example, the default property of a TextBox is its text property. If you have a TextBox called Text1, you can either type

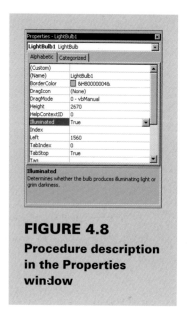

FIGURE 4.8
Procedure description in the Properties window

```
MyString = Text1.Text
```

or

```
MyString = Text1
```

and the two lines of code will mean the exact same thing.

> **Note** *The default property is not to be confused with the Default property (also referred to in VB5 as the user interface default). The Default property is a property of command buttons and similar controls. When the Default property is set to true, striking the Enter key triggers the command button's Click event.*

To designate a property of your control as its default property, do the following:

1 With the control designer open, choose the menu command Tools, Procedure Attributes.

2 The Procedure Attributes dialog box appears. In the Name combo box, select the property you want to designate as the default, then click on Advanced.

3 In the Procedure ID combo box, select (Default). The screen will look like Figure 4.9.

You can test your new default property by entering code in the Immediate window while the form is running. To do this:

1 Close the control designer, if it is still open.

2 Return to frmLBTestForm. Create a LightBulb control there, if one does not already exist.

3 Run the EXE project by choosing the menu command Run, Start or using the function key F5.

4 Pause execution by typing Ctrl+Break or clicking on the Break button on the toolbar (see Figure 4.10).

5 Open the Immediate window, if it's not already open. (To open the this window, choose the menu command View, Immediate Window or use the keystroke shortcut Ctrl+G.)

6 In the Immediate window, type the following code:

```
Print LightBulb1
```

and press Enter. The value of LightBulb1's Illuminated property appears in the Immediate window. Now when you type

```
LightBulb1 = True
```

LightBulb1 illuminates.

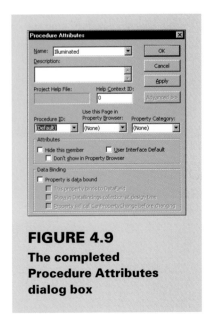

FIGURE 4.9
The completed Procedure Attributes dialog box

FIGURE 4.10
The toolbar Break button

Grouping Properties

You can organize properties into groups in order to make it easier for users to find them in the Properties windows. It's particularly useful to do this if your control exposes a large number of properties.

For example, you might want to create a bunch of electricity-related properties together in one group. The Wattage and Illuminated properties would be more easily accessible if they belonged to this group. To place the LightBulb control's Illuminated property in a property group, do the following:

1 Open the HappyHour control's designer, if it's not open already.

2 From the menu, choose the command Tools, Procedure Attributes.

3 The Procedure Attributes dialog box appears. Select the Illuminated property from the Name combo.

4 Click on Advanced. The dialog box expands.

5 The Property Category combo determines which category the property is placed in. You can select from one of the choices in the list (Appearance, Data, Font, and so forth) or you can create your own. To create your own property category, type the word Electrical in the Property Category box. The dialog box will look like Figure 4.11.

6 Click on OK to apply the changes.

To see that the Illuminated property has been assigned to a category, do the following:

1 Open the test form frmLBTestForm.

2 An instance of the LightBulb control should already be on the form. Click on it to select it.

3 In the Properties window, click on the Categorized tab. Scroll through the list of properties; you should be able to see that Illuminated now falls under the Electrical category, as illustrated in Figure 4.12.

FIGURE 4.11
Custom property category

Synchronizing a Property with Properties of Its Container

You can use the AmbientProperties object to gain access to information about the properties of your control's container. You do this in order to synchronize your control's properties with those of its container.

For example, when you set a form's Font property to Times New Roman 12 Bold and then place a Label control on the form, the Font property of the label is automatically set to Times New Roman 12 Bold as well. The default properties of the Label are synchronized with the properties of its container.

When you write properties, consider whether it is appropriate to synchronize properties of your control with properties of its container. For more information on the container, including an example of how to use the AmbientProperties object, see Chapter 7, "Interacting with the Container."

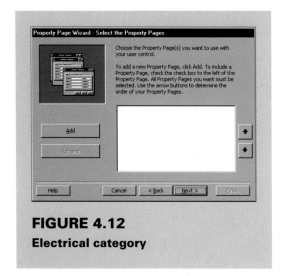

FIGURE 4.12
Electrical category

Creating Custom Property Pages

A custom property page can go a long way toward making the properties of your control easier to manipulate at design time. This is particularly true if your control has numerous properties or an otherwise complicated interface. You can assign a property page to your entire control or to a particular property in your control.

In this section you'll step through the construction of a simple property page using a wizard, then you'll write code to create a property page manually.

Using the Property Page Wizard

You can use the Property Page Wizard as a quick way to set up a basic property page for your control. After you've created a property page using the wizard, you can further customize the property page using the same visual design techniques you'd use to create Visual Basic applications and ActiveX controls.

Begin by setting up a minimal property page for the LightBulb control.
To do this:

1 Open the LightBulb control project in LightBulbGroup.vbg, if it is not open already.

2 Choose the menu command Add-Ins, Property Page Wizard.

3 The first Property Page Wizard screen appears. Click on Next.

4 As in Figure 4.12, the screen labeled Select the Property Pages appears. Here you have the option to designate an existing property page for your control or to create a new page.

5 The Property Page Wizard starts by allowing you to select the property pages to use for your control.

6 Click on Add to create a new page.

7 The Property Page Name dialog box appears, prompting you to name your new property page (see Figure 4.13). In place of PropertyPage1, type **LightBulbPage**, then click on **OK**.

8 The new page is added to your project and you are returned to the Select the Property Pages dialog box. Click on Next.

9 The Add Properties window appears. This window lets you add properties from your UserControl to the property page.

10 Double-click on Illuminated in the Available Properties list. The Illuminated property moves to the LightBulbPage page. Click on Next.

11 The Finished! window appears. Click on Finish.

12 The Property Page Created dialog box appears. Click on OK.

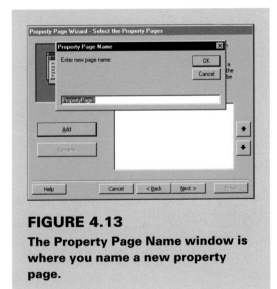

FIGURE 4.13

The Property Page Name window is where you name a new property page.

13 A report appears giving you information on what else needs to be done to make your property page functional (see Figure 4.14). Click on Close when you're done reading it.

Your property page is now functional. To test it:

1 Close the LightBulb control's designer, if it is open.

2 Open the EXE project form. There should be an instance of the LightBulb control there already.

3 Right-click on LightBulb1. A pop-up menu appears. Click on Properties. As in Figure 4.15, your custom property page appears.

You should also be able to see that a new file has been added to your project, a custom property page called LightBulbPage. Locate it in the Project Explorer and double-click it to open it.

You can see that at design time, a property page looks not unlike a control designer; in fact, they are called *property page designers*. You can manipulate this designer and add controls and code to it just like a control designer or a form. You'll do that in the next section.

Programming the PropertyPage Object

The PropertyPage object is a fully programmable Visual Basic object similar to a Form or a UserControl object. Tables 4.3 and 4.4 describe the important properties and events of the PropertyPage.

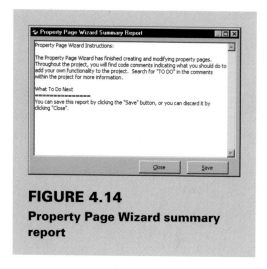

FIGURE 4.14
Property Page Wizard summary report

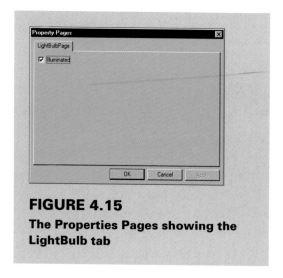

FIGURE 4.15
The Properties Pages showing the LightBulb tab

TABLE 4.3   IMPORTANT PROPERTIES OF THE PROPERTYPAGE OBJECT

Property	Description
ActiveControl	This is the control that has the focus. You can use this property to determine which type of control the user has selected when the PropertyPage is displayed.
Changed	This is a flag that indicates whether the user changed a property through the PropertyPage.
SelectedControls	This is a collection containing all the controls selected when the PropertyPage was activated.

TABLE 4.4 IMPORTANT EVENTS OF THE PROPERTYPAGE OBJECT

Event	When Triggered
ApplyChanges	This is triggered when the user clicks on the Apply or OK button or switches tabs in a PropertyPage comprised of multiple pages.
EditProperty	When the user clicks on the ellipsis button in the Properties window, the property page is opened. It exists so you can set the focus to the appropriate control.
SelectionChanged	This is triggered when the PropertyPage is first opened and when you select or deselect one or more controls while the page is still open.
Unload	This is triggered when the PropertyPage is about to be unloaded (usually as a result of the user closing the page). This is similar to the Unload event of a form.
Terminate	This event occurs after the Unload event. All references to the PropertyPage control go out of scope (or are set to Nothing).

Modifying the Property Page

Property pages created by the Property Page Wizard are generally adequate for most types of properties. But you might want to take your control's properties sheet further by applying additional code and custom controls to the property page's interface.

To demonstrate this, you'll convert the check box that controls the Illuminated property to a group of option buttons with graphical representations of the "on" and "off" states of the light bulb. To do this:

1 Open the property page designer LightBulbPage. There should be a single checkbox there for the Illuminated property; this checkbox was created by the Property Page Wizard in the preceding demonstration of property pages.

2 Beneath the Illuminated checkbox, create a Frame control.

3 Inside the Frame control, create two PictureBoxes and two OptionButton controls. Make sure that all the controls are contained inside the Frame control or the option buttons won't work properly.

4 Give one OptionButton the name optBulbOff. Name the other one optBulbOn.

5 Assign the properties shown in Tables 4.5-4.9 to the controls Picture1, Picture2, optBulbOff, optBulbOn, and Frame1, respectively.

TABLE 4.5 PICTURE1 CONTROL PROPERTIES

Property	Value
Picture	slite-off.bmp (on the CD-ROM)
AutoSize	True

TABLE 4.6 PICTURE2 CONTROL PROPERTIES

Property	Value
Picture	slite-on.bmp (also on your CD-ROM)
AutoSize	True

6 Delete chkIlluminated. The graphical interface of your property page should look like Figure 4.16.

7 Double-click on the property page designer to open its code window. You should be able to see existing code for changing the Illuminated property using the checkbox, chkIlluminated.

8 Delete the procedure chkIlluminated_Click and replace it with the following code. This code provides Click events for the two option buttons:

TABLE 4.7   OPTBULBOFF PROPERTIES

Property	Value
Caption	Off
Value	True

TABLE 4.8   OPTBULBON PROPERTIES

Property	Value
Caption	On
Value	False

TABLE 4.9   FRAME1 CONTROL PROPERTIES

Property	Value
Caption	Illuminated

```
Private Sub optBulbOff_Click()
    Changed = True
End Sub


Private Sub optBulbOn_Click()
    Changed = True
End Sub
```

This code flags the property page as "dirty," meaning that the user has altered a property in the page. When the property page is dirty, the Apply button is enabled; the property page then knows to apply the property changes to the control when the user clicks on Apply or OK.

Next you'll need to alter the ApplyChanges event of the PropertyPage so the page applies the property change appropriately. To do this, make the following changes to the code in the property page's ApplyChanges event:

```
Private Sub PropertyPage_ApplyChanges()
    SelectedControls(0).Illuminated = optBulbOn.Value
End Sub
```

Finally, you'll have to alter the property page's SelectionChanged event so it accurately reflects the state of the selected control when the property page was opened. This code is in the SelectionChanged event because this event is triggered when the property page is first opened. It is also triggered when the user changes the control that is selected. However, the event is *also* triggered when you click on the property sheet's Apply button, which is bad, because when you change the property to Off and press Apply, the code will change the property sheet to indicate that the property has been set to On. We'll include a workaround for this puzzling anomaly by placing a flag in the ApplyChanges event.

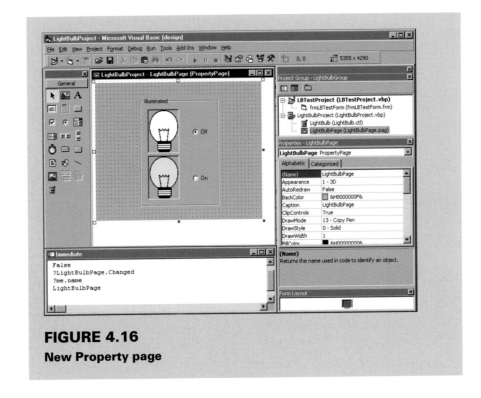

FIGURE 4.16
New Property page

Tip *It's important to remember that the set of selected controls can change after the user has brought up the Property sheet. This is the case because property pages are modeless (meaning that users can access windows in the background while the Property page is still being displayed).*

To make this change, start by creating the flag in the Declarations section of the code:

```
Private mApplyingFlag As Boolean
```

Next, alter the ApplyChanges event so it sets the flag. Its code should look like this:

```
Private Sub PropertyPage_ApplyChanges()
    mApplyingFlag = True
    SelectedControls(0).Illuminated = optBulbOn.Value
End Sub
```

Finally, alter the code in the SelectionChanged event as follows:

```
Private Sub PropertyPage_SelectionChanged()
    If mApplyingFlag = False Then
        optBulbOn.Value = SelectedControls(0).Illuminated
```

```
        Else
             ' do nothing
             mApplyingFlag = False
        End If
End Sub
```

To test your new Property page, do the following:

1 Close the Property page designer.

2 Open frmLBTextForm, the EXE project form that contains an instance of the LightBulb control.

3 Right-click on LightBulb1. From the pop-up menu, select Properties.

4 Your Property page appears. Using the Property page, change the Illuminated property of the selected control, then click on Apply. You should be able to see the control change.

Summary

This chapter discussed how to create properties in the ActiveX controls you create. Using an example project, you created properties, wrote validation procedures, and developed custom property pages.

In the next chapter, you'll learn about another new element of control interfaces: custom events.

Creating Custom Events

Events of the UserControl Object

Chapter 5
Handling and Raising Events

When your control raises an event, it gives programmers an opportunity to do something interesting. Controls with rich event models represent the difference between a do-nothing file viewer and a fully-featured piece of component software. This chapter discusses how to create custom events in your ActiveX control.

Additionally, this chapter discusses the events triggered by the UserControl object itself.

Creating Custom Events

Unlike custom properties, which were available in VB 4.0 classes, custom events are a new feature in Visual Basic 5.0. Events are a way to permit users to write code to hook into things that your control does.

For example, consider the HappyHour control we started building in Chapter 3. This control, which is comprised of a PictureBox and a Caption control, is designed to reside in a Web page. In order to receive regularly updated graphical and textual information, the HappyHour control might be modified to reload picture or text information on a regular basis—every fifteen minutes, for example. In order to give users of your control the ability to run other code in response to this, you instruct your control to raise an event, called Updated, to be triggered every time the control has finished re-downloading new data.

The user could then hook into the Updated event to cause some other action to take place in her program; an audio beep, or perhaps a pop-up dialog box or other interface element to let the user know that the data has been updated.

Understanding the Syntax of Event and RaiseEvent

You create a custom event using an event declaration in the Declarations section of a code module. Similar to a variable declaration, an event declaration denotes the name of the event procedure and, optionally, any parameters that are passed to it.

After you've declared a custom event, you can trigger the event using the RaiseEvent statement. The syntax of an event declaration looks like this:

```
Public Event EventName([ByVal variable As datatype])
```

Once you've declared an event, you can refer to it in your code by using the RaiseEvent statement. The syntax of the RaiseEvent statement looks like this:

```
RaiseEvent event_name
```

The argument event_name must, of course, be the same as the name of the event in the event declaration.

Creating an Event

In this section you'll add an event to the HappyHour project. This project is an updated version of the HappyHour control discussed in Chapter 3. (In case you skipped over the walk-through in Chapter 3, the HappyHour control is designed to provide graphical and textual notification to members of a company that it is time for happy hour.)

The major change in this version of the HappyHour control is the addition of a Timer control and two new properties, HappyHourStart and HappyHourEnd. Since the addition of these new elements of the control don't introduce any significant new elements to the HappyHour control, I've included them for you in the updated version of the HappyHour control on your CD-ROM.

The HappyHourStart and HappyHourEnd properties store user-defined start and end times for HappyHour. For the purposes of our demonstration, we'll assume that happy hour begins at 5:00 PM and ends at 6:00 PM (although the way it's set up, the user can change that to any values she wants).

In order to implement this, the user sets the HappyHourStart property to 5:00 PM and the HappyHourEnd property to 6:00 PM.

The Timer control checks the system time once per second, comparing the current time against the user-set values for HappyHourStart and HappyHourEnd. If it's happy hour, the control fires the HappyHourStart event. The user can then use the HappyHourStart event to do anything she wants—make the computer play a sound or change the Picture and Caption properties of the control. To do this:

1 Open the control designer for the HappyHour control. (This control project is on the CD-ROM that accompanies this book.) You should be able to see that in this version of the control, a Timer has been added to the control (Figure 5.1).

2 Double-click on the control designer to open its code window.

3 Using the Object combo box at the top of the code window, switch to the General section of the code. This should move your cursor to the top of the code window, if you're in Full Module view.

4 Insert the HappyHourStart event declaration by writing the following code in the Declarations section of the code window:

```
' Declarations

Public Event HappyHourStart()
```

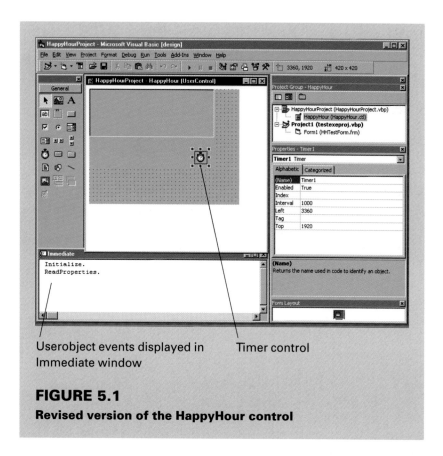

Userobject events displayed in   Timer control
Immediate window

FIGURE 5.1
Revised version of the HappyHour control

Your event has now been declared and is eligible to be used in your code. Since this event will be raised as a condition of the current time, you'll write code to raise the event in the Timer event of the Timer control. To do this:

1 Using the Object combo box, switch to the code for Timer1.

2 The Timer event procedure appears. (This is the only event raised by the Timer control.) Add the code in the listing below.

```
Private Sub Timer1_Timer()
' Triggered once per second.
' Compares current time to
' happy hour time. If it's happy
' hour, raise the HappyHourStart event.

' bail out if it's already happy hour
    If mHappyHour Then
        Exit Sub
    End If
```

```
' bail out if happy hour hasn't
' been defined yet
    If mHappyHourBegin = "" Or mHappyHourEnd = "" Then
        Exit Sub
    End If


' check to see if it's happy hour now
    If Time > CDate(mHappyHourBegin) And Time < CDate(mHappyHourEnd)_
Then
        mHappyHour = True
        RaiseEvent HappyHourStart
    Else
        mHappyHour = False
    End If

End Sub
```

The variable mHappyHour is an internal flag that indicates to the Timer event whether it's currently happy hour or not. This flag exists because it wouldn't make sense for the HappyHour control to raise the HappyHourStart event once per second during happy hour; instead, if the Timer event sees that it is happy hour already, it aborts without raising the HappyHourStart event.

Testing The HappyHourStart Event

Once you've entered the above code, you can test it by going through the following steps:

1 Set your computer's system clock to 5:00 PM. You can do this by using the Date/Time settings in Control Panel.

2 Close the HappyHour control designer, if it is open.

3 Open HHTestForm.frm, the EXE project test form for the HappyHour project.

4 Double-click on HappyHour1. The HappyHourStart event should appear in the code window. Enter the following code:

```
Private Sub HappyHour1_HappyHourStart()
    HappyHour1.Caption = "It is now happy hour!"
    Set HappyHour1.Picture = LoadPicture("d:\Code\Chapter 05\_
HappyHour2\After\happy.bmp")
End Sub
```

5 Launch the program by clicking on the Run button on the toolbar, or by pressing the function key F5.

6 As soon as the program runs, the HappyHour control should immediately trigger the HappyHourStart event and change the picture and caption. The running program should look like Figure 5.2.

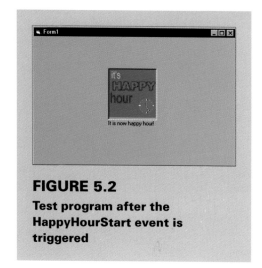

FIGURE 5.2

Test program after the HappyHourStart event is triggered

Creating an Event That Includes a Parameter

Sometimes it's useful for events raised by a control to pass additional information to event procedures. Controls do this in the form of *event parameters*. Most events do not have parameters, but it's useful to include them when necessary.

For example, consider the MouseDown event of most interface controls. It is not enough that Visual Basic simply indicates that the user has pressed the mouse key. Your program must also know where and how the mouse was clicked.

This is why the MouseDown event receives the parameters of Button, Shift, X, and Y. You should be familiar with these types of events already, but to illustrate this more clearly, the code below gives an example of the first line of a MouseDown event procedure for a PictureBox control.

```
Private Sub Picture1_MouseDown(Button As Integer, Shift As Integer, _
    X As Single, Y As Single)
```

The Button parameter tells the event which mouse button was pressed. The Shift parameter tells whether a key on the keyboard (either Shift, Ctrl, Alt, or some combination of these) was pressed. The X and Y parameters tell the event where on the PictureBox control the user pressed the mouse.

When events raised by your control pass arguments in this way, the RaiseEvent procedure specifies what the parameters are. To create an event that passes parameters in your example project, begin by declaring a HappyHourChanged event:

```
Public Event HappyHourChanged (bHappyHourStatus As Boolean)
```

Next, modify the Timer event of Timer1 to raise the new HappyHourChanged event, rather than the HappyHourStart event, using this code:

```
Private Sub Timer1_Timer()
' Triggered once per second.
' Compares current time to
' happy hour time. if it's happy
' hour, raise the appropriate event.
```

```
' happy hour hasn't been set yet
If mHappyHourBegin = "" Or mHappyHourEnd = "" Then
    Exit Sub
End If


' check to see if it's happy hour now
    If Time > CDate(mHappyHourBegin) And Time < CDate(mHappyHourEnd)_
Then

        If mHappyHour = False Then
            RaiseEvent HappyHourChanged(True)
            mHappyHour = True
        Else
            ' it's already happy hour
        End If
    Else
        If mHappyHour = True Then
            RaiseEvent HappyHourChanged(False)
            mHappyHour = False
        End If
    End If

End Sub
```

The Timer event still evaluates whether it's happy hour, but now instead of merely triggering the HappyHourStart event (which would lock the employees of our company into a perpetual state of happiness), it calls the HappyHourChanged event, passing the event the Boolean parameter of True or False depending on whether it's happy hour or not.

You can now take advantage of that Boolean parameter in the HappyHourChanged event. To do this:

1 Close the control designer and open the HHTestForm project on the CD-ROM that accompanies this book.

2 Double-click on HappyHour1 to open its code window.

3 Delete the event procedure HappyHourStart.

4 In the HappyHourChanged event procedure, enter the following code:

```
Private Sub HappyHour1_HappyHourChanged(HappyStatus As Boolean)

Select Case HappyStatus
    Case True
    HappyHour1.Caption = "It is now happy hour!"
    ' Change the following filename to match your system's configuration
    Set HappyHour1.Picture = LoadPicture("d:\Code\Chapter 05\HappyHour2\After\_
happy.bmp")

    Case False
    HappyHour1.Caption = "It is not happy hour yet. Get back to work."
    ' Change the following filename to match your system's configuration
    Set HappyHour1.Picture = LoadPicture("d:\Code\Chapter 05\HappyHour2\After\_
work.bmp")

End Select

End Sub
```

(You'll want to change the filename "d:\work\work.bmp" to reflect the location of the file work.bmp on your system.)

5 Using the Date/Time icon in the Control Panel, set your system clock to 5:59 PM.

6 Run the program. You should be able to see the control change to the happy hour state as soon as the program runs. When your system clock changes to 6:00 PM, the control should change back to its work state.

Raising Events of Constituent Controls

The preceding example demonstrates how to modify the Timer event of the constituent Timer control for a specific purpose. But if you are interested in simply passing a constituent control's event through to your UserControl, it's easy to do. Simply raise the constituent control's event to the UserControl level by using the RaiseEvent statement.

Events that are passed through to constituent controls are said to be *forwarded*. Here is an example of how a forwarded event might work in the HappyHour control. In this case, we're forwarding the Click event of PictureBox control:

```
Public Event Click()     ' This goes in the Declarations section

Private Sub Picture1_Click()
    RaiseEvent Click
End Sub
```

Note that as written, this code will only raise the Click event if the user clicks on the PictureBox portion of the HappyHour control; it will not raise the event if the user clicks on the Label portion. To cause the Click event to be raised when the user clicks on any portion of the control, add a RaiseEvent to the Label's Click event as well (thereby forwarding the Click event of the Label control):

```
Private Sub lblCaption_Click()
    RaiseEvent Click
End Sub
```

Providing Standard Events

There is a set of events that users expect in practically every control. These events are:

▶ Click

▶ DblClick

▶ KeyDown

▶ KeyPress

▶ KeyUp

▶ MouseDown

▶ MouseMove

▶ MouseUp

Providing this core set of recommended events will go a long way toward making your control's programmable interface more intuitive. And, of course, providing more than this basic set of events will make your control more flexible for the programmers that use it.

Of course, you're not required to provide any of these events if they don't make sense in the context of your control. For example, a control that is meant to be clicked (such as a CommandButton) doesn't need to have a DblClick event (indeed, it would be difficult to implement a DblClick event in such a control, since its Click event would be triggered the first time a user clicked it).

Specifying a Default Event

You can specify that a particular event in your control's event model is the *default event* for that control. The default event is the first event that appears in a code window.

For example, consider the PictureBox control. When you instantiate a PictureBox on a form at design time and double-click on it, the code window opens to the picture box's Click event. This happens because Click is the default event for a PictureBox control. To designate a default event for your control:

1 Select the menu commands Tools, Procedure Attributes.

2 The Procedure Attributes dialog box appears. In the Name combo box, select the event you want to serve as your control's default event.

3 Click on the Advanced button.

4 The Procedure Attributes dialog expands. Activate the User Interface Default box.

5 Click on OK.

It's never mandatory to provide a default event for your control, but it makes things a little easier on your users. Most commercial controls designate a default event, so your users will expect you to provide one, too. If you don't provide an event, the first event to be displayed in the code window is the event that comes first in alphabetical order.

Understanding Container-Provided Events

The Extender object of your control's container can automatically provide a number of events for your control. However, bear in mind that not all containers are the same. In Visual Basic, the container provides the following events:

▶ GotFocus

▶ LostFocus

▶ DragOver

▶ DragDrop

Because they are provided by the container, you don't have to write any code to enable the user to hook into these events; they're there inherently.

However, you need to remember that you can't count on these events being provided by the container. If you raise an event that you expect to be provided by the container's Extender object, use error-trapping just in case your control is placed into a container that doesn't raise the event you expected.

See Chapter 7, "Interacting with the Container," for more details on the container. See Chapter 15, "Debugging and Error Trapping," for more information on error-trapping.

Events of the UserControl Object

In order to be able to provide a number of standard features of an ActiveX control, it's important to understand the events that it triggers during its lifetime. This is different than the events that your control raises; the events of the UserControl object are analogous to events of the Visual Basic form such as Load, Unload, and Activate.

The events of the UserControl object are summarized in Table 5.1.

TABLE 5.1   EVENTS OF THE USERCONTROL OBJECT

Event	Occurs When
InitProperties	The user places the control on the container for the first time. This event is only triggered once in the lifetime of the control. It is used to set the initial values for a control's properties.
Initialize	An application creates an instance of a UserControl. The Extender and Ambient objects are not available to this event. This is the first event triggered by a control; it is triggered numerous times in the control's lifetime.
ReadProperties	An old instance of a control is re-instantiated. This is where you read design-time properties from the PropertyBag and reassign them to your control.
Resize	This occurs after the control appears and whenever its size is changed.
Paint	This occurs when the control needs to redraw itself.
WriteProperties	The design-time properties of the control need to be saved using the PropertyBag object. This event is only triggered at design time (because run-time properties of the control aren't saved via the PropertyBag).
Terminate	All references to a UserControl are set to Nothing or when the last reference to the object falls out of scope. This occurs as the control is about to be destroyed.

Tip *The Load and Unload events you're accustomed to working with in Visual Basic forms aren't present in control designers. The analogous events of the UserControl are the ReadProperties and WriteProperties events.*

Although the table makes the chain of events look deceptively simple, bear in mind that these events get triggered numerous times—often in seemingly counter-intuitive ways—during the development and deployment of your control. Part of the reason why the events are triggered in ways you might not expect is because the UserControl is destroyed and re-created by Visual Basic behind the scenes while you move through the development-testing-debugging-refinement cycle of control creation.

For example, if you create a UserControl, then instantiate it on an EXE project form, go back to the control designer in order to make changes to it, then return to the EXE project form, the control will have been destroyed and re-created by Visual Basic. This is to insure that the changes to the control are reflected in the instantiation of the control on your EXE project form.

Controls that are placed on a form at design time are destroyed, then re-created, when the user runs the Visual Basic EXE project. Because this process is performed seamlessly behind the scenes by Visual Basic, it might seem strange that so many Terminate events occur in your UserControl.

Table 5.2 provides a step-by-step narrative that should give you a better idea of how and when these events are triggered.

The example project HappyHour2 on your CD-ROM has Debug.Print statements in all the important UserControl events, so you can see the events explained in Table 5.2 in action.

TABLE 5.2   EVENTS IN THE LIFETIME OF A TYPICAL USERCONTROL OBJECT

Action	Events Triggered
You instantate a control on an EXE project form.	Initialize InitProperties
You open a form containing a previously-instantiated control.	Initialize ReadProperties
You alter the control's designer, then return to the EXE project form.	Initialize ReadProperties
You run the EXE program.	WriteProperties Terminate Initialize ReadProperties
You halt the EXE program.	Initialize ReadProperties
You delete the instance of the control from the form.	WriteProperties Terminate

Note *Because there is no such thing as "design-time" on a Web page, controls that reside on Web pages don't go through the same life cycle as controls that reside in Visual Basic applications. Controls that live in Web pages are always treated as if they are newly instantiated each time they appear; consequently, they trigger Initialize, InitProperties, Resize, and Paint events. For more information on how your controls behave in Web pages, see Chapter 13, "Deploying Your Control on the Web."*

Summary

This chapter explored how to raise events in your control. We covered both event declaration and implementing a real-world event in a control.

We also covered the event model of the UserControl object itself. In addition, we went over how you can use such events to manage properties and other run-time and design-time attributes of your control.

In the next chapter, you'll learn how to provide custom methods in your controls.

Chapter 6
Control Methods

You can create a method in your ActiveX control as easily as you create a function or subroutine in Visual Basic; the syntax is the same, because any public function or subroutine in your control is exposed as a method.

Methods are the verbs of your control, just as properties are the adjectives. Users expect methods to perform processing or other actions. Accordingly, you should carefully consider whether the method you're looking to implement should really be implemented as a property. Putting yourself in the user's shoes and comparing your control to other controls that provide similar functionality will go a long way toward resolving the way your interface should be presented.

Bear in mind that it is permissible for methods to automatically adjust properties, although you should avoid doing this if it makes your interface incomprehensible. One example of a method that can change a property is the Move method, which most controls expose. The Move method not only determines where a control is positioned relative to its container, but it can also alter the control's size. The Move method has the ability, then, to change the Top, Left, Height, and Width properties of a control. Giving your methods the ability to alter properties of your control isn't always necessary to do, but it can make your control easier to program.

Creating a Method

This section demonstrates how to implement a simple method in your control. For this demonstration, we'll use a new version of the HappyHour control you worked on in previous chapters. You'll find this control on your CD-ROM.

The procedure you'll create will display the amount of time between now and happy hour. This procedure will be exposed in the HappyHour control as the WatchClock method. When this method is executed, the control will display a message box informing the user how much time remains until happy hour. To add this method to the HappyHour control:

1 Open the project group HappyHour.vbg in the HappyHour3 folder.

2 In the Project Explorer, open the HappyHour control designer.

3 Double-click on the HappyHour control designer to open its code window.

4 Enter the code in the following listing.

```
Public Sub WatchClock()
Dim lMinutesLeft As Long

    If mHappyHourBegin = "" Or mHappyHourEnd = "" Then
        MsgBox "I have no idea when happy hour is.", _
                            vbExclamation, _
                            "Something's Wrong"

        Exit Sub
    End If


    If Time > mHappyHourBegin And Time < mHappyHourEnd Then
        ' it's already happy hour
        MsgBox "It's happy hour! What are you doing here?", _
                            vbExclamation, _
                            "Party Time!"

        Exit Sub
    Else
        ' calculate and display the number
        ' of hours until happy hour
        lMinutesLeft = DateDiff("n", Time, mHappyHourBegin)
        MsgBox "Happy hour is in " & lMinutesLeft _
                            & " minutes!", _
                            vbInformation, _
                            "Get Back To Work!"

    End If
End Sub
```

Caution *Be very careful that you declare this sub as Public. Subs declared as Private aren't exposed as methods of the property.*

What the WatchClock Method Does

The code you just entered does the following:

▶ It verifies that the properties HappyHourStart and HappyHourEnd have been initialized. (If they aren't set to anything, the procedure informs the user. In real life, you'd probably instead want to formally raise an error and let the user determine whether a message should be displayed or not. For more information on this, see Chapter 15, "Debugging and Error Trapping.")

▶ The code determines if it's happy hour already. If it is happy hour, the procedure notifies the user with a message box urging them to get out there and party.

▶ If it's not happy hour, the procedure uses the Visual Basic DateDiff function to determine how many minutes there are until happy hour. The procedure then displays this information to the user using a message box.

Testing the WatchClock Method

Since methods are only executable at runtime, you will have to put the EXE project form into run mode and use the Immediate window to test your new method. To do this:

1 Close HappyHour's control designer.

2 Open the EXE project form frmHHTestForm and add an instance of the HappyHour control.

3 Run the project by clicking on the Start button, using the Run, Start menu commands, or pressing the function key F5.

4 Pause the program by clicking on the Break button on the toolbar or by using the keystroke combination Ctrl+Break.

5 Make sure the Immediate window is visible. If it isn't, choose the menu commands View, Immediate Window or use the keystroke shortcut Ctrl+G.

6 Click in the Immediate window.

7 Set the happy hour start time by typing in the following code into the Immediate window:

```
HappyHour1.HappyHourBegin = #11:49:00 AM#
```

8 Next, set the happy hour end time by typing in the following code into the Immediate window:

```
HappyHour1.HappyHourEnd = #12:30:00 PM#
```

9 Finally, execute your method by typing in the following code:

```
HappyHour1.WatchClock
```

The message box displayed by the HappyHour control depends on what time it is. If it is currently happy hour, you'll see the message box displayed as in Figure 6.1.

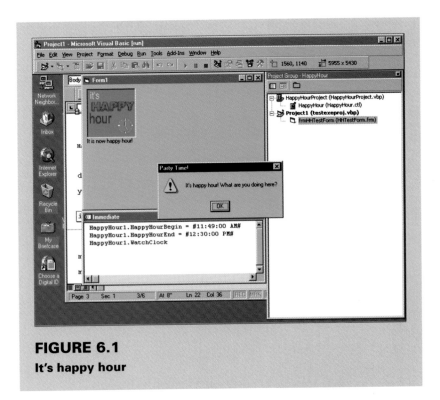

FIGURE 6.1
It's happy hour

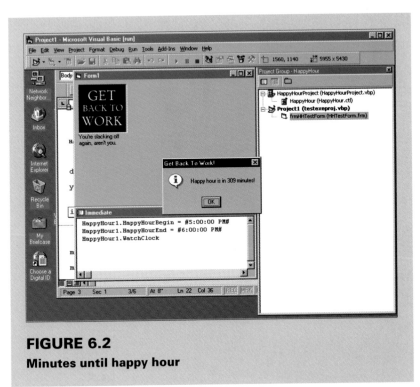

FIGURE 6.2
Minutes until happy hour

If it's not happy hour, the control will determine how many minutes until it's happy hour and display the message shown in Figure 6.2.

> **Note** *You'll recall that in Visual Basic, the standard delimiter for date and time values is the pound sign (#). This is analogous to the double-quotation sign that delimits a string.*

Creating a Method That Takes an Argument

You can pass an argument to a method the same way you pass an argument to any other procedure. Passing an argument to a procedure gives the procedure additional information about how to perform its processing.

For example, consider the Move method that exists in most controls. The syntax of this method is:

```
object.Move [left, top, width, height]
```

To use this method to move a command button called cmdSpeedy, you'd use the code:

```
cmdSpeedy.Move 100, 100
```

(The *width* and *height* arguments are omitted in this code because you're only looking to move, rather than resize, the control.)

You can add arguments to your event procedures to make them work the same way the Move event does. In the following example, you'll learn how to create a method that takes an argument by adding another method to the HappyHour project. This method, called HappyAlert, generates one or more audible tones that get the user's attention. The number of audible tones generated by the HappyAlert event is determined by the integer argument passed to it; if you write the code HappyHour1.HappyAlert 5, the control will beep five times.

Here's the code for the HappyAlert method. This code is designed to be included in the HappyHourChanged event; to include it, type the following code in the code window of the HappyHour user control:

```
Public Sub HappyAlert(iAlertNumber As Integer)
    Dim iCounter As Integer


    For iCounter = 1 To iAlertNumber
        Beep
    Next iCounter
End Sub
```

Testing the Parameterized Event Procedure

To test this code, do the following:

1 Close the HappyHour control's designer and return to frmHHTestForm.

2 Run the EXE project by clicking on the Start button on the Toolbar, choosing the Run, Start commands from the menu, or pressing the function key F5.

3 Pause execution by clicking on the Break button on the Toolbar, or by using the keystroke shortcut Ctrl+Break.

4 In the Immediate window, type the code:

```
HappyHour1.HappyAlert 5
```

You should be able to hear your computer beep five times.

> **Note** *If your computer uses a .WAV file as standard system beep, you may not hear exactly five beeps. This is because the Beep statement isn't capable of beeping synchronously; it simply tells the operating system to beep as fast as it can. If you don't hear five beeps, the system may be playing them so fast that the first beep doesn't have a chance to finish before the second and third beeps get going. You have the ability, however, to make the operating system play sounds in a more intelligent manner through the use of API calls. We'll discuss how to make API calls in Chapter 11, "Windows API and DLL Calls."*

Creating a Method That Returns a Value

Just as functions return values, methods can return values as well. Methods that return values don't occur very frequently in the Visual Basic world, but when they do, they can be very powerful.

If your method returns a value, you can use the value it returns in other code. For example, consider the OpenRecordset method of the Database object. This method is used to return a reference to a table, query, or another set of records in a database. The method takes a table name or query name as a parameter and returns a Recordset object variable.

A typical OpenRecordset method looks like this:

```
Dim MyDatabase As Database
Dim MyRecordset As Recordset
Set MyRecordset = MyDatabase.OpenRecordset("tblAddress")
```

The whole purpose of the OpenRecordset method, then, is to put the object that represents the table called tblAddress into the object variable MyRecordset.

This brings up an interesting point about methods that return values: If a method can act like a function and return a value, what is the difference between a method that returns a value and a property?

It makes sense that a database would have an OpenRecordset method rather than a Recordset property, since a single database can produce a potentially infinite number of recordsets. (This is not only because databases can have multiple tables, but because a Recordset object can point to any subset of records in a single table.)

To my way of thinking, for most purposes you're likely to run across, there isn't much functional difference between a property and a method that returns a value, except that a method that returns a value is a strange animal. Most Visual Basic programmers aren't expecting your methods to return values, so if you write a bunch of methods that return values, most Visual Basic programmers are going to become confused.

This means if you're ever tempted to include a property-like method in your control, you should strongly consider writing the procedure as a property instead. Properties are much easier for the average Visual Basic user to understand, they're much more commonly used, and they're generally more hygienic and morally upright.

Because you might have a case where you want to write a method that acts as a property, I'll toss out a demonstration of how to do it. The demonstration will calculate the number of minutes between now and happy hour in the form of a method called TellHowLong. Bear in mind this method could just as well be written as a read-only property.

The CalculateHowLong method won't be nearly as complicated to call as the OpenRecordset method of the Database object; in fact, it will be nearly identical to the WatchClock method. But instead of notifying the user with a message box saying how many minutes until happy hour, it will return the number of minutes as a long integer to the calling procedure (rather than displaying it on the screen, as in the previous example). If it is currently happy hour, the method returns the value True (or -1). To do this:

1 Open HappyHour's control designer.

2 Double-click on its control designer to open its code window.

3 Enter the following code:

```
Public Function CalculateHowLong()
' Returns the number of minutes
' until happy hour (similar to
' WatchClock).

    If mHappyHourBegin = "" Or mHappyHourEnd = "" Then
        CalculateHowLong = False
        Exit Function
    End If
```

```
        If Time > mHappyHourBegin And Time < mHappyHourEnd Then
            ' It's already happy hour
            CalculateHowLong = True
            Exit Function
        Else
            ' Calculate and return the number
            ' of minutes until happy hour
            CalculateHowLong = DateDiff("n", Time, mHappyHourBegin)
        End If
    End Function
```

Tip *Don't forget to declare methods that return values as Public Functions.*

You can see this code does almost the same thing as the WatchClock method, except instead of displaying a message box, it returns a value. The user could then use that value to take an action (such as displaying a message, updating a status label, or running some other code). Limiting the actions of your control in this way gives the user more flexibility.

Testing the CalculateHowLong Method

To demonstrate that your new method returns the number of minutes until happy hour, do the following:

1   Close the HappyHour control designer and open frmHHTestForm.

2   Run the EXE project by clicking on the Start button on the toolbar, choosing Run, Start from the menu, or pressing the function key F5.

3   Pause execution by clicking on the Break button on the toolbar or by using the keystroke combination Ctrl+Break.

4   In the Immediate window, set the beginning time of happy hour by typing the code:

```
HappyHour1.HappyHourBegin = #5:00:00 PM#
```

5   Set the ending time of happy hour by typing the following code:

```
HappyHour1.HappyHourEnd = #6:00:00 PM#
```

6   Execute your method by typing the following code:

```
Print HappyHour1.CalculateHowLong
```

The number of minutes between now and happy hour should be displayed in the Immediate window, unless it is currently happy hour, in which case the value True will be displayed.

Implementing Standard Methods

Although methods tend to be used less often than properties, certain methods should always be available. As a minimum, you should consider exposing the following methods in any control you create:

- ▶ Click
- ▶ DblClick
- ▶ KeyDown
- ▶ KeyPress
- ▶ KeyUp
- ▶ MouseDown
- ▶ MouseMove
- ▶ MouseUp

In general, you should think about controls that are similar to your control and expose as many methods as similar controls expose. For example, if your control works like a command button, consider exposing as many of the command button's methods as possible (such as Move, Drag, and SetFocus). In general, try to surprise the user of your control as little as possible; if you leave something out, have a good reason for doing so.

If your control is comprised of constituent controls, you should consider exposing as many methods of those constituent controls as possible, as long as it makes sense to do so.

For example, in order to control the height, width, and placement of your control, you should expose a Move method. (You can simply expose Height, Width, Top, and Left properties, but a Move method is faster to execute and easier to code.)

Often, you'll find yourself merging the methods of two or more constituent controls embedded in your control. For example, if the HappyHour control had a Move method, it would control the Height and Width properties of both its constituent Label control as well as its PictureBox control.

Any method can be mapped from a constituent control to your UserControl, either manually or through the ActiveX Control Interface Wizard. See Chapter 2, "Control Basics," for information on how to use the ActiveX Control Interface Wizard.

As a bare minimum, if your control is visible at runtime, it should expose a Refresh method. You can implement the Refresh method using the Refresh method of the UserControl object.

Using Methods Supplied by the Container

Just as properties and events are provided by the Extender object of the container, a number of methods are provided by the container as well. Because these methods are provided by the container, users can call them to manipulate your control; you do not have to write code to expose these methods.

In Visual Basic, the following methods are provided by the container:

▶ Drag

▶ Move

▶ SetFocus

▶ ShowWhatsThis

▶ ZOrder

Because they are supplied by the container, you do not need to write any code to make these methods available in your control; they are always available when your control is placed in a Visual Basic form. Remember, though, that because these methods are provided by the control's container, you cannot depend on these methods being available to you in all containers.

For more information on the container, see Chapter 7, "Interacting with the Container." For information on error-handling, see Chapter 15, "Debugging and Error Trapping."

Summary

In this chapter, you learned how to write public subroutines and functions that are exposed as methods in your control. In the next chapter, you'll learn how to take advantage of the container to provide additional functionality to your ActiveX control.

What Is a Container?

Using the Extender Object

Chapter 7
Interacting With the Container

ActiveX controls can't exist on their own. In order to function, they must be deposited into some other element of a running application, referred to as a *container*.

Often it is necessary to obtain information about or alter properties of the container. You can query the container in order to keep your control's properties in synch with the properties of its container; you can even alter certain properties of the container from your control.

What Is a Container?

A container can be a Visual Basic form, but it can also be any number of other things, including a Microsoft Access form, a Microsoft Excel spreadsheet, or a Web page displayed in Microsoft Internet Explorer. Other ActiveX controls can act as containers. A container can also be an application you've never even heard of at the time you authored your ActiveX control.

You have to refrain from overly-ambitious assumptions about what your control's container can do, because the ActiveX specification sets out few hard-and-fast requirements for what containers can be expected to do.

You can use the container to provide a number of handy features for your control. However, failing to plan for the various implementations of ActiveX control containers can leave your control without a leg to stand on, so to speak.

Visual Basic Containers

The most commonly used container in a Visual Basic project is the form. Virtually every Visual Basic application has at least one form, and almost every form contains at least one control.

In addition, Visual Basic controls can contain other controls. For example, PictureBox controls are sometimes used solely as containers, without even utilizing their primary property, the Picture.

The Visual Basic Frame control can also be a container; it is most commonly used as a container for OptionButton controls, although you can use it as a container for your controls as well.

Interacting with Non-VB Containers

As the number of applications that use Visual Basic for Applications (VBA) increases, you'll find there are more and more places in which ActiveX controls can be found. Now that Microsoft has licensed VBA version 5.0 to third-party developers, you'll likely start seeing ActiveX controls popping up in unexpected places, such as Microsoft Office applications, Visio drawing documents, and Adobe Photoshop. This is because support for ActiveX control hosting is a feature of VBA 5.0. For more information on the applications in which ActiveX controls can be used today, see Chapter 2, "Control Basics."

For a demonstration of how to embed an ActiveX control in a non-VB container (specifically, Microsoft Access) see Chapter 12.

> **Tip** *You can see a complete list of the companies that have licensed VBA 5.0, and are presumably going to adapt their applications to serve as ActiveX control hosts, on the Microsoft Web site, http://www.microsoft.com/vba/vbawho.htm.*

Using Microsoft Internet Explorer as a Container

Microsoft Internet Explorer's browser window is a container of its own, with its own effects on a control's behavior.

You use the Microsoft ActiveX control pad to embed an ActiveX control in a Web page. For more information on how to embed and program ActiveX controls in a Web page, see Chapter 13, "Using Your Control on the Web."

Using the Extender Object

The Extender object is your primary interface with the container. The properties exposed by the Extender object are the way you gain information about the container and alter its properties (for those container properties that are allowed to be changed by controls they contain).

The Extender object becomes available when the InitProperties or ReadProperties event is raised in your UserControl. It is not available in your control's Initialize event.

For more information on events in the UserControl object, see Chapter 5, "Handling and Raising Events."

Properties Exposed by the Visual Basic Extender Object

The Extender object of a container exposes a set of standard properties described in Table 7.1.

In addition to the standard Extender properties described in the preceding table, Visual Basic exposes an additional set of Extender properties listed in Table 7.2.

TABLE 7.1 STANDARD EXTENDER PROPERTIES

Property	Description	Data Type	Availability
Name	The name given to the control by the user (not the name of the container)	String	Read-only
Visible	Specifies whether the control is visible	Boolean	Read-write
Parent	An object that represents the control's container. You can get the name of the container (for example) by using the syntax Extender.Parent.Name.	Object	Read-only
Cancel	Specifies whether the control acts as the cancel button for the form; only used with command button-like controls	Boolean	Read-only
Default	Specifies whether the control acts as the default button for the form; only used with command button-like controls	Boolean	Read-only

TABLE 7.2 ADDITIONAL VB EXTENDER PROPERTIES

Property	Description	Data Type	Availability
Container	An object that represents the control's container. You can use this object to get additional properties of the container; for example, Extender.Container.Name will return the name of the container on which the control resides	Object	Read-only
DragIcon	A Picture object; the icon displayed when the control is being dragged	Object	Read-write
DragMode	Specifies manual or automatic drag-and-drop	Integer	Read-write
Enabled	Specifies whether the control can be accessed as an element of the user interface. This property requires special implementation.	Boolean	Read-only
Height	The height of the control	Integer	Read-write
HelpContextID	The ID of the help topic that is displayed when the user requests online help and the focus is on the control	Integer	Read-write
Index	The position this control occupies if it is in control array; if the control is not in an array, the property is not available	Integer	Read-write
Left	The position of the control in terms of how far it is from the left edge of its container	Integer	Read-write
TabIndex	The control's position in the tab order	Integer	Read-write
TabStop	Determines whether the control takes the focus when the user presses Tab to change the focus from one control to the next	Boolean	Read-write
Tag	A text string stored by the control and accessible in code	String	Read-write
ToolTipText	Text that appears when the user positions the mouse on top of the control for one second	String	Read-write
Top	The position of the control in terms of how far it is from the top edge of its container	Integer	Read-write
WhatThisHelpID	The ID of the control's What's This pop-up help topic	Integer	Read-write
Width	The width of the control	Integer	Read-write

In addition to these properties, the Visual Basic Extender object provides the following standard methods:

- ▶ Drag
- ▶ Move
- ▶ SetFocus
- ▶ ShowWhatsThis
- ▶ ZOrder
- ▶ DragDrop
- ▶ DragOver
- ▶ GotFocus
- ▶ LostFocus

All of these methods are similar to other standard methods you should be familiar with in Visual Basic controls.

Providing an Enabled Property

The Enabled property is a special case, since it is technically a container-supplied property, but it doesn't function until you write code for it. This has to do with the fact that controls that provide the Enabled property have both runtime and design-time behaviors that need to be managed by the Visual Basic IDE.

The code to add an Enabled property to your control is fairly simple:

```
Public Property Get Enabled() As Boolean
    Enabled = UserControl.Enabled
End Property


Public Property Let Enabled(ByVal NewValue As Boolean)
    UserControl.Enabled = NewValue
    PropertyChanged "Enabled"
End Property
```

Using the AmbientProperties Object to Synchronize Properties

The AmbientProperties object is another way for your control to interact with its container. You can inspect the properties of the AmbientProperties object to get cues about how your control's default properties should be set. You synchronize your control's properties with that of its container in your control's InitProperties event.

For example, to make the default BackColor of your control the same as the form on which it resides, you'd write the following code in your control's InitProperties event:

```
Private Sub UserControl_InitProperties()
    Debug.Print "InitProperties."
    BackColor = Ambient.BackColor
End Sub
```

To test this code, switch to an EXE project form, change the form's BackColor property to some color other than the default, then place the control on the form. You should be able to see that the control is the same color as the form (as shown in Figure 7.1).

The control's AmbientProperties object is typically accessed through the use of the Ambient property of the UserControl. For example, to determine whether the control is in design mode or run mode, you might use the following code. Ambient properties are always read-only.

```
If Ambient.UserMode = True Then
    Label1.Caption = "Running."
Else
    Label1.Caption = "Design mode."
End If
```

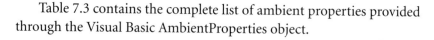

FIGURE 7.1
The control is the same color as the form.

Table 7.3 contains the complete list of ambient properties provided through the Visual Basic AmbientProperties object.

Using the AmbientChanged Event

The AmbientChanged event of the UserControl enables your control to keep up with changes in the container's properties. For example, you might want the background color of your control to always be the same as the background color of its container. To do this, you write code in the AmbientChanged event to make the BackColor property of your control the same as the ambient BackColor property. To see how to use the AmbientChanged event, do the following:

1 Create a new control project. Add the following code to the UserControl:

```
Private Sub UserControl_AmbientChanged(PropertyName As String)
    Debug.Print "AmbientChanged: " & PropertyName
    BackColor = Ambient.BackColor
End Sub
```

2 Close the code window and the control designer, then switch to the EXE test form. Add the control to an EXE project form.

3 Using the Properties window, change the BackColor property of the EXE project form. The background color of the UserControl will change to match the color you selected.

Using Extender Properties with the Containerator Project

The Containerator project exists on the CD-ROM that accompanies this book. This project is designed to test which container-provided properties are available in a container.

The Containerator control is comprised of a single text box. The control exposes one custom method, ShowContainerProperties. This method displays a list of the container properties accessible by the control.

TABLE 7.3   PROPERTIES OF THE AMBIENTPROPERTIES OBJECT

Property	Description
BackColor, ForeColor	Standard color properties
DisplayAsDefault	Determines if the control is the container's default button
DisplayName	Returns a string used as the name displayed in the control's error messages
Font	Standard font property
LocaleID	Used for internationalization purposes
MessageReflect	Indicates whether the container can handle message reflection. This property is ignored in a Visual Basic ActiveX control
Palette	Standard palette property
RightToLeft	Determines the text input method on a bidirectional system
ScaleUnits	A string that indicates the container's coordinate measurement system (such as points, pixels, or twips). This property is ignored in a Visual Basic ActiveX control.
ShowGrabHandles	Indicates whether the control should display grab handles in design mode. This property envisions a container that handles control resizing in some custom manner unlike that of Visual Basic; consequently this property is ignored in a Visual Basic ActiveX control.
ShowHatching	Indicates whether the control should display hatching around its edges when it is in design mode in a container designed to accommodate hatching. Visual Basic does not support design-mode hatching, but Microsoft Access, for example, does. Consequently, this property is ignored in a Visual Basic ActiveX control.
SupportsMnemonics	Indicates that the container supports access keys. This property is ignored in a Visual Basic ActiveX control.
TextAlign	Indicates the manner in which the container would like the control to align text. Values are 0 (general alignment), 1 (left), 2 (center), 3 (right), 4 (fill justify).
UIDead	Indicates whether the control should respond to user input. This property is ignored in a Visual Basic ActiveX control.
UserMode	Indicates whether the control is in a container that is in run mode (True) or design mode (False)

To build this control, do the following:

1 Start a new control project. Give the UserControl the name Containerator.

2 Place a text box on the control designer. Make the text box about the same size as the designer.

3 Give the text box the name txtInfo, set its Text property to nothing, and set its MultiLine property to True.

4 Double-click on the control designer to open its code window. Enter the code in Listing 7.1.

LISTING 7.1   The Containerator Control

```
Public Sub ShowContainerProperties()
' sticks info on container properties into
' txtInfo.


On Error Resume Next        ' very important

    txtInfo.Text = txtInfo.Text & "*Cancel: " & Extender.Cancel & vbCrLf
    If Err Then
        txtInfo.Text = txtInfo.Text & "*Cancel: Not available." & vbCrLf
        Err.Clear
    End If


    ' Container is an object, so use its Name
    txtInfo.Text = txtInfo.Text & "Container: "_
                    & Extender.Container.Name & vbCrLf
    If Err Then
        txtInfo.Text = txtInfo.Text & "Container: Not available." & vbCrLf
        Err.Clear
    End If


    txtInfo.Text = txtInfo.Text & "*Default: " & Extender.Default & vbCrLf
    If Err Then
        txtInfo.Text = txtInfo.Text & "*Default: Not available." & vbCrLf
        Err.Clear
    End If
```

LISTING 7.1   The Containerator Control (Continued)

```vb
' DragIcon can't be displayed textually

txtInfo.Text = txtInfo.Text & "DragMode: " & Extender.DragMode & vbCrLf
If Err Then
    txtInfo.Text = txtInfo.Text & "DragMode: Not available." & vbCrLf
    Err.Clear
End If


' Enabled requires some special fiddling around
txtInfo.Text = txtInfo.Text & "Enabled: " & Extender.Enabled & vbCrLf
If Err Then
    txtInfo.Text = txtInfo.Text & "Enabled: Not available." & vbCrLf
    Err.Clear
End If


txtInfo.Text = txtInfo.Text & "Height: " & Extender.Height & vbCrLf
If Err Then
    txtInfo.Text = txtInfo.Text & "Height: Not available." & vbCrLf
    Err.Clear
End If


txtInfo.Text = txtInfo.Text & "Index: " & Extender.Index & vbCrLf
If Err Then
    txtInfo.Text = txtInfo.Text & "Index: Not available." & vbCrLf
    Err.Clear
End If


txtInfo.Text = txtInfo.Text & "HelpContextID: "_
              & Extender.HelpContextID & vbCrLf
If Err Then
    txtInfo.Text = txtInfo.Text & "HelpContextID: Not available."_
                  & vbCrLf
    Err.Clear
End If


txtInfo.Text = txtInfo.Text & "Left: " & Extender.Left & vbCrLf
```

LISTING 7.1   The Containerator Control (Continued)

```
If Err Then
    txtInfo.Text = txtInfo.Text & "Left: Not available." & vbCrLf
    Err.Clear
End If


txtInfo.Text = txtInfo.Text & "*Name: " & Extender.Name & vbCrLf
If Err Then
    txtInfo.Text = txtInfo.Text & "*Name: Not available." & vbCrLf
    Err.Clear
End If


' Parent is actually an object, so you have to get its Name
txtInfo.Text = txtInfo.Text & "*Parent: " & Extender.Parent.Name_
                & vbCrLf
If Err Then
    txtInfo.Text = txtInfo.Text & "*Parent: Not available." & vbCrLf
    Err.Clear
End If


txtInfo.Text = txtInfo.Text & "TabIndex: " & Extender.TabIndex & vbCrLf
If Err Then
    txtInfo.Text = txtInfo.Text & "TabIndex: Not available." & vbCrLf
    Err.Clear
End If


txtInfo.Text = txtInfo.Text & "Tag: " & Extender.Tag & vbCrLf
If Err Then
    txtInfo.Text = txtInfo.Text & "Tag: Not available." & vbCrLf
    Err.Clear
End If


txtInfo.Text = txtInfo.Text & "TabStop: " & Extender.TabStop & vbCrLf
If Err Then
    txtInfo.Text = txtInfo.Text & "TabStop: Not available." & vbCrLf
    Err.Clear
End If
```

LISTING 7.1 **The Containerator Control (Continued)**

```
txtInfo.Text = txtInfo.Text & "ToolTipText: " & Extender.ToolTipText_
            & vbCrLf
If Err Then
    txtInfo.Text = txtInfo.Text & "ToolTipText: Not available." & vbCrLf
    Err.Clear
End If


txtInfo.Text = txtInfo.Text & "Top: " & Extender.Top & vbCrLf
If Err Then
    txtInfo.Text = txtInfo.Text & "Top: Not available." & vbCrLf
    Err.Clear
End If


txtInfo.Text = txtInfo.Text & "*Visible: " & Extender.Visible & vbCrLf
If Err Then
    txtInfo.Text = txtInfo.Text & "*Visible: Not available." & vbCrLf
    Err.Clear
End If


txtInfo.Text = txtInfo.Text & "WhatsThisHelpID: "_
            & Extender.WhatsThisHelpID & vbCrLf
If Err Then
    txtInfo.Text = txtInfo.Text & "WhatsThisHelpID: Not available."_
                & vbCrLf
    Err.Clear
End If


txtInfo.Text = txtInfo.Text & "Width: " & Extender.Width & vbCrLf
If Err Then
    txtInfo.Text = txtInfo.Text & "Width: Not available." & vbCrLf
    Err.Clear
End If


End Sub
```

5 Close the code window and close the control designer.

6 Switch to the EXE test form. Place an instance of the Containerator on the EXE test form.

7 Run the EXE test project by choosing the menu commands Run, Start (or by using the function key F5).

8 The project runs. Pause the project by selecting the menu command Run, Break, or by using the keystroke shortcut Ctrl+Break.

9 The EXE project pauses. In the Immediate window, type the code:

```
Containerator1.ShowContainerProperties
```

10 The Containerator displays a list of Extender properties it was able to retrieve.

There's a bunch of code in the Containerator control, but it all does pretty much the same thing: tests the properties of the Extender object to see if they're available. The code uses error-trapping to keep from crashing the host application in the (very likely) case where a particular property of the Extender object isn't available. For more information on error-trapping in a control, see Chapter 15, "Debugging and Error Trapping."

To test the Containerator control, drop it into an EXE project form and add a command button to the form. In the command button's Click event, write the code:

```
Containerator1.ShowContainerProperties
```

Run the EXE project, then click on the command button to execute the ShowContainerProperties method. Your form should display something similar to Figure 7.2.

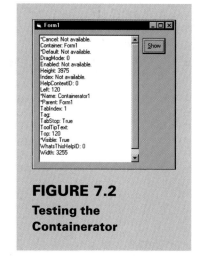

FIGURE 7.2

Testing the Containerator

The Container Property

The Container property of a control is not to be confused with the concept of the container. Visual Basic provides the Container property so you can change the container that a control is associated with.

For example, consider a form that contains three controls: two PictureBoxes and a Label control contained in the first PictureBox. You could cause the Label to jump from the first PictureBox to the second by writing the code:

```
Label1.Container = PictureBox2
```

The Container property doesn't have a direct bearing on control creation, although there's no reason why you couldn't build a control to take advantage of this property. (This property existed in versions of Visual Basic prior to version 5.0.) Hopefully with this short explanation of this property you won't furrow your brow, as I did, when you run across it in online Help.

Summary

In this chapter, you learned about the properties of the Visual Basic container and how non-Visual Basic containers differ from Visual Basic forms. We covered ambient properties supplied by the container, as well as using the Extender object as a way to interact with the container.

In the next chapter, you'll explore the concept of constituent controls in depth, putting together what you've learned in the last few chapters into one big mega-control of doom.

Inherent Controls

Acting on All the Constituent Controls in Your Control

Third-Party Controls

Locating Commercial Controls

Chapter 8
Using Constituent Controls

Although previous chapters have demonstrated how to create a control using other controls and how to use constituent controls' properties, events, and methods in your UserControl, a few issues remain.

You understand how to use constituent controls, but how do you know what controls are available? And if the controls provided by the Windows operating system and Visual Basic don't quite fit the bill, where can you turn to uncover more options? This chapter answers those questions.

Inherent Controls

Inherent controls are controls that exist as part of Windows. These controls exist on every user's machine and are generated in Visual Basic by the VB run-time module you distribute with every VB application you create. Consequently, inherent controls do not have OCX files.

> **Note** *If you're a seasoned Visual Basic veteran but you haven't used VB in a while, note that the number of inherent controls has increased since the release of Windows 95 and Windows NT 3.5. These controls are the ImageList, ListView, ProgressBar, RichTextBox, Slider, StatusBar, TabStrip, Toolbar, and TreeView controls.*

Here is a complete list of inherent controls in Visual Basic 5.0:

▶ CheckBox

▶ ComboBox

▶ CommandButton

▶ Data

▶ DriveListBox; DirListBox; FileListBox

▶ Frame

▶ HScrollBar; VScrollBar

▶ Label

▶ ListBox

105

▶ OptionButton

▶ PictureBox; Image

▶ Shape; Line

▶ TextBox

▶ Timer

The OLE container control does not appear in this list because while you can use an OLE container control in an EXE project, you can't use the OLE container control as a constituent control in your application, so distributing it is not an issue.

In addition to using inherent controls, you can use OLE controls (known as OCX controls) that predate the current ActiveX specification as constituent controls in your control project. So you can draw on the large market of third-party Visual Basic control vendors to provide constituent controls for your control projects, whether or not the vendor has positioned their controls as being explicitly ActiveX or not. The rule is: if it's a 32-bit OCX control, it should work in Visual Basic 5.0.

See "Locating Commercial Controls" later in this chapter for information on third-party control vendors.

Acting on All the Constituent Controls in Your Control

Occasionally you may wish to perform an action on all the constituent controls in your UserControl. To do this, you can use a With block with the controls collection. Here is an example of how this works:

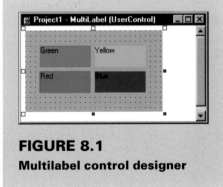

FIGURE 8.1
Multilabel control designer

1 Create a UserControl with a number of Label controls, all of different colors. The layout for this control is illustrated in Figure 8.1.

2 Write the following code in the UserControl's Click event:

```
Private Sub UserControl_Click()
    Dim c As Control
    For Each c In UserControl.Controls
        c.Caption = "Changed"
        c.BackColor = &H808000
    Next
End Sub
```

3 To test this code, you must place an instance of the control on an EXE project form, run the application, then click on a part of the control's background (not on one of the labels). You should be able to see the control change to resemble Figure 8.2.

You can see from this demonstration that you can use a For Each block to iterate through all of the constituent controls in your UserControl. You can use this same technique to apply changes to all the controls in your UserControl no matter how many controls your control project contains.

The code for this example is on the CD-ROM that accompanies this book.

FIGURE 8.2
Multilabel control after clicking

Third-Party Controls

There is no reason why you can't take existing ActiveX controls and extend their functionality by making them constituent controls of your controls. The problem with doing this is the same problem you face when you use an ActiveX control to begin with: when you use a third-party custom control, you put yourself at the mercy of the developer who created it. Be sure to bear this in mind before adding dozens of third-party controls to your project.

For example, let's say your control project uses a third-party ActiveX control designed to handle a number of different graphic formats. If you design your project around this control only to discover late in the project that the control doesn't handle a particular graphic format subtype in quite the way you expected, you'll be forced to work around the problem or compromise your project's feature set.

Third-party controls represent project dependencies that you have little or no control over. This is the case because with controls you purchase, you usually don't have access to the control's source code. And even if you had access to the control's source code, there's no guarantee that the control is written in a language you can deal with (many ActiveX controls are written in C++).

> **Note** *If you're considering using a third-party control as a part of your control, you may want to instead consider writing your own code to provide the same functionality. Things that seem impossible to do in Visual Basic, such as multimedia and Internet access, can often be accomplished with calls to the Windows API. For more information on this, see Chapter 11, "Making Windows API and DLL Calls."*

That said, using a third-party control can save you a great deal of development time, particularly if you're attempting to delve into a complex area of programming.

For example, in Chapter 14, you'll see an example of how to create a control project that is capable of sending electronic mail over the Internet. In order to do this with code, you'd need to know not only the Internet SMTP mail protocol, but the Winsock

API that enables a Windows application to send and receive data using the TCP/IP networking protocol (an API that is very poorly documented and very difficult to call from a VB perspective).

Using a constituent control resolves all those problems by wrapping them up in a programming paradigm that is easy to understand and consistent.

Licensing Considerations Applicable to Third-Party Controls

Whenever you use a commercial, third-party control in your Visual Basic application, you must have a license to use it. In most cases, an improperly installed or unlicensed ActiveX control won't be usable in Visual Basic, because the IDE won't let you instantiate a control unless the appropriate licensing information has been inserted into your computer's system registry.

But what happens when you purchase an off-the-shelf control from a software vendor, incorporate it into an ActiveX control project of your own, add a few enhancements to it, and redistribute the control to other programmers for their use? Are the other programmers–the users of your new, improved ActiveX control–also required to have a license for the third-party constituent control?

The answer is yes. The reason is simple: when a software company grants you a license to redistribute their ActiveX control, they're granting you a *runtime* license, not a *design-time* license. If you had the right to redistribute a runtime license, the control developer would be giving the control away. There'd be nothing to stop you from writing a wafer-thin wrapper that exposed 100% of the functionality of the constituent control, adding nothing new of your own, and reselling the knockoff version of the control on the street corners of America for $1.98.

> **Note** *Special considerations apply to the issue of licensing when you're sending a control over the Internet. In a nutshell, the license for a control you distribute resides on the Web server, and a temporary copy of the license is passed to each Web browser that encounters it. If your control supports licensing, then users who receive your control through a Web page do not have the ability to use your control at design time, unless they have purchased and installed a licensed copy of your control. For more information on licensing Web-distributed controls, see Chapter 13, "Using Your Control On The Web." For information on how to add licensing to controls you create, see Chapter 12, "Distributing Your Control."*

Locating Commercial Controls

There are a number of companies that specialize in selling ActiveX components; many of these companies have been around for years, having built their businesses on the 16-bit VBX market, switching over to OCXes and ActiveX controls as Microsoft goes through its seemingly annual paradigm revisions.

There are also quite a number of free controls out there. The number of freeware and shareware controls available will undoubtedly increase dramatically now that Visual Basic can be used to create controls.

Many sites permit you to download versions of controls for evaluation before you purchase them. Some of these controls are fully functional, others are demo versions that stop working after a period of time or display a message when they aren't fully licensed.

There are a number of Web sites that make information on ActiveX controls available for free. Here is a listing of the best among them, ranked in descending order of indispensability:

Microsoft

The Microsoft Web site, at http://www.microsoft .com/activex/gallery/, is the first place to look for ActiveX resources.

As of this writing, the site has over 100 controls available for download. Many of them are geared toward use in Web pages, but they'll work in VB applications as well.

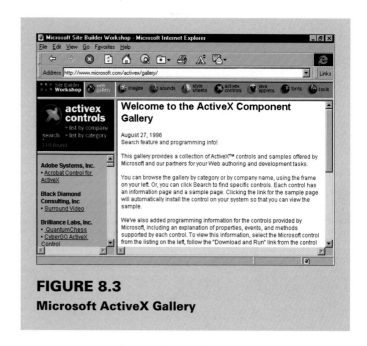

FIGURE 8.3
Microsoft ActiveX Gallery

CNET ActiveX.com

Found at http://www.activex.com, this site is the only ActiveX site to rival Microsoft's in terms of completeness and ease of navigation. It features a library of downloadable ActiveX controls and Visual Basic utilities divided into categories. It is extremely well-maintained and well-organized.

The site uses ActiveX controls for navigation, and it serves as a good example of how to use ActiveX to enhance your Web site. (The site works perfectly fine with Netscape as well as Internet Explorer.)

CNET's activex.com also contains links to news articles on ActiveX technology from CNET's techie news site, news.com.

TechWeb ActiveXpress

Found at http://www.techweb.com/activexpress/, this site has original articles and tutorials on how to use ActiveX technology on the Web, as well as a large download area with links to controls divided into categories. The full-text search feature is fast

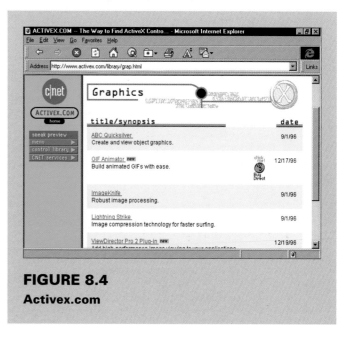

FIGURE 8.4
Activex.com

and easy to use, displaying only ActiveX-related information.

Like the CNET site, this site has a link to a daily news section (http://www.techweb.com/activexpress/xnews/xnews.html), that has a new story on ActiveX-related issues every two or three days.

Dave Central

Who is this Dave person and why does he have a Web site (at http://www.davecentral.com/activex.html) devoted to Microsoft development tools? I couldn't figure out the answer to that question, but he does have a pretty decent site.

The layout isn't quite as nice as the CNET site, and the number of ActiveX resources isn't nearly as extensive, but the purpose is pretty much the same: provide a library of downloadable software, mainly focusing on Internet-related tools, including ActiveX controls.

The site lets you do keyword searches to look up information but doesn't let you search by category or product. This means that when you do a search on the keyword "database," for example, you get a long list of database products (rather than a list of Visual Basic database products). This can be a bit inundating, but it's not impossible to navigate around.

BrowserWatch ActiveX Arena

At the time I hit their page (at http://browserwatch.iworld.com/activex.html),

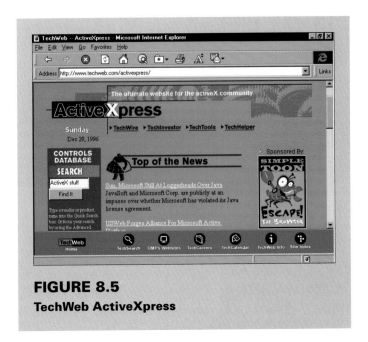

FIGURE 8.5
TechWeb ActiveXpress

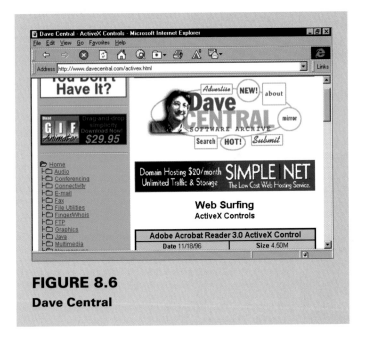

FIGURE 8.6
Dave Central

their big list of ActiveX controls (at http://browserwatch.iworld.com/activex/activex-big.html) was formatted a little funny and hard to read in MS Internet Explorer. Also, their search engine is confusing and returned way too much information. I got a few crazy error messages when performing searches, and it never returned anything useful.

The site seems fairly comprehensive, though, containing capsule descriptions of controls broken into categories, so if you don't mind navigating with links instead of a search engine, this is a good resource.

Catalog Resellers Specializing in VB Controls and Add-Ons

There are a number of resellers that specialize in selling Visual Basic add-ons, including ActiveX controls, that can be used as constituent controls in your control projects. Here (in no particular order) is a list of some retailers specializing in VB components.

Programmer's Paradise

1163 Shrewsbury Avenue
Shrewsbury, NJ 07702-4321
Voice: 800-445-7899
Fax: 908-389-9227
Fax-back (product information): 908-389-8173
Web: http://www.pparadise.com

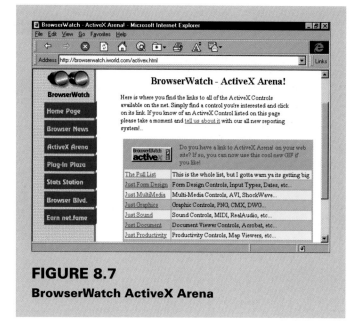

FIGURE 8.7
BrowserWatch ActiveX Arena

The Programmer's Paradise Web site offers online ordering. There are a few products that you can purchase online, then download immediately. They also have a fax-back server that can send information on products to your fax machine.

ActiveXtras

1905 Powers Ferry Road, Suite 100
Atlanta, GA 30339
Voice: 1-800-788-4794
Fax: 1-770-952-6388
Web: http://www.vbxtras.com, http://www.xtras.com/activex

The VBXtras Web site offers online ordering and downloading of controls. They have a great search engine that enables you to search for products by product name, keyword, category, or vendor. They also provide invariably flattering "evaluations" of the controls they sell, which can be helpful, I guess, if you're good at translating from the native Marketingese.

VB only Tools/Zachary Software

1090 Kapp Drive
Clearwater, FL 34625
Voice: 1-800-GO-BASIC
Fax: 813-461-2743
Web: http://www.zaccatalog.com/VBASIC/VBASIC.HTM
E-mail: sales@zaccatalog.com

The VB *only* Tools Web site permits you to perform keyword searches to find information on products you're interested in. You can download demo versions of some controls, but as of this writing there was no way to order online. They seem a little too proud of the fact that their Web site is rather rudimentary.

Summary

This chapter delved deeper into the perils of including constituent controls in the controls you develop. The chapter also provided information resources that should help you locate ActiveX resources you can use in your control.

In the next chapter, you'll look at controls you draw yourself, without any constituent controls.

Chapter 9
User-Drawn Controls

Until now, all of the example controls in this book have been comprised of one or more constituent controls. But that does not mean that all your ActiveX controls must be based on existing controls. Using Visual Basic's graphics methods, you have the ability to create controls that have totally unique graphical appearances. It's possible that you may already be familiar with these graphics methods; you'll find that implementing them in the context of a UserControl is quite straightforward.

A control that does not use constituent controls is referred to as a *user-drawn control*. (This is something of a misnomer, since the control isn't technically drawn by the *user*, it's drawn by your code, but we'll let that slide for now.)

When your control project is user-drawn, there are a number of things to watch out for. This chapter will take a look at those considerations and summarize the Visual Basic graphic methods available to you when you're creating your user-drawn control.

Graphics Methods

You can use Visual Basic's graphics methods to draw the interface and appearance of your control.

The graphics methods discussed in this section apply to forms and form-like objects, such as property pages, as well as your UserControl object. You can also use these graphics methods with the PictureBox control. In this chapter, I'll refer to any component of the Visual Basic interface that can be drawn on as a *Painting object*.

> **Note** *For experienced users of Visual Basic, much of this section will be review, but I'm including it here because I wanted all the important stuff to be in the same place, thereby satisfying my need for tidiness and organization. If you understand VB's graphics methods, you may wish to skim this section and skip to the middle of the chapter, where I'll relate it all back to control creation.*

Addressing the Coordinate System

When you're using any of these graphics methods, you are drawing in a coordinate system. Everything you do in this coordinate system must be addressed to a point in the system. In Visual Basic, the coordinate system of any Painting object has its origin in the upper-left corner of the Painting object; coordinates increase as you go down and to the right. Horizontal dimensions are expressed along the X axis, while vertical dimensions are expressed along the Y axis. This is illustrated in Figure 9.1.

So, for example, to draw a line from the upper left corner of the form to the lower right corner of the form, you'd instruct the graphics method to draw a line from point (0,0) (that is, zero units on the X axis, and zero units on the Y axis) to point (Me.Width, Me.Height). If the Painting object were 2000 units wide and 3000 units high, the destination point for your line would be (2000, 3000).

> **Note** *In Visual Basic, the keyword Me refers to the currently executing form (or other class). In the code examples in this book, it's invariably used as shorthand in situations where you don't care to specify (or don't know) the name of the form that contains the control.*

Visual Basic's standard method of measurement is the *twip*. There are 1,440 twips to the inch, although the actual size of a twip on your screen will vary according to the resolution of your screen and the size of your monitor.

Since a twip is much smaller than the resolution of a pixel on any computer monitor you're likely to run across in your lifetime, it makes sense to express on-screen graphics methods in another measurement system. Visual Basic gives you the ability to express units on the coordinate system in inches, points (there are 72 points to the inch), millimeters, and so forth.

You can change the measurement system of a Painting object by using its ScaleMode property. For example, the code:

```
Me.ScaleMode = vbCentimeters
```

sets the coordinate system of the current form to centimeters.

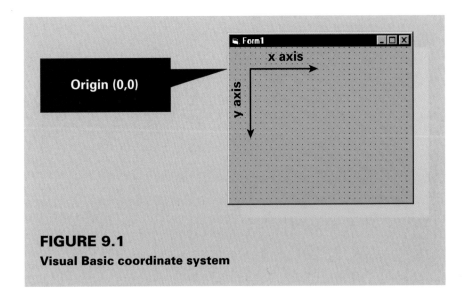

FIGURE 9.1
Visual Basic coordinate system

Visual Basic Painting objects also provide graphics properties (TwipsPerPixelX and TwipsPerPixelY) that enable you to convert between twips and pixels. For simplicity's sake, in this chapter I'll use pixels (signified by the Visual Basic ScaleMode constant vbPixels).

The Line Method

The Line method draws a line between two points. The syntax of this method is:

```
object.Line (startX, startY) - (endX, endY)[, color, BF]
```

The parameters startX and startY designate the starting point of the line you're drawing. The values *endX* and *endY* indicate where the line ends. The optional *color* argument is a long integer corresponding to a Windows color. If you include the B argument, then the Line method will draw a box instead of a line. If you include the F argument, then the Line method will draw a filled box. (Of course, it's only meaningful to include the F argument if you also include the B argument.)

> **Note** *The syntax of this method is a little kooky, as you might have noticed, mainly because it's a throwback to the early days of Basic. The funny syntax is retained for compatibility with earlier versions of the language.*

To see how the Line method works, try this example. The code draws a simulated text box on the center of the form. You might find this code helpful as an example of how to create 3-D user interface effects for your controls.

To see how this works, create a command button on the EXE project form. In the button's Click event, type the following code:

```
Private Sub Command2_Click()

    Me.ScaleMode = vbPixels


    lngStartX = 20
    lngStartY = 20
    lngEndX = 200
    lngEndY = 35

' white box
Line (lngStartX, lngStartY)-(lngEndX, lngEndY), _
    RGB(255, 255, 255), BF

' ** black lines
' vertical
```

```
Line (lngStartX - 1, lngStartY - 1)-(lngStartX - 1, lngEndY + 1), _
    RGB(0, 0, 0)
' horizontal
Line (lngStartX - 1, lngStartY - 1)-(lngEndX + 1, lngStartY - 1), _
    RGB(0, 0, 0)

' ** dark grey lines
' vertical
Line (lngStartX - 2, lngStartY - 2)-(lngStartX - 2, lngEndY + 2), _
    RGB(128, 128, 128)
' horizontal
Line (lngStartX - 2, lngStartY - 2)-(lngEndX + 2, lngStartY - 2), _
    RGB(128, 128, 128)

' ** white lines
' vertical
Line (lngEndX + 2, lngStartY - 2)-(lngEndX + 2, lngEndY + 3), _
    RGB(255, 255, 255)
' horizontal
Line (lngStartX - 2, lngEndY + 2)-(lngEndX + 2, lngEndY + 2), _
    RGB(255, 255, 255)

End Sub
```

This code gives you a feel for the different flavors of the Line method. The first Line method takes the optional BF parameter, drawing a white box on the form. The remaining Line methods draw lines in black and gray around the box in order to give it that three-dimensional look that the kids are so crazy about these days.

The Circle Method

The Circle method draws a circle. Its syntax looks like this:

```
object.Circle (x, y), radius, [color, start, end, aspect]
```

The x and y arguments determine the midpoint of the circle. The radius argument sets the radius of the circle. The optional *color* argument is a long integer corresponding to a Windows color. The optional *start* and *end* arguments are single values that determine the start and end points for an arc (rather than a complete circle). The optional *aspect* argument determines the aspect ratio for the circle. Setting an aspect ratio other than 1 will produce an ellipse rather than a perfect circle.

To see how the Circle method works, try the following code. This code draws a bulls-eye on the center of the a form:

```
Private Sub Command3_Click()


    Me.ScaleMode = vbTwips


    lngCenterX = Me.Width / 2
    lngCenterY = Me.Height / 2
    Me.FillStyle = vbFSSolid    ' constant from VB's object library


    Me.FillColor = RGB(0, 0, 255)
    Circle (lngCenterX, lngCenterY), Me.Width / 5, Me.FillColor


    Me.FillColor = RGB(255, 255, 255)
    Circle (lngCenterX, lngCenterY), Me.Width / 10, Me.FillColor


    Me.FillColor = RGB(255, 0, 0)
    Circle (lngCenterX, lngCenterY), Me.Width / 20, Me.FillColor


End Sub
```

When you run this code and click on the button, the form should look something like the one in Figure 9.2.

The PSet Method

You can use the PSet method to draw an individual pixel on an object. The syntax of the PSet method looks like this:

```
object.PSet (x, y) [, color]
```

The *x* argument represents a horizontal position of the point in the coordinate system. The *y* argument represents the vertical position. The optional *color* argument is a long integer corresponding to a Windows color.

FIGURE 9.2
Example of Circle method

To test how the PSet method works, create an EXE project form with a command button. In the command button's Click event, type the following code:

```
Private Sub Command1_Click()


intMaxX = Me.Width
```

```
intMaxY = Me.Height

For x = 1 To 5000
    intX = Int(intMaxX - 1) * Rnd
    intY = Int(intMaxY - 1) * Rnd
    Me.PSet (intX, intY)
Next x


End Sub
```

This code demonstrates the PSet method by painting the form with random pixels. To see how it works, run the EXE project, then click on the button. The form should look like the one shown in Figure 9.3. Because of the way this code is written, the density of the pixels drawn on your screen will be a function of the dimensions of your Form1.

The Print Method

The Print method renders text on the target object. Here is the Print method's syntax:

```
object.Print text
```

The *text* argument represents the text to be printed. It can be any string.

FIGURE 9.3

Example of PSet method

Tip *There are additional, seldom-used arguments to the Print method that are included primarily for compatibility with older versions of Visual Basic. For example, the Print method provides support for printing tabulated lists in columns. See the Print method topic in Visual Basic online help for more information on these arguments.*

Here is an example of code that uses the Print method. This code displays a word on the form over and over, in a range of colors (or, rather, shades of gray):

```
Private Sub Command5_Click()
    Me.FontBold = True
    Me.Font = "Arial"
    Me.FontSize = 36


    Randomize Timer


    For x = 1 To 255
        Green = Int(255 * Rnd + 1)
        Blue = Int(255 * Rnd + 1)
```

```
        Me.CurrentX = x
        Me.CurrentY = x
        Me.ForeColor = RGB(x, Green, Blue)
        Print "Spoon!"
    Next x


End Sub
```

The effect this code produces when run is illustrated in Figure 9.4

The font face and style used by the Print method is a function of the Drawing object's font properties (such as FontSize and FontBold). These properties must be set before you use the Print method, because you can't change the way the text is rendered once it's been placed on the painting object.

The Cls Method

You can clear the painting area by using the Cls method. The Cls method takes no arguments; its syntax is:

```
object.Cls
```

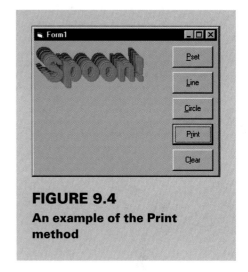

FIGURE 9.4
An example of the Print method

To see how this works, add a command button to your example form. In the command button's Click event, add the code:

```
Me.Cls
```

Then run the EXE project. Click on one of the buttons that generates graphics on the form, then click on the Cls button. You should be able to see that the Cls method clears all the graphics on the form.

The Paint Event

In a user-drawn control, the graphics methods that comprise the control's appearance are placed in the control's Paint event.

Here are some things to watch out for when writing code in the Paint event of a UserControl:

▶ Don't set the BackStyle property of your user-drawn UserControl to True. Doing this will short-circuit the code you place in the Paint event and cause your control to be invisible.

▶ Don't place a DoEvents statement in the Paint event.

▶ Setting the AutoRedraw property of your UserControl to False will result in faster performance.

Example of a User-Drawn Control: The Hexagon Control

Let's put all that together in an example. The Hexagon control is similar to the Shape control that comes with Visual Basic, except it draws a regular, six-sided figure. It is a completely user-drawn control; the code to draw the hexagon is in the UserControl's Paint event. The code for this control is on the CD-ROM that accompanies this book. To create the Hexagon control, insert the following code in a control designer called Hexagon:

```
' Declarations section

Private lngSideLength As Long
Private lngXPoint0 As Long, lngXPoint1 As Long
Private lngXPoint2 As Long, lngXPoint3 As Long
Private lngYPoint0 As Long, lngYPoint1 As Long
Private lngYPoint2 As Long

' The business end of the code

Private Sub UserControl_Paint()

    lngSideLength = (UserControl.Width / 2)
    lngXPoint0 = 0
    lngXPoint1 = lngXPoint0 + (lngSideLength / 2)
    lngXPoint2 = lngXPoint1 + lngSideLength
    lngXPoint3 = lngXPoint2 + lngXPoint1 - 10


    lngYPoint0 = 0
    lngYPoint1 = CLng(lngSideLength * (Sqr(3) / 2))
    lngYPoint2 = lngYPoint1 * 2


    DrawWidth = 1
    Line (lngXPoint1, lngYPoint0)-(lngXPoint2, lngYPoint0)
    Line (lngXPoint2, lngYPoint0)-(lngXPoint3, lngYPoint1)
    Line (lngXPoint3, lngYPoint1)-(lngXPoint2, lngYPoint2)
    Line (lngXPoint2, lngYPoint2)-(lngXPoint1, lngYPoint2)
    Line (lngXPoint1, lngYPoint2)-(lngXPoint0, lngYPoint1)
    Line (lngXPoint0, lngYPoint1)-(lngXPoint1, lngYPoint0)
```

```
End Sub


Private Sub UserControl_Resize()
    ' Make sure the control always
    ' fits dimensions of the hexagon
    UserControl.Height = UserControl.Width * (Sqr(3) / 2) + 20
End Sub
```

You can see that the Paint event is responsible for drawing the appearance of the control.

One cool thing about this code is that because the drawing in the Paint event is based on the dimensions of the UserControl, the hexagon always fills the available area of the control. If you resize the control, the hexagon redraws so it's exactly the right size.

The Refresh Method

Anytime you change the appearance of your user-drawn control, the control must execute the Refresh method. The Refresh method causes the code in your control's Paint event to run, thereby redrawing the control.

For example, let's say you want to enable the Hexagon control to draw in a color chosen by the user. To do this, you create a ForeColor property for the control and execute the Refresh method in the ForeColor's Property Let procedure. Here are the steps to implementing this feature in the Hexagon control:

1 Add the following code to the declarations section of the Hexagon control. This variable stores the state of the control's foreground color.

```
Private mlngForeColor As Long
```

2 Alter the code in the control's Paint event so that it takes advantage of the new property. The code should look like this:

```
Private Sub UserControl_Paint()
    .
    .
    .
    Line (lngXPoint1, lngYPoint0)-(lngXPoint2, lngYPoint0), mlngForeColor
    Line (lngXPoint2, lngYPoint0)-(lngXPoint3, lngYPoint1), mlngForeColor
    Line (lngXPoint3, lngYPoint1)-(lngXPoint2, lngYPoint2), mlngForeColor
    Line (lngXPoint2, lngYPoint2)-(lngXPoint1, lngYPoint2), mlngForeColor
    Line (lngXPoint1, lngYPoint2)-(lngXPoint0, lngYPoint1), mlngForeColor
    Line (lngXPoint0, lngYPoint1)-(lngXPoint1, lngYPoint0), mlngForeColor
```

3   Next, add Property Let and Property Get procedures for the new property:

```
Public Property Get ForeColor() As OLE_COLOR
    ForeColor = mlngForeColor
End Property


Public Property Let ForeColor(ByVal NewValue As OLE_COLOR)
    mlngForeColor = NewValue
    PropertyChanged "ForeColor"
    Refresh    ' this redraws the control with the new color
End Property
```

Note *Don't forget to declare color properties as type OLE_COLOR so a color palette is displayed in the Properties window when the user changes the ForeColor property.*

If you place an instance of the Hexagon control onto an EXE project form and then change its ForeColor property, you should be able to see that you can change the color of the control to any Windows color. The control should look like Figure 9.5.

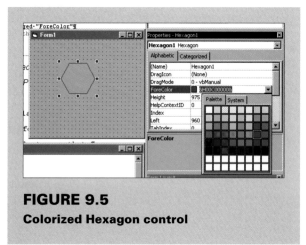

FIGURE 9.5
Colorized Hexagon control

Displaying Your Control As Disabled

If your control has an Enabled property and that property has been set to False, you should provide some graphical indication that the control is disabled. You do this by providing logic in the control's Paint method.

There is no standardized way of graphically indicating that a control is disabled, but in general, drawing a disabled control involves graying out the colored portions of the control. For ideas on how to do that, take a look at some existing controls. Figure 9.6 shows some standard Windows controls in their disabled state.

In order to implement a graphical display of Enabled = False, you need to inspect the Enabled property in the Paint event using an If...Then statement. If Enabled is False, the Paint event draws the disabled version of the control. If Enabled is True, the Paint event draws the enabled version of the control.

FIGURE 9.6
Disabled controls

Displaying the Default Property

A control is said to be the *default control* when its Default property is set to True. This control will always be given the focus when the form it resides on is first displayed.

You see this most frequently in situations where the user is confronted with a dialog box containing OK and Cancel buttons; assuming the user does not move the focus to some other control in the dialog box, the user can either click on OK or press the Enter key to quickly confirm the dialog box settings.

You should draw a thick black line around your control when all of the following things are true:

▶ Your control acts as a command button

▶ Your control has a Default property

▶ The Default property is set to True

▶ No other control has the focus

The tricky part about this is determining whether another control residing on the same form as your control has the focus. Fortunately, Visual Basic helps you out here, through the DisplayAsDefault property of the AmbientProperties object. The DisplayAsDefault property is a Boolean property that tells your control whether it should draw itself as the default button.

> **Note** *Exactly how thick the line should be is an aesthetic choice you'll make depending on what your control looks like; take a look at some existing controls for hints. In a user-drawn control, you'll use Visual Basic graphics methods to draw the border.*

As an example, let's say you want to change the Hexagon control into a hexagonal button control. To do this:

1 Open the control's designer. In the Properties window, change the DefaultCancel property to True. This tells Visual Basic that the control is capable of acting as a default or cancel button. Because the Cancel and Default properties are provided by the container, you don't have to write any code to implement these properties; they appear automatically when you set the DefaultCancel property to True.

2 Change the control's Paint property as follows:

```
Line (lngXPoint1, lngYPoint0)-(lngXPoint2, lngYPoint0), _
    RGB(255, 255, 255)
Line (lngXPoint2, lngYPoint0)-(lngXPoint3, lngYPoint1), _
    RGB(128, 128, 128)
Line (lngXPoint3, lngYPoint1)-(lngXPoint2, lngYPoint2), _
    RGB(128, 128, 128)
```

```
Line (lngXPoint2, lngYPoint2)-(lngXPoint1, lngYPoint2), _
    RGB(128, 128, 128)
Line (lngXPoint1, lngYPoint2)-(lngXPoint0, lngYPoint1), _
    RGB(128, 128, 128)
Line (lngXPoint0, lngYPoint1)-(lngXPoint1, lngYPoint0), _
    RGB(255, 255, 255)

If Extender.Default = True Then
    Line (0, 0)-(Width - 20, Height - 20), 0, B
End If
```

3 To redraw the control when the user changes the Default property at design time, insert the following code in the AmbientChanged event of the UserControl:

```
Private Sub UserControl_AmbientChanged(PropertyName As String)
    If PropertyName = "DisplayAsDefault" Then
        Refresh
    End If
End Sub
```

4 To trap the user action when the Default or Cancel properties have been set to True, use the following code:

```
Private Sub UserControl_AccessKeyPress(KeyAscii As Integer)

    Select Case KeyAscii
        Case 13  ' user hit enter when Default property True
        MsgBox "Default."

        Case 27  ' user cancelled when Cancel property True
        MsgBox "Cancel."
    End Select

End Sub
```

You will, of course, want to replace the MsgBox statements in the AccessKeyPress event with something more meaningful. Typically, when the AccessKeyPress event of a command button detects that the user has pressed Enter when the Default property is True, it triggers the Click event.

To test the new version of the Hexagon control, do the following:

1 Switch to the EXE project form that contains an instance of the Hexagon control.

2 In the Properties window, set the Default property of Hexagon1 to True.

3 Run the EXE project by pressing F5.

4 After the program runs, press Enter. The MsgBox statement in the UserControl's AccessKeyPressed event is triggered, producing the message box illustrated in Figure 9.7.

The fact that the control has been set as the default means that it responds to the user pressing the Enter key. In this case, pressing Enter causes the message box to be displayed.

Showing That Your Control Has the Focus

If your control can take the focus, then it should graphically display that is has the focus. Standard Windows controls show that they have the focus by drawing a thin, dotted line around themselves. In Figure 9.8, the command button with the caption "Martini" has the focus.

The thin dotted line drawn around a control to indicate that it has the focus is called the *focus rectangle*. You can write custom graphics methods to draw the focus rectangle, or you can use a standard Windows API function called DrawFocusRect. This function only works for rectangular controls; if you create a non-rectangular control (such as our hexagonal button), you must manage the focus rectangle yourself.

For more information on making Windows API calls, see Chapter 11, "Making Windows API and DLL Calls."

Summary

This chapter explored the triumphs and pitfalls of rendering your control's appearance using Visual Basic graphics methods. In addition, we covered how you can use VB's graphics methods to render your control, including methods to display controls as disabled and in focus.

In the next chapter, you'll delve into a mixed bag of miscellaneous control features, effects, and tricks to give your control the kind of full-featured interface that users expect.

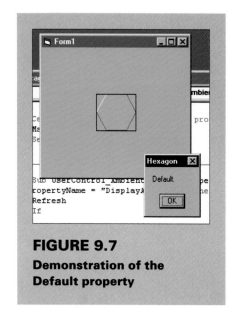

FIGURE 9.7
Demonstration of the Default property

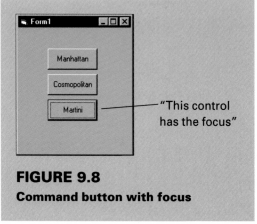

FIGURE 9.8
Command button with focus

Giving Your
Control a
Transparent
Background

Design Time,
Runtime, Read-Only
Properties

Permitting Your Control
to Act as a Container

Implementing Access Keys

Controls That Are Invisible
at Runtime

Controls That Align
to the Edges of Forms

Adding an About Box

Project Templates

Adding a Toolbox Bitmap

Chapter 10
Window Dressing

This chapter covers a mixed bag of ActiveX control features. Many of these features are cosmetic in nature, but even the seemingly superficial features can be crucial if you want to give your control the feature set and interface that users expect.

This chapter is chock-full of demonstrations that show how each feature works; many of the demonstrations include information on non-obvious techniques you can use to achieve a number of interesting effects in your ActiveX control project.

Giving Your Control a Transparent Background

Enabling your control to show the background of its container is a feature that's particularly useful when your control is based on several constituent controls.

You can make the background of your UserControl property transparent by setting its BackStyle property to 0 - Transparent. Bear in mind that making the background of your control transparent creates a significant performance hit on your control because it must do much more calculation in order to redraw itself.

Design Time, Runtime, Read-Only Properties

Although some properties are design-time-only or runtime-only, most properties can be set at any time. The nature of each property will help you determine whether your control should expose properties that can't be set at runtime or design time. You should obviously avoid restricting user access to properties if you can help it.

You can make a property design-time-only or runtime-only by inspecting the UserMode property of the Ambient object in the Property Let procedure. If the UserMode property is True, then it is runtime. If the property is False, the control is in design mode.

Demonstration

Here's a demonstration of a property that can't be set at runtime.

1   Create a new control project. Give the UserControl the name ArkeyMalarkey.

2 Enter the following code in the ArkeyMalarkey control's code window:

```
' Declarations


Private mlngArkeyMalarkey As Long



Public Property Get ArkeyMalarkey() As Long
    ArkeyMalarkey = mlngArkeyMalarkey
End Property



Public Property Let ArkeyMalarkey(ByVal lngNewValue As Long)

    If Ambient.UserMode = True Then
        ' It's runtime.
        MsgBox "You ninny! You can't set this at runtime!"
    Else
        mlngArkeyMalarkey = lngNewValue
    End If


End Property
```

3 To test this code, close the code window, close the control designer, and switch to the EXE project test form. Create an instance of the ArkeyMalarkey control on the form.

4 You should be able to see the control's ArkeyMalarkey property in the Properties window. Change it to some other value. You should be able to do this with no problem. This demonstrates that the property can be changed at design time.

5 Now run the project by choosing the menu command Run, Start. Pause execution by clicking on the Pause button on the toolbar (or by pressing Ctrl+Break on your keyboard).

6 If the Immediate window isn't already visible, press Ctrl+G to make it visible. In the Immediate window, enter the code

```
ArkeyMalarkey1.ArkeyMalarkey = 14
```

7 When you press Enter, the message box should pop up, as illustrated in Figure 10.1. The property will be left unchanged. This property cannot be changed at runtime.

> **Note** *When the user attempts to set a design-time-only property at runtime, your control should raise an error, rather than display a message box, as this simplified demonstration does. For more information on raising errors, see Chapter 15, "Debugging and Error Trapping."*

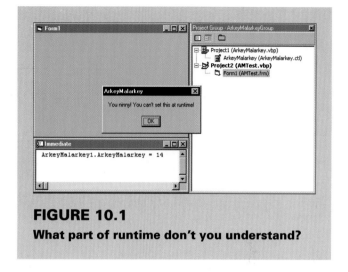

FIGURE 10.1
What part of runtime don't you understand?

Permitting Your Control to Act as a Container

Just as a Visual Basic form can contain one or more ActiveX controls, a control can also contain one or more ActiveX controls. Not all controls can act as containers for other controls; examples of controls that can contain other controls include the PictureBox control and the Frame control.

Controls are contained in other controls for a variety of reasons. For example, the Frame control gives end users a choice of options, usually presented in the form of multiple OptionButton controls.

Sometimes controls are contained in other controls for cosmetic purposes. A PictureBox grouping of a collection of controls enables you to place a different color or bitmap behind the control group. Additionally, when you move the PictureBox control, all the controls contained in it move along with it, which can be a real help when you're coding complicated Resize events.

To let your UserControl contain other controls, you set its ControlContainer property to True. Once you do that, users can deposit a hypothetically unlimited number of controls in it. The only problem with this, as the following demonstration shows, is writing code to handle them.

Demonstration

To see how to program a control that has the ability to host other controls, you'll create a control called ViewPort. This control is designed to conserve screen space by housing a large number of controls in a very small space on the screen. It can do this because not all of the controls are visible at once; the user must scroll left or right to locate the correct control within the ViewPort control. So, this control trades off ease of use for the end user with conservation of screen space.

The ViewPort control consists of nothing more than some code and a constituent horizontal scroll bar control. The scroll bar enables the user to scroll left and right to view all the controls.

To create this control:

1 Start a new control project. Give the UserControl the name ViewPort.

2 Add a horizontal scroll bar control (HScroll) to the UserControl. It doesn't matter where you place the scroll bar, since its dimensions and position on the control will be determined by the UserControl's Resize event. The control designer will look like Figure 10.2.

3 In the Properties window, set the UserControl's ControlContainer property to True.

4 Set the HScrollBar's LargeChange property to 100, and its SmallChange property to 20.

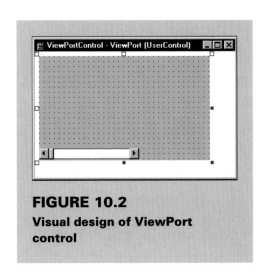

FIGURE 10.2
Visual design of ViewPort control

5 You'll need to write some code to make the scroll bar stretch to fill the width of the UserControl. The code looks like this:

```
Private Sub UserControl_Resize()
    HScroll1.Move 0, Height - HScroll1.Height, Width
End Sub
```

6 Next, you need to create a new property for the control. This property will dictate the scrollable area of the control (as opposed to the *visible* width of the control, which is determined by the control's Width property). Call this property VirtualWidth. To implement it, enter the following code:

```
' Declaration
Private mlngVirtualWidth As Long
Private Sub UserControl_WriteProperties(PropBag As PropertyBag)
    PropBag.WriteProperty "VirtualWidth", mlngVirtualWidth, Width
End Sub

Private Sub UserControl_ReadProperties(PropBag As PropertyBag)
    mlngVirtualWidth = PropBag.ReadProperty("VirtualWidth", Width)
End Sub

Public Property Get VirtualWidth() As Long
    VirtualWidth = mlngVirtualWidth
```

```
End Property

Public Property Let VirtualWidth(ByVal lngNewValue As Long)
    mlngVirtualWidth = lngNewValue
    HScroll1.Max = lngNewValue
End Property
```

7 In the Declarations section of the code, declare an internal variable that stores the value of the horizontal scroll bar. You'll use this variable in the next step.

```
Private mlngPreviousScroll As Long
```

8 Add the following code to the horizontal scroll bar's Change event. This code moves all of the controls contained in the control to the left or right whenever the scroll bar is changed. This will give the end user the impression that she is panning left or right when she clicks on the scroll bar, when in fact the controls are physically being moved each time she clicks.

```
Private Sub HScroll1_Change()
    Dim c As Control
    For Each c In UserControl.ContainedControls
        c.Left = c.Left + (mlngPreviousScroll - HScroll1.Value)
    Next
    mlngPreviousScroll = HScroll1.Value
End Sub
```

This is the trickiest piece of code in the control. It uses the ContainedControls collection of the UserControl object to iterate through all the controls contained in the control, adjusting their Left properties so it appears as if the control is panning across them. In fact, though, the control isn't panning at all; the controls themselves are moved left or right.

9 The control is ready to be sited on the form. Close the control designer and return to the test EXE project form.

10 Create an instance of the ViewPort control on the EXE project form. Resize the control so it's big enough to accommodate three CommandButton controls.

11 Create a new CommandButton on the form.

12 With the CommandButton still selected, choose the menu command Edit, Cut (or use the keyboard shortcut Ctrl+X).

13 Select the ViewPort control and select the menu command Edit, Paste (or use the keyboard shortcut Ctrl+V). This causes the command button to be contained by the ViewPort control.

14 Repeat the process for two more command buttons, and adjust their position and Caption properties so they look like Figure 10.3.

15 Resize the ViewPort control so that only one of the three buttons is visible.

16 Before you run the EXE project, you must add one line of code to the EXE project form. This code sets the VirtualWidth property as a function of the width of the control. Enter the following code in the Load event of the form:

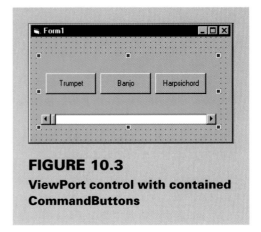

FIGURE 10.3
ViewPort control with contained CommandButtons

```
Private Sub Form_Load()
    ' Set virtual width of view port to
    ' the right side of the rightmost command button
    ViewPort1.VirtualWidth = Command3.Left + Command3.Width
End Sub
```

17 Run the EXE project by choosing the menu command Run, Start (or by using the function key F5). You should be able to use the scroll bar to scroll back and forth to see all of the buttons contained in the ViewPort control.

The ViewPort control should work for an unlimited number of contained controls, as long as the code you entered in the Load event of Form1 that sets the control's VirtualWidth property takes all the controls stored in the control into account; the property must always be large enough to store the rightmost control contained within.

> **Note** *If you feel like getting a little more show-offy, you might consider adding a vertical scroll bar and some more code to this control to make it scroll in two dimensions, both horizontally and vertically. Such a control would be a very handy way to view large graphics in a small area on screen.*

Implementing Access Keys

An *access key* is a key that the user presses in combination with the Alt key. Controls can be programmed to respond to access keys. A typical use for this feature is for a control to take the focus in response to an access key, but you could have a control respond by executing a method.

Controls that can respond to access keys have a Caption property that responds to the ampersand (&) character in a special way. When the user assigns a caption that contains an ampersand, it means that the next character in the caption string is to be treated as that control's access key. A control with a caption of ABC&DEFG would then have an access key of d (and the caption would display as ABC<u>D</u>EFG). So, to produce the result specified in this caption, the user would press ALT+D.

For example, let's say you have a form with a frame and two option buttons. The first option button has the caption &Jes, and the second button has the caption &Ne. (I'm talkin' Esperanto here; try to keep up with me.) Pressing Alt+J on your keyboard is the equivalent of clicking the Jes button, while pressing Alt+N is the equivalent of clicking Ne, as illustrated in Figure 10.4.

On the other hand, if you create a CommandButton control and give it the Caption property of J&erky, the control's access key becomes Alt+E. If you run the program and press Alt+J, the CommandButton's Click event is triggered.

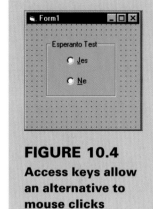

FIGURE 10.4

Access keys allow an alternative to mouse clicks

Access Keys with Constituent Controls

If you rely on the behavior of constituent controls to provide access key behavior, you don't have to write any code at all. To see how this works, do the following:

1 Set up a new control project with constituent Label and TextBox controls. Be sure to add the Label first, and then the Text Box.

2 Give the UserControl the name TextLabel.

3 Set the Text property of the constituent TextBox to nothing. The control should look like Figure 10.5.

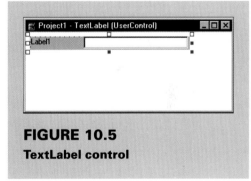

FIGURE 10.5

TextLabel control

4 Insert the following code to delegate a Caption property to the Label control:

```
Property Get Caption() As String
    Caption = Label1.Caption
End Property


Property Let Caption(NewCaption As String)
    Label1.Caption = NewCaption
End Property


Private Sub UserControl_ReadProperties(PropBag As PropertyBag)
    Caption = PropBag.ReadProperty("Caption")
End Sub
```

```
Private Sub UserControl_WriteProperties(PropBag As PropertyBag)
    PropBag.WriteProperty "Caption", Label1.Caption
End Sub
```

5 Close the form designer and switch to the EXE project form.

6 Place a normal TextBox control on the form, then place an instance of your TextLabel control on the form.

7 Set the Caption property of TextLabel1 to &Punkinhead. Make sure you include the ampersand, because that's the character that designates the access key. The form should look like Figure 10.6.

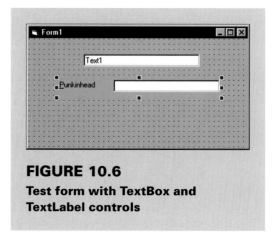

FIGURE 10.6

Test form with TextBox and TextLabel controls

8 Run the EXE project. You can see that the normal TextBox takes the focus, because its TabIndex property is zero. (This is the case because you added it to the form first.)

9 Press the access key for the TextLabel control, Alt+P. You should be able to see that the focus changes–not to the Label, but to the TextLabel's constituent TextBox control.

Relying on a Label to serve as an access key for another control is a neat (albeit not-entirely-obvious) trick. It works because the Label can't take the focus itself, so instead, the next control in the tab order (in this case, the constituent text box) is given the focus instead.

Using the AccessKey Property and AccessKeyPress Event

Hijacking the Label control's access key works well when you have a Label in your control. But what happens when you want to (for example) build your own avant-garde command button out of a constituent PictureBox control? A PictureBox control doesn't respond to an access key, so you have to build that functionality into your control manually.

You can build manual access key functionality into your control by using the AccessKeys property and AccessKeyPress event of the UserControl. The AccessKeys property denotes the key or keys that will cause the AccessKeyPress event to be raised. The AccessKeyPress event enables you to write code that will take an action based on the end user pressing the control's access key. Whether the code in the AccessKeyPress event simply moves the focus onto your control or initiates an action (such as another event) is up to you. To see how this works:

1 Create a new control project. Give the UserControl the name ClickyPicture.

2 Add a constituent PictureBox control to the designer and make it roughly the same height and width as the designer.

3 Set Picture1's AutoRedraw property to True.

4 Create a Click event for the control by adding the following code:

```
' Declarations
Public Event Click()


Private Sub Picture1_Click()
    RaiseEvent Click
End Sub
```

5 Give your PictureBox a textual component in its Paint event by entering the following code:

```
Private Sub UserControl_Paint()
    Picture1.Font.Bold = True
    Picture1.Font.Size = 24
    Picture1.Font.Underline = True
    Picture1.Print "C";
    Picture1.Font.Underline = False
    Picture1.Print "lick me!"
    Picture1.CurrentX = 0
    Picture1.CurrentY = 0
End Sub
```

6 In order to show that the control has responded to your pressing of the access key, enter the following code in the UserControl's AccessKeyPress event:

```
Private Sub UserControl_AccessKeyPress(KeyAscii As Integer)
    SetFocus
    Debug.Print "You sunk my battleship."
End Sub
```

7 Finally, in the Properties window, change the UserControl's AccessKeys property to the letter c, as illustrated in Figure 10.7.

This will cause the control's AccessKeyPress event to be triggered when the end-user presses the keystroke combination Alt+C.

To test the control, place an instance of it on an EXE project form, along with a normal control such as a text box. The EXE project form should look like Figure 10.8. Then run the EXE project by clicking in the normal text box, then pressing Alt+C. You should be able to see the focus move off of the text box. The Immediate window will also indicate that the control's AccessKeyPress event was run.

So you can see in this example how to provide an access key through the AccessKeyPress event. Providing such shortcuts can make your control easier to use, providing users with the kind of interface they expect from controls.

FIGURE 10.7
AccessKeys property

Controls That Are Invisible at Runtime

Not too many controls are invisible at runtime. This is because the vast majority of controls provide user-interface elements, and as every user-interface designer knows, an invisible user interface is an unhappy user interface.

Controls that are invisible at runtime usually provide some sort of calculation, or they're used as wrappers to Windows API calls. The Timer control is the most common example of this. Because it only serves to tick off time, the Timer doesn't need to have a visual interface; instead, it serves only to generate events after a certain period of time has passed.

Creating a control that is invisible at runtime is simplicity itself–simply set the control's InvisibleAtRuntime property to True.

FIGURE 10.8
ClickyPicture control

> **Note** *Controls that are invisible at runtime do not generate Paint events. This seems like a no-brainer (because nothing that's invisible ever needs to be painted) but it's worth mentioning. In Chapter 11 you'll see an example of a control that is desperately crying out for a Paint event, but simply can't have one because it's invisible at runtime.*

Demonstration

To set up a control that is invisible at runtime:

1 Create a new control project. Give the UserControl the name AnnoyingPing.

2 Add a Timer control to the UserControl.

3 Set the UserControl's InvisibleAtRuntime property to True.

4 Set the Timer's Interval property to 5000. Because the Interval property is measured in milliseconds, this will cause the Timer to raise its Timer event every five seconds.

5 Double-click on the Timer control to get to its code window. In the code window, write the following code:

```
Private Sub Timer1_Timer()
    If Ambient.UserMode = True Then
        Debug.Print "This has been an annoying ping."
        Beep
    End If
End Sub
```

(You're beginning to see why we call this control AnnoyingPing. You're also beginning to see why I live in a two-bedroom apartment all by myself.)

One interesting thing about the AnnoyingPing control is the fact that it only beeps when the program it's in is running (that is, Ambient.UserMode) is True. This conditional test is necessary because the Timer control will happily continue to tick off Timer events no matter what–whether it's runtime or design-time. If only my dad's old Ford Pinto were that reliable.

Anyway, to test this control, close the form designer, create an instance of the control on an EXE project form, then run the EXE project. The AnnoyingPing control will start pinging wildly. You may wish to consider dropping this program off on the doorstep of any cranky old men (or ladies) you have living in your neighborhood. Try as they might, they won't be able to figure out what's causing the AnnoyingPing control to annoy them, because it has no visual interface. Science marches on.

> **Note** *It's a good idea to consider placing the functionality of an invisible control in some other Visual Basic component, such as a class or an ActiveX DLL (formerly referred to as an OLE DLL). This is because an ActiveX control can have greater overhead (in terms of distributables and potentially also in terms of run-time resources) than a code module or a DLL. You can't create DLLs with the Control Creation Edition, but you can create them with the Professional or Enterprise edition of Visual Basic.*

Controls That Align to the Edges of Forms

Some controls, such as the PictureBox control, have the ability to automatically align themselves to the edge of their containers. Such controls can be set to align themselves to either the top, left, right, or bottom of the form on which they reside. Such controls also automatically resize themselves when their parent form is resized.

Controls that are alignable expose an Align property. The Align property can be set to None (meaning the control's alignment feature is disabled), Top, Bottom, Left, or Right.

Alignability is used most often to implement a status bar that sits at the bottom of the form. You can make a control align to the edge of its container by setting the Alignable property of the UserControl to True.

Since status bars usually have textual and graphical components to inform the user of what's going on in the application, it would make sense to create a status bar control out of a PictureBox control. But because a PictureBox control doesn't have a Caption property, you'll have to create one yourself.

Demonstration

To demonstrate how to implement the UserControl's Alignable property, you'll create a status bar control that can align itself to the edge of the form it resides on and can resize automatically to match the form. To do this:

1 Create a new Visual Basic control project.

2 Add a constituent PictureBox control to the UserControl. Set the PictureBox's Height property to about 375 twips. (It does not matter how wide the control is, because its width will adjust automatically to the width of its parent form.)

3 Give the UserControl the name StatusBar.

4 Set the UserControl's Alignable property to True.

5 To enable the control's Caption property and drawing events, enter the following code:

```
Private mstrCaption As String

Private Sub UserControl_InitProperties()
    mstrCaption = Extender.Name
End Sub

Private Sub UserControl_Paint()
    Picture1.Cls
    Picture1.Font.Name = "MS Sans Serif"
    Picture1.Font.Size = 10
    Picture1.CurrentX = 0
    Picture1.CurrentY = 0
    Picture1.Print mstrCaption
End Sub
```

```
Private Sub UserControl_Resize()
    Picture1.Move 0, 0, ScaleWidth, ScaleHeight
    UserControl_Paint
End Sub


Private Sub UserControl_ReadProperties(PropBag As PropertyBag)
    mstrCaption = PropBag.ReadProperty("Caption", Extender.Name)
End Sub


Public Property Get Caption() As String
    Caption = mstrCaption
End Property


Public Property Let Caption(ByVal strNewValue As String)
    mstrCaption = strNewValue
    UserControl_Paint
End Property


Private Sub UserControl_WriteProperties(PropBag As PropertyBag)
    PropBag.WriteProperty "Caption", mstrCaption, Extender.Name
End Sub
```

6 Close the control designer and switch to the text EXE project form.

7 Place an instance of the StatusBar control on the form.

8 Set StatusBar1's Align property to 2—vbAlignBottom.

9 Notice how the control snaps to align itself with the bottom of the form.

10 Set StatusBar1's Caption property to the text "Spoon." The form should look like Figure 10.9.

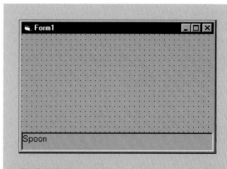

FIGURE 10.9
Form with StatusBar control

Adding an About Box

An About box is a way to stamp your control with your name or your company's name, as well as other information about your control. Including this information has become more important now that ActiveX controls are downloadable over the Internet. It's possible that users will download your control and scarcely pay attention to where it came from. Which means that when they want to pay you big bucks for the licensed version of your control (or harass your tech support people because the control doesn't work right) they have no idea whom to call. Providing an About box resolves that dilemma by including a sort of electronic business card with every control you create.

In addition to information about your control and your company, you might also consider adding information on your online presence in an About box, including your company's Web page, if you have one. You can add anything to the About box you can add to a normal Visual Basic form.

The standard Visual Basic way to provide an About box in a control is to attach the About box to the control's About property. This "property" can't be set, so it really acts like a method, but it's customarily implemented as a property so that users of your control can access it easily through the About property in the Properties window. The About property in the Properties window is illustrated in Figure 10.10.

FIGURE 10.10

AboutBox property in the Properties window

> **Note** *It's common for licensed, commercial controls to display their About boxes every time the control is run on a system that does not have a license to run the control. This enables unlicensed users to play with the control and see how it works, even though they haven't paid for it yet. But it discourages them from redistributing the control in the applications they build, because, you know, who wants to see your goofy About box every time the control runs? For more information on licensing your control, see Chapter 12, "Distributing Your Control."*

To create your own About box, do the following:

1 In the Project Explorer, right-click on Project1.

2 Project1's Context menu appears. Click on Add.

3 The Context menu's submenu appears. Click on Form.

4 The Add Form dialog pops up. Click on Form, if it is not selected already, then click on Open.

5 A new form is added to Project1. Change the form's properties as shown in Table 10.1.

6 Add whatever other visual elements you want to the About box. (In my About box, for example, I chose to include a graphic promoting the virtues of cheese.)

7 When you're done designing the About box, close it and return to your control designer.

TABLE 10.1 FORM PROPERTIES

Property	Setting
Name	frmAbout
BorderStyle	3 - Fixed Dialog
Caption	About
StartUpPosition	2 - CenterScreen

If you don't care to create your own About box for this demonstration, you can instead add the About box About.frm (from the CD-ROM that accompanies this book) to your template project. To add this About box to your project:

1 Right-click on Project1 in the Project Explorer. Project1's context menu pops up. Select Add. Then, from the submenu, choose Add File (as pictured in Figure 10.11).

2 The Add File dialog appears. Locate the file About.frm on the CD-ROM, select it, and click on Open.

3 The file is added to Project1.

> **Note** *Be sure you've added the About box to Project1, your control project, not Project2, your test EXE project.*

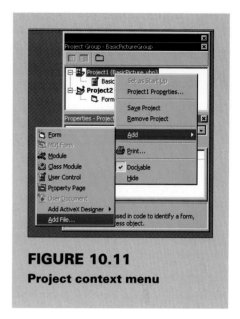

FIGURE 10.11
Project context menu

Now that your project contains an About box, you need to enable it. To do this:

1 In your UserControl, write the following code:

```
Public Sub AboutBox()
    frmAbout.Show vbModal
    Unload frmAbout
    Set frmAbout = Nothing
End Sub
```

> **Note** *The code Set frmAbout = Nothing is used to remove the form from memory.*

2 Select the menu command Tools, Procedure Attributes. The Procedure Attributes dialog box appears.

3 Choose AboutBox from the Name combo box, if it isn't already selected.

4 Click on Advanced. The Procedure Attributes dialog box expands.

5 In the Procedure ID combo box, select AboutBox. This designates your AboutBox subroutine as the official AboutBox procedure for this control. As you'll see later, Visual Basic treats the AboutBox procedure in a special way.

6 Click on OK.

7 Close the code window, close the control designer, and place an instance of the control on Form1.

8 In the Properties window, you should be about to see an About property at the top of the list. Click on the property, then click on its ellipsis button.

9 The About box is displayed, as illustrated in Figure 10.12.

FIGURE 10.12
About box

Project Templates

If you find yourself creating the same type of project again and again, you should consider setting up a *project template*. Project templates are a new feature of Visual Basic that let you create a prefabricated set of visual design and code elements that are included in every project you create.

It's worth noting that the CtlGroup project you've been basing most of your Visual Basic control projects on is itself a template. You can modify that template as well. For example, if your control projects always contain a certain set of API declarations, ActiveX controls (built by you or somebody else), a custom class library you've devised, or a third-party add-in, you can alter the standard project templates to load these automatically every time you create a new project.

> **Note** *Project templates take the place of the autoload.vpj file in Visual Basic 4.0 that loaded a programmer-defined set of custom controls each time you launched VB.*

Demonstration

Let's say you work for a software company that makes ActiveX controls that enable users to create custom charts and other graphics. Your company's standards dictate that every control have a similar About box with your company's logo. Additionally, since all your company's controls have to do with charting, you want all of your new controls to contain a PictureBox control with the appropriate resize code already included.

Start by creating the visual design of the project that will become your template. To do this:

1 Create a new control project based on the template CtlGroup. Give the UserControl the name BasicPicture.

2 Add a PictureBox control to the control designer.

3 Double-click on the UserControl to open its code window. In the UserControl's Resize event, type the following code:

```
Private Sub UserControl_Resize()
```

```
' The Move method is the fastest and most
' sanitary way to resize a control
    Picture1.Move 0, 0, ScaleWidth, ScaleHeight


End Sub
```

4 Close the code window, then close the BasicPicture control's form designer.

At this point, you could have added more code to expose the constituent Picture property of Picture1 and take care of PropertyBag operations (for example), but we've proven our point for the time being.

Now it's time to take the skeletal project group you've created and move it into the Visual Basic templates directory so you can use it as a template. The trick here is that you're going to save the control *group* (that is, the .VBG file) into the templates folder, but you're going to save the individual elements of the project into a separate folder alongside the templates folder. That way, only the project group becomes a template. To do this:

1 Select the menu command File, Save Project Group.

2 Visual Basic will offer to save the control file, BasicPicture.ctl, first.

3 Use the file dialog box to switch to the \vb\template folder.

4 Click on Create New Folder, to create a new folder alongside the template folder. Call this new folder BasicPicture. The CreateNewFolder button is illustrated in Figure 10.13.

5 Double-click on the new BasicPicture folder, then click on Save to save the file.

6 Next, Visual Basic will offer to save the control project file. Save it as BasicPicture.vbp in the BasicPicture folder.

7 Visual Basic will then offer to save the EXE project test form. Name this file BPTest.frm and save it in the BasicPicture folder.

8 The next file to save is the EXE project file. Call this BPProject.vbp and save it in the BasicPicture folder.

9 Finally, you are ready to save the project group. But don't save it into the BasicPicture folder. Instead, back up one folder level by clicking on Up One Level, as illustrated in Figure 10.14.

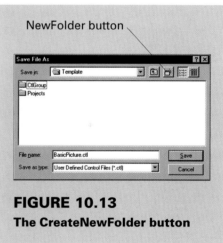

FIGURE 10.13
The CreateNewFolder button

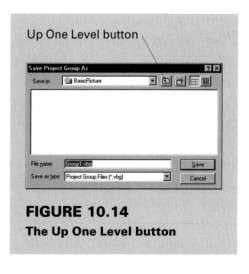

FIGURE 10.14
The Up One Level button

10 Next, double-click on the Projects folder. This is where Visual Basic saves project templates. Give your project group the name Picture.vbg, then click on Save.

11 The project is saved. Just in case you lost track of what just happened, Table 10.2 contains a handy summary of the filenames and where they should be stored.

To see that your project has been made into a template, start a new project by choosing the menu command File, New Project. The New Project dialog box appears. You should be able to see your BasicPicture template in the dialog box, as illustrated in Figure 10.15.

TABLE 10.2 FILENAMES FOR TEMPLATE PROJECT

Project Group	\vb\template\projects\Picture.vbg
Project1	\vb\template\BasicPicture\BasicPicture.vbp
BasicPicture control	\vb\template\BasicPicture\BasicPicture.ctl
Test project	\vb\template\BasicPicture\BPTest.vbp
Test form	\vb\template\BasicPicture\BPTest.frm

Changing the Default Templates Folder

If for some reason you don't care to store your templates under the VB folder, you can change it to whichever directory you like. For example, if you are part of a team of developers, you might want to store a collection of templates on a file server accessible to everyone in your work group. In this case, you'd want all the developers in your work group to use the same templates folder.

To do this, choose the Tools, Options menu command, then select the Environment tab. The dialog box looks like Figure 10.16.

Enter your preferred directory in the Templates Directory area, then click OK. The directory you chose will be the directory Visual Basic will look in to find templates. If you're working in a group, each member of the group must set this option in their copy of Visual Basic.

Adding a Toolbox Bitmap

You can add a bitmap to your UserControl. This bitmap represents your control in the Visual Basic toolbox.

Adding a bitmap that will represent your control in the Visual Basic toolbox is similar to setting the Picture property of a PictureBox control.

FIGURE 10.15

New Project dialog box

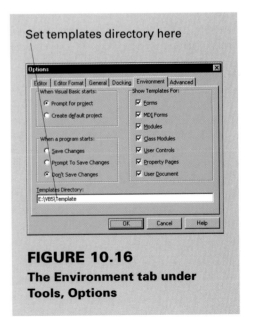

FIGURE 10.16

The Environment tab under Tools, Options

You add a toolbox bitmap by assigning a bitmap to the ToolboxBitmap property of your UserControl. The bitmap you assign can be of any size. However, you should tailor your toolbox bitmaps to the standard size of 16 pixels wide by 15 pixels high. If you make your bitmaps any bigger than that, Visual Basic will automatically scale them down and they'll look heinous.

Demonstration

To add a bitmap to a control project:

1 Open or create a new control project.

2 Open the control designer.

3 In the control designer's Properties sheet, click on the ToolboxBitmap property, then click on its ellipsis button.

4 The Load Bitmap dialog box appears. Locate and select the file tombo.bmp, which is on the CD-ROM that accompanies this book. When you've located it, click on Open.

5 Close the form designer.

6 Open Form1. You should be able to see that the nice new bitmap appears in the toolbox (as in Figure 10.17) and the stinky old generic toolbox bitmap is nowhere to be seen.

> **Note** *Paint Shop Pro is a righteous tool for creating goofy little bitmaps like this. It's orders of magnitude better than Windows Paintbrush. Better yet, it's shareware, so you can torture it before you purchase it. You can get a copy from the good folks as JASC, Inc. by visiting their web site at http://www.jasc.com.*

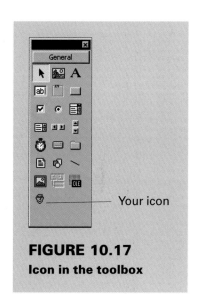

Your icon

FIGURE 10.17
Icon in the toolbox

Summary

In this chapter, you learned probably more than any human being should be permitted to learn about a smattering of varied yet vital features of a well-crafted ActiveX control. In the next chapter, you'll learn how to take advantage of the Windows API to enable your control to perform tasks not available in Visual Basic.

Declaring DLL
Calls

Sample Project:
The SoundButton
Control

Sample Project:
The MenuPic Control

Chapter 11
Making Windows API and DLL Calls

Visual Basic is easy to learn because it takes difficult Windows concepts and reduces them to easy-to-understand abstractions. Similarly, ActiveX controls are easy to program because they wrap program complexity in the easy-to-understand Visual Basic paradigm of properties, events, and methods.

There is a price to pay for this simplification, though. Using Visual Basic represents a trade-off between ease of use and programming power. Fortunately, Visual Basic enables you to delve deeper into the world of Windows through the use of the Windows Application Programming Interface, or API.

Most of the topics surrounding low-level programming with the Windows API are beyond the scope of this book. The quintessential reference to the Windows API for Visual Basic users clocked in at over 1500 pages in its last incarnation. But hopefully this chapter will point you in the right direction and give you an idea of what's possible outside the realm of plain vanilla Visual Basic.

> **Note** *If you've used Visual Basic to make calls to the Windows API before, congratulations. You'll have a leg up on this chapter. But whether you've used the Windows API or not, I have tried to include examples in this chapter that will be meaningful and relevant to control creation.*
>
> *For VB programmers, the best reference to the Windows API is Daniel Appleman's Visual Basic Programmer's Guide to the Win32 API (Ziff-Davis Press, 1996). If you ever plan on doing serious work with Visual Basic, you need this book. (There is also a 16-bit version of the book if you're still working with 16-bit Windows.)*

Declaring DLL Calls

Anything that happens in Windows ultimately takes place as a result of a program calling an element of the Windows API.

The Windows API is comprised of a number of *dynamic-link libraries*, or DLLs. In 32-bit Windows, the core Windows API DLLs are:

▶ gdi32.dll–The graphic display interface API

▶ kernel32.dll–The API that handles low-level stuff like memory and task management

▶ user32.dll–The API that handles windows and messages (some of which are accessible to the Visual Basic programmer as events)

There are a few other APIs, and more are being added all the time to handle new operating system extensions such as e-mail, networking, and new types of hardware peripherals.

In order to use a Windows API procedure in Visual Basic, you must first declare it. API calls are declared in the Declarations section of a module. The generic syntax of an API call looks like this:

```
Declare Function TheAPICall "gdi32" (param1 As String) As Long
```

This made-up example is a declaration to an API function called TheAPICall. This function exists in the file gdi.dll. It is a function that returns a long integer. And it takes one parameter, called param1, a String.

> **Tip** *By convention, you do not spell out the entire name of the DLL in which the API is contained for Windows system APIs. However, for calls to functions in non-system DLLs, you usually will spell out the full DLL filename and, optionally, a directory path to the DLL. By the way, there's no difference between calling a Windows API DLL and calling a DLL that is not a part of the Windows DLL. The Declare statement works for both types of calls.*

One thing you notice fairly quickly about Windows DLL calls is that they're usually quite strongly typed; that is, all the parameters and function calls have data types. This is because the language they're written in (C or C++) is itself strongly typed. Additionally, there is no such thing as a variant in the world of DLLs; the variant is a Visual Basic animal.

You want to double- and triple-check your function declarations when placing calls to DLLs in Visual Basic. Mistakes in the declaration of API calls is one of the fastest ways to crash your program.

> **Tip** *The wise Visual Basic programmer almost never types API function declarations in directly. Instead copy and paste them in as needed from a reference library of DLL calls. Windows 4.0 contains a utility called API Viewer that enables you to list, view, and copy Visual Basic declarations for Windows API calls. The beta version of Visual Basic 5.0 used for this book did not contain a new version of this utility, but it's a safe bet that Microsoft will include it in the final release. There are also third-party component libraries that expose the Windows API in an object-oriented fashion. I haven't used any of these extensively, so I can't recommend any of them, but if you're interested, you might want to check out Sheridan Software's WinAPI Oblets (http://www. shersoft.com/products/oblets/obgen.htm) or Desaware's Spyworks (http://www.desaware.com/desaware/spyhome.htm). Desaware, by the way, is Daniel Appleman's company; he's the guy who wrote the tremendous book on using Windows API calls in Visual Basic that I plugged earlier in this chapter.*

Sample Project: The SoundButton Control

To get you started on a project that makes a simple API call, you'll create an enhanced command button control. The button you create will make a clicking sound (using Windows' multimedia API) whenever it is clicked. To do this:

1 Create a new control project. On the control designer, add a single command button control. Set the command button's Top and Left properties to zero.

2 In the UserControl's Properties window, change the name of the UserControl object to SoundButton.

3 Double-click on the UserControl to open a code window. The first code you'll enter will be the API call to play a sound. This code requires a few constant declarations as well. Enter the following code:

```
Const SND_SYNC = &H0
Const SND_ASYNC = &H1
Const SND_NODEFAULT = &H2
Const SND_LOOP = &H8
Const SND_NOSTOP = &H10


Private Declare Function sndPlaySound Lib "WINMM.DLL" _
    Alias "sndPlaySoundA" _
    (ByVal lpszSoundName As String, ByVal uFlags As Long) As Long
```

4 Add a Click event by placing the following declaration in the Declarations section of the UserControl code window:

```
Public Event Click()
```

5 Make the Click event the default event for your control by selecting the menu command Tools, Procedure Attributes. Select the Click event from the Name combo box, then click on Advanced. Activate the User Interface Default checkbox. The dialog box will look like Figure 11.1.

6 Click on OK.

7 Next, enter the code that will play the sound whenever the button is clicked. Be sure to replace the filename c:\windows\clicksnd.wav

FIGURE 11.1
Procedure Attributes screen

with the correct path to the file clicksnd.wav on the CD-ROM that accompanies this book.

```
Private Sub Command1_Click()
SoundName$ = "c:\windows\clicksnd.wav"
    wFlags% = SND_ASYNC Or SND_NODEFAULT
    x% = sndPlaySound(SoundName$, wFlags%)
End Sub
```

8 Finally, add some standard code to handle resizing and the control's Caption property.

```
Private Sub UserControl_InitProperties()
    Caption = Extender.Name
End Sub


Public Property Get Caption() As String
    Caption = Command1.Caption
End Property


Public Property Let Caption(ByVal NewCaption As String)
    Command1.Caption = NewCaption
End Property


Private Sub UserControl_Resize()
    Command1.Width = Width
    Command1.Height = Height
End Sub
```

To test the enhanced button control, close the designer and place an instance of the control on an EXE project form. Run the EXE project, then click the button. You should be able to hear a clicking sound each time you click the button (assuming your PC has a sound card installed).

> **Note** *The clicking sound, incidentally, was made by me. I did it by clucking into a microphone. I'm a master of the stupid sound effect. Impressed? I knew you would be.*

Using Resources

You may find it useful to include *resource files* along with your control. A resource file is a file containing one or more *resources*–a piece of data that is compiled along with your control or VB application. A resource can be a string, a bitmap, a sound file–nearly any kind of data.

Because it requires a sound file to work properly, the SoundButton control is a prime candidate for the use of a resource file. If the .WAV file it uses for its click sound is ever moved or deleted, the control will bite the dust. Including the sound as a resource, rather than a file, means that it will be far less likely that the control will fail to make its pleasant, soothing click sound each time it is clicked.

Using the Resource Compiler

In order to provide a resource for use with your application, you must first compile it with a special utility called a *resource compiler.*

The full version of Visual Basic 4.0 contains a resource compiler, rc.exe. (It doesn't get copied to your hard disk when you install VB; it resides on the Visual Basic CD-ROM in the \tools\resource folder.) There are 16- and 32-bit versions of this compiler; make sure you use the 32-bit one when creating resources to be included in your ActiveX control.

> **Note** *It's likely that rc.exe or a tool like it will be included with the full version of Visual Basic 5.0, although I can't tell you for sure whether that's the case, because as I write this, the full version of VB 5 hasn't been released yet. (By the way, hello all you people in the future! How's the weather up there?) A resource compiler was not scheduled to be included with the Control Creation Edition of VB5 as of this writing. However, the compiler that ships with Visual C++ is the exact same one that ships with Visual Basic, so if you have access to VC++, you can use those and everything should work just peachy.*
>
> *Also note that resource files created by 16- and 32-bit compilers are different. This means that you won't be able to use resource files created in the resource compiler of the 16-bit version of Visual C++ in Visual Basic.*

Creating a Resource Script

In order to compile a resource, you must have a script that describes what should go into the file. This file can be created in a text editor such as Notepad. The file can contain references to more than one resource, although this example only requires the sound file clicksnd.wav.

The resource file is on the CD-ROM that accompanies this book as clicksnd.rc. Here's what's in the file:

```
// clicksnd.rc
// Jeffrey P. McManus (jeffreyp@sirius.com)
// December 12, 1996


// WAV resources
```

```
CLICKSND        WAVE      DISCARDABLE      "Clicksnd.wav"
```

The first few lines of the .RC file are comments, set off by double slashes. The last line of the file indicates which file to include in the compiled resource file. CLICKSND is the *resource ID* of the resource; it's what you'll later use to retrieve the resource from the compiled resource file in your program.

Although our example .RC file only contains one resource, you can add as many more resources as you want, as long as each one has its own description in the .RC file and no two resources have the same resource ID.

The next entry, WAVE, indicates that the file that's being included is a .WAV audio resource. If this resource were a string, you'd use the descriptor STRING.

DISCARDABLE indicates to the host application that it is OK to remove this resource from memory during the course of the program's execution.

Finally, Clicksnd.wav is the name of the sound file that is to be compiled into the resource file.

Compiling Your Resource File

Now that you have your sound file and your resource script set up, you need to compile it into a resource file. To do this:

1 On the Windows taskbar, click on Start.

2 On the taskbar menu, select Run.

3 Type the path and filename to the 32-bit resource compiler, the switch -r, and the path and filename of your resource script. For example, if you're running the resource compiler directly from the Visual Basic CD-ROM and your system recognizes the CD-ROM as drive F:, the command line is:

```
f:\tools\resource\rc32\rc.exe -r c:\resource\clicksnd.rc
```

Note *The file clicksnd.wav needs to be in the same folder as the resource script clicksnd.rc.*

4 Click on OK. A command prompt window briefly pops up, then disappears. A new file, Clicksnd.res, appears in the folder along with the resource script. This is the resource file you'll use in your control.

Using the Resource in Your Control

To use the resource in your control, you must first add it to your control's project. To do this:

1 In the Project Explorer, right-click on Project1.

2 Project Explorer's context menu pops up. Click on Add, then click on Add File.

3 The Add File dialog box appears. Select the file Clicksnd.res on the CD-ROM that accompanies this book (or the one you just compiled, if you followed the previous demonstration), then click on Open.

4 The resource appears in the Project Explorer, as illustrated in Figure 11.2.

Next, you'll have to change the declaration you used for the API call sndPlaySound previously. This is because you're going to pass a byte array to it instead of a string (the name of the .WAV file on disk). So the parameter should be declared As Any instead of As String.

Additionally, you remove the ByVal before the SoundName because you're no longer passing the parameter by value; instead, you're passing a reference to the array that contains the actual data. (In the declaration, I changed the name of the parameter from SoundName to SoundData to reflect this.) The new version of the declaration should look like this:

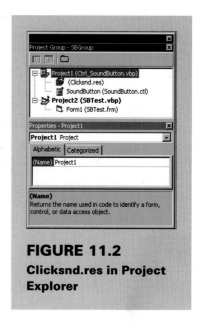

FIGURE 11.2
Clicksnd.res in Project Explorer

```
Private Declare Function sndPlaySound _
    Lib "winmm" Alias "sndPlaySoundA" _
    (SoundData As Any, _
    ByVal uFlags As Long) As Long
```

Next you need to write code to access the sound file compiled in the resource file. To begin, you'll need to declare a variable to store it in. Type the following code in the Declarations section of the UserControl's code module:

```
' byte array for storing binary file


Private bSound() As Byte
```

The variable bSound is a byte array. The byte array stores the return value of the Visual Basic LoadResData function. LoadResData retrieves a binary resource from a compiled resource file and returns a byte array.

The reason bSound is declared at the module level is because it must not go out of scope before the sound is done playing. If the user chooses to play the sound asynchronously, the sound could go on for hours, long after the PlayRes procedure and all of its variables have gone out of scope.

Here's the code that actually plays the sound. The code belongs in the Click event of the constituent CommandButton in your control; you should delete or comment out the existing code before adding the new code. When you're done, the event procedure will look like this:

```
Private Sub Command1_Click()


' ***** vastly inferior version
```

```
'      SoundName$ = "c:\windows\clicksnd.wav"
'      x% = sndPlaySound(SoundName$, wFlags%)
' ***** end of vastly inferior version


     bSound = LoadResData("Clicksnd", "WAVE")
     wFlags% = SND_NODEFAULT Or SND_SYNC Or SND_MEMORY


     sndPlaySound bSound(0), wFlags%


End Sub
```

Voila. If you run the EXE project test form and click, it should make the clicky sound just like it did before. But the difference is, this time the sound file does not have to exist on disk–it exists in your project, ready to be compiled into an EXE or OCX. The project no longer requires that the file clicksnd.wav exist on disk anywhere.

Beyond Clicksnd

There are a number of other uses for resource files beyond embedding a sound file in your application. You can use resources to store graphics, for example, although it might make more sense to store graphics in a PictureBox control, since Visual Basic has many features for handling graphics built into the language.

You can also use resource files to store strings. This makes particular sense in situations where your control must be *localized*, or translated into international languages. For more information on localization, see Chapter 12, "Distributing Your Control."

Sample Project: The MenuPic Control

The SoundButton control is a fairly simple demonstration of how to use a Windows API call to perform a task not normally available to a Visual Basic programmer. In this next section you'll create a control that makes use of several calls to the core Windows API.

The MenuPic control acts as a wrapper for a set of Windows API functions that control the drawing of menus. The purpose of the control is to replace a particular menu with a bitmap of your choice. This mimics the functionality of the menus in the new Visual Basic 5.0 IDE, which includes bitmaps that serve as a cue to toolbar buttons. The MenuPic control exposes three main properties:

▶ Picture, which is delegated to its single constituent PictureBox control

▶ Menu, a long integer that designates the menu you wish to change

▶ MenuItem, a long integer that designates the item in the menu you wish to change.

To use the MenuPic control, you place an instance of the control on a form that has a menu, then you set the control's Menu and MenuItem properties to tell it which menu to change. Finally, you assign a graphic to the control's Picture property. The existing menu item will be replaced by the graphic of your choice (both at design-time and at runtime).

Designing the MenuPic Control

The visual design of the MenuPic control consists of nothing more than a constituent PictureBox control, called Picture1. In order to make the control appear invisible at runtime, you set the UserControl's InvisibleAtRuntime property to True.

The MenuPic's Picture property is delegated to Picture1's Picture property; the picture stored in the PictureBox is assigned to the menu through an API call.

Once you've created the MenuPic control with its constituent PictureBox control, you can begin entering code. Begin by entering a code module to the project. Code modules are where you store global declarations (such as API declarations) that are accessible from any part of your project.

To add a code module to your project:

1 In the Project Explorer, right-click on your control project.

2 From the Context menu, select the menu command Add, Module.

3 A code module is added to your project.

4 In the Properties window, give this code module the name MenuAPIs.

5 Double-click on the MenuAPIs module in the Project Explorer to open its code window.

You can now begin entering API call declarations in the MenuAPIs code window. Here are the API call declarations for the MenuPic project:

```
Public Const MF_BITMAP = &H4
Public Const MF_BYPOSITION = &H400


Declare Function GetMenu Lib "user32" (ByVal hwnd As Long) As Long
Declare Function GetSubMenu Lib "user32" (ByVal hMenu As Long, _
    ByVal nPos As Long) As Long
Declare Function GetMenuItemID Lib "user32" (ByVal hMenu As Long, _
    ByVal nPos As Long) As Long
Declare Function ModifyMenuByNum Lib "user32" Alias "ModifyMenuA" _
    (ByVal hMenu As Long, ByVal nPosition As Long, _
    ByVal wFlags As Long, ByVal wIDNewItem As Long, _
    ByVal lpstring As Long) As Long
```

Here's a brief summary of what these API calls do:

▶ GetMenu gets a *handle* to a menu bar given a particular window. You can think of a handle as the internal name of an element of the window's interface. Windows, bitmaps, hardware devices, and menus, as well as other things, all have handles.

▶ GetSubMenu gets a handle to a particular menu in a menu bar (such as the File menu, for example). You make this API call after making the GetMenu call.

▶ GetMenuItemID returns the unique internal identification number of a *menu item*. (A menu item is one particular element in a menu; for example, the File menu is a *submenu*, and the File Print command is a menu item.) You need the menu item ID to make a change to the menu item.

▶ ModifyMenuByNum is the procedure that does most of the work. The function takes a menu item ID (as well as a number of other parameters) and modifies it, either changing its text, or, in the case of the MenuPic control, replacing it with a bitmap.

Because it has to be called from several places in the control, I put the menu-changing code into a private subroutine, called ChangeMenu. This code belongs in the UserControl's code window. Here is the code for the ChangeMenu subroutine:

```
Private Sub ChangeMenu()
    If Picture1.Picture = 0 Then
        'nothing to do yet
        Exit Sub
    End If


    Dim lngTopMenuHandle As Long
    Dim lngSubMenuHandle As Long
    Dim lngMenuID As Long
    Dim result As Long

    ' Get a handle to this form's top menu
    lngTopMenuHandle = GetMenu(Extender.Parent.hwnd)


    ' Get a handle to its submenu
    ' Syntax: GetSubMenu(top_menu_handle, entry_position)
    lngSubMenuHandle = GetSubMenu(lngTopMenuHandle, mlngMenu)


    ' Gets the menu ID
```

```
' Syntax: GetMenuItemID(menu_handle, entry_position)
lngMenuID = GetMenuItemID(lngSubMenuHandle, mlngMenuItem)


' Stick the picture in the menu
' Syntax: ModifyMenuBynum(menu_handle, entry_position, _
'    flags, ID_new_item, string)
result = ModifyMenuBynum(lngSubMenuHandle, mlngMenuItem, _
                         MF_BITMAP Or MF_BYPOSITION, _
                         lngMenuID, _
                         Picture1.Picture)


Debug.Print "ChangeMenu: Success: " & result


End Sub
```

Tip *When you're writing subroutines like ChangeMenu, remember to make them private, rather than public. When you make a public subroutine in a UserControl, it is exposed to the user as a method of your control.*

How ChangeMenu Works

In order to get access to a menu item so the ModifyMenuByNum function can do its work, ChangeMenu has to do the following, in order:

1 Get a handle to the form that the control resides on.

2 Given that handle, get a handle to that form's menu bar.

3 Given that handle, get a handle to the menu you want to alter.

4 Given that handle, get the menu item ID of the menu item you want to alter.

You can see that the ChangeMenu procedure starts by getting the window handle of the control's parent by inspecting the HWnd property of the Extender's Parent object. This is a powerful trick that enables you to access properties of the form on which your control resides.

After ChangeMenu has retrieved the window handle of your control's parent form, it feeds it to the GetMenu API call. GetMenu returns the handle to the menu that resides on the form.

Once you've got a handle to the menu, you can feed that to the GetSubMenu API, which returns a handle to the individual menu.

You then feed GetSubMenu's return value to the GetMenuItemID API call, which gives you the ID number of the item in the submenu you're interested in messing with.

Finally you can do the actual work–calling the ModifyMenuByNum function to make the change to the menu.

Complicated, ain't it? Almost makes you wish there were an ActiveX control to encapsulate all these hairy function calls.

Implementing MenuPic's Properties

The Menu and MenuItem properties are simple long integers that have no direct effect on the control's appearance (they serve only to supply parameters to the ModifyMenuByNum API call; there are no new concepts here, so they shouldn't require any explanation).

To implement these properties, enter the following code into MenuPic's code window::

```
' Declarations
Private mlngMenu As Long
Private mlngMenuItem As Long


' The meat and potatoes
Public Property Get Menu() As Long
    Menu = mlngMenu
End Property


Public Property Let Menu(ByVal New_Menu As Long)
    mlngMenu = New_Menu
    PropertyChanged "Menu"
```

More Fun with ModifyMenuByNum

By the way, ModifyMenuByNum can be used to make other kinds of changes to menus, as well. For example, you can use it to change the text of a menu. But you probably wouldn't want to do that, and here's why: changes you make to menus using the Windows API short-circuit the Visual Basic Menu object you normally use to create and manage menus in VB.

To demonstrate this, create a menu with the caption Ringbo, then use the MenuPic control to assign the Photon Lock graphic to it. Then use the Immediate window to inspect the Caption property of the menu. You should be able to see that the caption is still officially Ringbo. Watch out for this little anomaly when you start monkeying with menus in Visual Basic forms.

```
        ChangeMenu
End Property


Public Property Get MenuItem() As Long
    MenuItem = mlngMenuItem
End Property


Public Property Let MenuItem(ByVal New_MenuItem As Long)
    mlngMenuItem = New_MenuItem
    PropertyChanged "MenuItem"
    ChangeMenu
End Property
```

There are, of course, a number of additional enhancements you could make to this control. For example, making the user choose what menu to change by having them type in a number isn't the most elegant way of going about it. Ideally, you'd let the user pick from a list of available menus; this might be best done in a custom property sheet.

Calling ChangeMenu

You've already placed calls to ChangeMenu in the Property Let procedure. This causes the menu to change when the user assigns a Picture to the MenuPic property. However, ChangeMenu must also be called in a few other situations as well.

The "normal" time when the menu needs to be changed is when the application is first started. If you were programming this as a normal VB application, you might put the ChangeMenu code in the form's Load event. But since you're working with a UserControl instead of a form, you have to do it a little differently.

If you put a call to ChangeMenu in the UserControl's Paint event, the menu will be changed at design time. But because the control is invisible at runtime, it raises no Paint events then. The menu won't be changed at runtime. So you have a problem.

My solution to this problem was to take advantage of the fact that the UserControl's container undergoes a palette shift at the time the container application is run. You can trap this event by placing code into the AmbientChanged event of the UserControl.

> **Note** *Using the AmbientChanged event in this way seems like an inelegant way to accomplish what you're trying to do with this control. There may very well be a better way to do it, but it worked reliably for me. Maybe a future enhancement to control creation in Visual Basic will include a new UserControl event that will correspond more closely with the initialization of the container application.*

The code looks like this:

```
Private Sub UserControl_Paint()
    ' changes the menu at design time only
    ChangeMenu
End Sub


Private Sub UserControl_AmbientChanged(PropertyName As String)
    ' this is a hack, but it works.
    If PropertyName = "Palette" Then
        ChangeMenu
    End If
End Sub
```

Testing MenuPic

To test the MenuPic control, do the following:

1 Close its code window and its control designer.

2 Open a test EXE project form. Name it frmMPTest.

3 Create a menu for the form by using the menu editor. To open the menu editor, use the menu command Tools, Menu Editor, or use the keyboard shortcut Ctrl+E.

4 The menu editor appears. Type in the name of the top-level menu, &Weapons, and its name, mnuWeapon, then click Next.

5 Click on the right-arrow button to indent the next entry into a submenu. Give this menu item the caption &Photon Lock, and name it mnuPhotonLock. Click on Next.

6 Give the next menu item the caption &Fire Photons and the name mnuFirePhotons. The menu editor should look like Figure 11.3.

7 Click on OK to close the menu editor. The Weapons menu appears on the form.

8 Place a MenuPic control on the form.

9 Assign the graphic photon.bmp (from the CD-ROM that accompanies this book) to the MenuPic control's Picture property. You can place the control anywhere on the

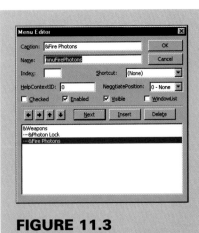

FIGURE 11.3
The completed Menu Editor window

form that's convenient, since it will be invisible at runtime. The form should look like Figure 11.4.

10 By default, MenuPic1's Menu property is set to 0 and its MenuItem property is set to 0, so it's going to affect the first menu item in the first menu on the form, which just so happens to be the menu you want to change. Click on the Weapons menu to confirm that this is the case. Your form should look like Figure 11.5.

11 Run the project using the Run, Start menu command or the function key F5. You should be able to see that the menu is still altered, but the MenuPic control itself is invisible.

This example gives you a sense of how easy you can make it for users to access advanced functionality. By wrapping the functionality of Windows API calls in an ActiveX control, you provide new features for users while keeping them rooted in the world of Visual Basic objects, properties, and methods.

Summary

In this chapter you learned how to place calls to the Windows API in Visual Basic, as well as some of the pitfalls of API calls particular to control creation. In the next chapter, you'll learn how to compile and distribute your control to users.

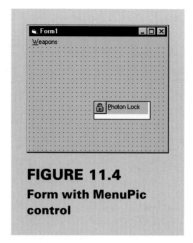

FIGURE 11.4
Form with MenuPic control

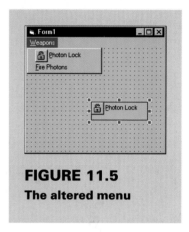

FIGURE 11.5
The altered menu

Compiling Your
Control

Binary
Compatibility

Naming Your
Control

Project Properties

Testing Your Compiled
Control in Microsoft Access

Using the Setup Wizard

Binary Licensing

Localization

Registering and
Unregistering Controls

Using Regclean

Chapter 12
Distributing Your Control

By this time, you've been exposed to most of the functionality of a typical control. Now it's time to kick your control out of the nest and unleash it on the real world.

Getting an ActiveX control to end users isn't as easy as it was in the old days. In the 16-bit world of VBXs, you could distribute a VBX to a user simply by putting a copy of it into their \windows\system directory.

Not so with ActiveX controls. ActiveX controls must be registered with the system in order to work properly. You can register controls manually (using a registration utility called regsvr32), but in all likelihood you'll want to distribute your control to users without forcing them to register the controls manually. A Setup application does this for you; you can create a Setup application with the Visual Basic Setup Wizard.

> **Note** *There is one situation in which you don't have to create a conventional Setup application: when you're distributing your control on the Web. Controls distributed via a Web page are downloaded and install themselves automatically on a user's machine, without a Setup application. For more information on Web-distributed controls, check out Chapter 13, which goes into more detail about how this works.*

Compiling Your Control

To get your control to users, you must first compile it. Compiling the control takes all of its code and other components and combines it into a .OCX file that you can distribute to users.

> **Note** *You can't use the Control Creation Edition of Visual Basic to create compiled executable (.EXE) files. This edition of Visual Basic can only be used to create compiled ActiveX (.OCX) files. In order to compile EXEs, you need to purchase one of the commercial versions of VB. You'd think this would be a no-brainer (as in, "What part of Control Creation Edition don't you understand?"). But you'd be surprised at how many people posted messages on the Net asking "Where's the make .EXE option in the Control Creation Edition?" during the beta.*

Demonstration

As a demonstration of how to compile and distribute your control, you'll compile a version of the HappyHour control you set up in a previous chapter. To compile this project, do the following:

1 Open the enhanced version of the HappyHour project on the CD-ROM that accompanies this book. Use the version in the Chapter 12 folder on the CD-ROM.

2 Select the menu command **File, Make HappyHourProject.ocx.**

> **Note** *If you don't see the Make .ocx command on the File menu, make sure that you've selected your control project (as opposed to the test EXE project) in the Project Explorer window.*

3 The Make Project dialog box will appear. Confirm that the name of the .OCX file you want is correct.

> **Note** *I still give my .OCX files conventional DOS/Windows 8.3 filenames (that is, filenames with a maximum of eight characters in their names and a maximum of three characters in their extensions). This may be sheer paranoia on my part; I dunno. At any rate, old habits die hard, and since most users will never have to deal with the .OCX file as a filename anyway, using the 8.3 convention doesn't hurt anything.*

4 Click on **OK**. The control will compile.

Confirming That It Worked

You'll be able to tell that your control is compiled because it will appear on the list of insertable controls in applications that support ActiveX controls. To see this list in Visual Basic 5.0, you use the Project, Components menu command. In Microsoft Access 95, you can see the list by opening a form in design view, then choosing the menu command Insert, Custom Control.

Binary Compatibility

When you compile your control, it is assigned a Globally Unique Identifier (GUID). A GUID is a 16-byte number that uniquely identifies your control to Windows. When your control is installed and registered on another user's system, the GUID is copied to that system's registry as part of the installation process.

Each time you compile your control, the random GUID generated by Visual Basic will be different, unless you have an option known as *binary compatibility* turned on.

Turning on binary compatibility means that you're almost ready to distribute your control (or you've already distributed a version of your control) and you want to make sure that the version you're about to build remains consistent with future versions. (A side effect of turning this option on is that the GUID remains stable from one build of your control to the next.)

> **Note** *Having a stable GUID from one version of your control to the next becomes particularly important when you're inserting controls on a Web page. See Chapter 13 for more information on this.*

When you turn binary compatibility on, you're making a formal commitment to your control's interface. You can add new elements to your control's set of properties, methods, and events, but if you remove any part of the existing interface, backward compatibility with earlier versions of your control will break. Visual Basic will issue a warning to you when this happens.

To activate binary compatibility, do the following:

1 From the menu, choose Project, <my control name> Properties.

2 The Project Properties dialog box appears. Choose the Component tab. The dialog box should look like Figure 12.1.

3 Click on **Binary Compatibility**, then click **OK**.

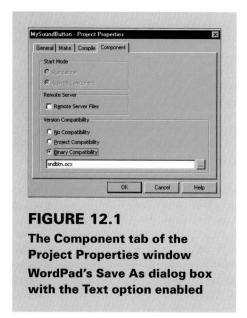

FIGURE 12.1

The Component tab of the Project Properties window

WordPad's Save As dialog box with the Text option enabled

Naming Your Control

The name you give your control project and your UserControl designer determines the name the user will see when he places the control into a project.

Consider the SoundButton control as illustrated in Figure 12.2.

When a user of your control inserts it into his project, the control will appear in the list of available controls as SoundButton. (However, in Microsoft Access 95, it will appear as MySoundButton.SoundButton; see the topic "Testing Your Compiled Control In Microsoft Access" later in this chapter for more information.)

The moral of the story is that you should give your control project and UserControl a name that is going to make sense when a user browses the list of insertable controls.

FIGURE 12.2

SoundButton project names

Project Properties

You can assign a number of properties to your control project. These properties are added to the .OCX file at compile time.

Some project properties can be viewed by users of your control whether or not the control is actually installed on their machine. Such information is nice to add, because it makes it easier for users to manage .OCX files. If you don't add version information, for example, your users will have a hard time figuring out what your .OCX file does or where it came from.

To set project properties for your control project, select the menu command Project, <my project> Properties. Then choose the Make tab.

The Project Properties dialog box is shown in Figure 12.3.

The following are some details on what each of the project properties do.

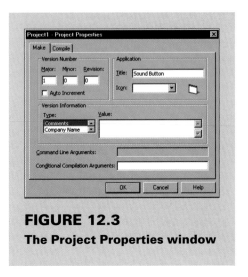

FIGURE 12.3
The Project Properties window

Version Number

The version number of your control is important in situations where a user is re-installing or upgrading the control on a particular system. Most Setup programs will refuse to overwrite an existing copy of a control if the existing control is of a later version than the one it's trying to install. (That is, the Setup program won't kill version 2.0 of your control in order to install version 1.0.)

For this reason, it's important that you keep the interface of your control consistent across versions. (And by interface, I'm referring here to its programmable interface–its properties, methods, and events.) If you don't do this, newer versions of your control will break applications built on earlier versions. Once you've implemented an element of your programmable interface, it should stay there forever, even if you've since come up with a much better way to implement something.

To enable version numbering in your control, do the following:

1 In the Project Properties dialog box, select the Make tab.

2 If you want the revision number of your control to be automatically incremented each time it is recompiled, activate the Auto Increment checkbox. Otherwise, you will need to remember to change the version number manually each time you recompile your project (which is perfectly fine, if that's the way you want to go about it).

Version Information

Version information enables you to add some textual information to your control. Even if the control is not installed, the user can use the Properties page in Windows Explorer to figure out what your control is and where it came from.

The version information categories that you can include with your control are:

▶ Comments

▶ Company Name

▶ File Description

▶ Legal Copyright

▶ Legal Trademarks

▶ Product Name

It's particularly important to supply version information in the Company Name category, because guess which company's name appears in that slot if you don't include your company's name? (I'll give you a hint: It's two words, and it begins with the word "Microsoft" and ends with the word "Corporation.")

To supply version information with your control:

1 In the Project Properties dialog box, click on the type of version information you wish to supply.

2 In the Value box, type the value to be assigned to the category of version information. For example, Figure 12.4 shows a comment assigned to the Comments category of the SoundButton control.

3 Continue to enter version information values for as many of the categories as you wish. When you're done, click on OK. You will, of course, need to recompile your control for the information to be included in the distributable .OCX file.

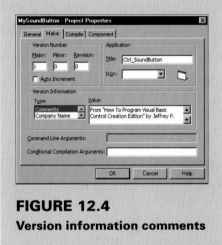

FIGURE 12.4
Version information comments

Checking Version Information

After you've compiled your control, you can inspect the version information compiled in with your control by doing the following:

1 Using Windows Explorer, locate your compiled .OCX file on disk.

2 Right-click on the file. The file's context menu pops up. Select Properties.

3 The control's Properties dialog box appears. Select the Version tab.

4 The control's version information is displayed, as illustrated in Figure 12.5.

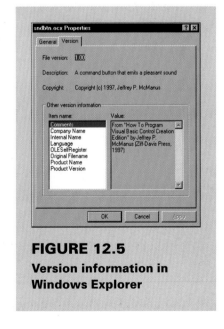

FIGURE 12.5
Version information in Windows Explorer

Application

The Application panel determines two properties of your compiled application: its name and its icon. However, these properties do not pertain to ActiveX controls; they are used for compiled EXE projects only.

DLL Base Address

The DLL base address is the part of memory that your control loads into by default. (The reason why it's called the DLL base address and not the ActiveX base address is because ActiveX controls are really just another type of DLL.)

It's important to choose a DLL base address for your control because if you don't, the DLL base address for your control will be the same as the controls created by the millions of yo-yos out there who didn't buy this book and read this chapter. When your control is loaded into memory on a system that already has a DLL in memory at its base location, the operating system has to find a new slot in memory in which to load your control. This makes your control load more slowly, although how much more slowly is anyone's guess. (My guess is, since we're talking about a memory operation here, not that much more slowly.)

The key to solving this problem is to pick a base address that is different from the default. Valid DLL base addresses are multiples of 65,536 that fall between the range 65,536 and 2,147,418,112.

> **Note** *Although the Visual Basic manuals and help files use hexadecimal notation for memory addresses, you're free to enter a DLL base address in either hex or decimal notation. By the way, you might find the Windows Calculator useful if you need to do hexadecimal calculations, since it has the ability to quickly switch back and forth between decimal and hex.*

One handy way to come up with a DLL base address for your control is to pick a random number between two and 32,000-ish, multiply that number by 65,536, and use that as your base address. For example, I set the DLL base address of the SoundButton control project to 1179648 decimal (&H120000 hex), which is 65,536 times 18.

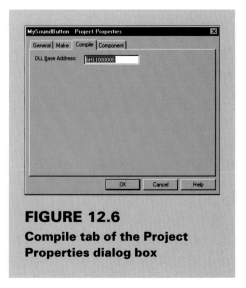

FIGURE 12.6
Compile tab of the Project Properties dialog box

Using this method, you might run into a base address used by some other control, but it's not terribly likely. And even if you do, it won't cause a fatal error, just a teensy performance degradation at runtime.

You can access the DLL base address setting in the Compile tab of the Project Properties dialog box, as illustrated in Figure 12.6.

Testing Your Compiled Control in Microsoft Access

Using Visual Basic to test your control is like driving a four-wheel-drive vehicle on the freeway on a sunny day. You might be able to verify that it works, but you won't have an idea of how it's going to perform in unexpected situations.

Testing your compiled control in a non-VB container such as this is like coating that sunny highway with a thin layer of tapioca pudding. Just as driving your Jeep down a pudding-covered highway gives you a sense of how it *really* handles, putting your control into a container other than VB, such as Microsoft Access 95, can give you important insights into how your control is going to behave in the real world.

Even if your control is destined for use in only one container (such as a Visual Basic project or a Web page) I'd recommend you test it in at least one other container, for no other reason than to gain a non-VB perspective on how your control will be used.

In this section, I'll demonstrate how a Microsoft Access user might use your compiled SoundButton control in an Access form.

> **Note** *I used Access 95 as an example because a lot of people have it and it's an application that I'm familiar with, and the fact that it's different enough from Visual Basic to make it an effective alternative test application. But it's no big deal if you don't have it on your machine. You should be able to follow along in whatever ActiveX container application you're most familiar with. (And by the time you read this, Access 97 will be out; you can of course use that for testing as well.)*
>
> *For a list of apps that support ActiveX controls, see Chapter 2. If you don't have any other ActiveX-capable apps on your system, don't sweat it–we'll go through this again in the next chapter, when I'll talk about embedding controls in Web pages. In that chapter, you'll use the ActiveX Control Pad to embed the SoundButton control in a Web page.*

To embed the SoundButton control in a Microsoft Access form, do the following:

1 Start Microsoft Access. You can either create a new database, use an existing database of your own, or use the example database provided on the CD-ROM that accompanies this book. The name of this database used in this example is example.mdb.

2 If you're using your own database or a new database, select the menu command **Insert Form**. The New Form dialog box appears (see Figure 12.7); select Design View, then click on **OK**. Or, if you're using the example database on the CD-ROM, locate the form called frmAddress in the database window, then click on **Design**. The form will appear in design mode.

FIGURE 12.7

Create New Form dialog box

3 To insert the control onto the form, select the menu command **Insert, Custom Control**. The Insert OLE Custom Controls dialog box appears (see Figure 12.8). Scroll down until you find the SoundButton control, which appears in the list as MySoundButton.SoundButton.

> **Note** *You can see that the control appears differently in Access than it does in Visual Basic. This is one of the reasons why it's good to test your control in a non-VB container, even if you don't really intend to use the control in a non-VB container.*

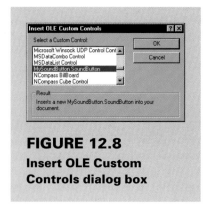

FIGURE 12.8

Insert OLE Custom Controls dialog box

4 Click on **OK**. The button appears on the form. To confirm that it works properly, put the form into run mode by selecting the menu command **View, Form**.

5 The form goes into run mode (see Figure 12.9). Click on the SoundButton. It should generate the soothing click sound you've come to appreciate.

> **Note** *Remember that property pages aren't just a good idea, they're the law, at least when you plan on using your ActiveX control in a non-Visual Basic container. If you don't provide a custom property sheet, users may not be able to get design-time access to its properties at all. Access 95 is a good example of an application in which this is the case.*

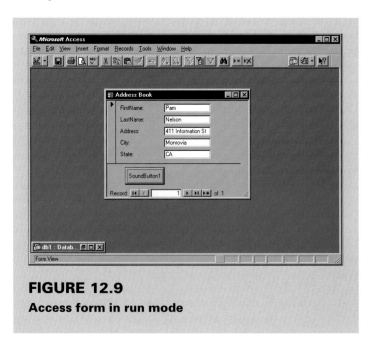

FIGURE 12.9

Access form in run mode

Using the Setup Wizard

If you're going to give your control to developers who are going to use it in Visual Basic or other development environments, you need to build a Setup application. The Setup application installs your control and, optionally, any attendant controls that are installed along with your controls, such as DLLs, constituent controls, help files, README files, and so forth.

Note *This chapter gives instructions on how to distribute your control to users via floppy disk or a shared disk drive on a local-area network (LAN). For instructions on how to distribute your control over the Internet, see Chapter 13.*

To use the Setup Wizard to create a setup program for your control, do the following:

1 If Visual Basic is open, close it.

2 From the Windows taskbar, select the Visual Basic 5.0 program group.

3 In the VB 5 program group, choose Application Setup Wizard. This is illustrated in Figure 12.10.

4 The Setup Wizard runs and displays an introductory screen. Click on **Next**.

5 The Select Project and Options screen appears. Choose the project file for your control by browsing the disk and selecting the .VBP file.

6 If your control needs to be rebuilt (that is, recompiled), then make sure the Rebuild the Project checkbox is selected.

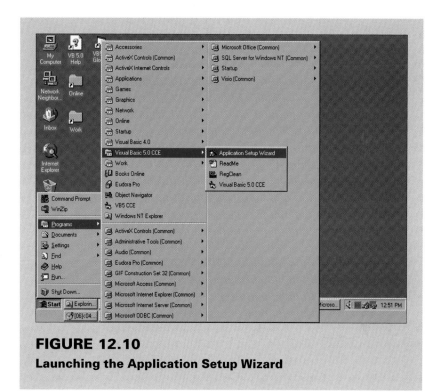

FIGURE 12.10
Launching the Application Setup Wizard

7 Finally, if you want the Setup Wizard to create a dependency file rather than a Setup program, make sure the Generate Dependency File Only button is selected. (A *dependency file* is a file that lists all the files that need to be distributed to users in order for your project to function.) The screen should look like Figure 12.11.

8 Click on **Next**. There will be a short delay while the Setup Wizard contemplates its navel. After a few seconds, the Distribution Method screen appears, as illustrated in Figure 12.12. Choose the option you want.

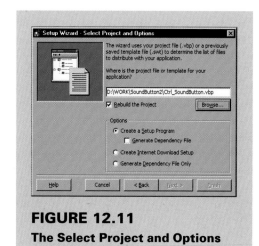

FIGURE 12.11
The Select Project and Options window

Tip *Selecting Floppy disk means that you want the Setup Wizard to create diskettes containing your code components. Choosing Single Directory means that the Setup program created by the Setup Wizard will occupy a single folder. (This type of program could conceivably be much larger than a 1.44 megabyte diskette but is appropriate for situations when you're distributing a control to users over a shared disk on a local-area network, for example.) For my money, the best type of Setup program is the third option, Disk Directories, because it offers the speed of the hard disk combined with the flexibility of a Setup program broken up into diskettes.*

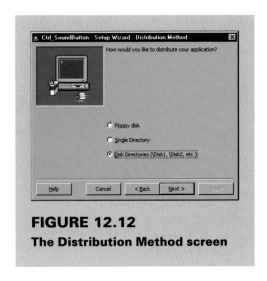

FIGURE 12.12
The Distribution Method screen

9 Click on **Next**.

10 If you chose the Disk Directories option, you're next confronted with the Multiple Directories screen. Choose the directory into which you'd like your Setup program installed, then click on **Next**. If the directory you denote doesn't exist, the Setup Wizard will create it; however, if the directory you choose already contains files, the Setup Wizard will not delete those files for you. (For this reason, you should create a new directory or choose a directory you know is empty.) The screen should look like Figure 12.13.

11 The ActiveX Components screen appears. In this screen, the Wizard determines whether your project uses any constituent controls. If you wish to add constituent controls to your Setup program, you can do so now by clicking on **Browse**. Otherwise, click on **Next**.

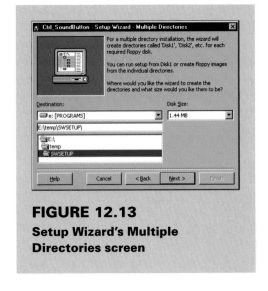

FIGURE 12.13
Setup Wizard's Multiple Directories screen

12 The Confirm Dependencies screen appears. This screen informs you of the files required for your project to run. If you want more information on any of these files, click on **File Details**. Otherwise, click on **Next**.

13 The Setup Wizard enters an additional period of contemplation, during which you may wish to go out to the kitchen and obtain yourself a tasty beverage.

14 For an ActiveX control project, you'll get the message pictured in Figure 12.14. Of course you wish to include the Property Page DLL, because if you don't,

your users will have a tough time gaining access to properties of your control at runtime. So if you plan on using your control in non-VB applications, click on Yes.

15 The File Summary screen (Figure 12.15) appears, showing a list of files that will be distributed along with your control project. If you need to add additional files to your installation (such as a readme file or a help file), now's the time to do it. Click on **Add** to add files.

16 Click on **Next**. The Setup Wizard is finished, so click on **Finish**. The Setup wizard dutifully collects and compresses files as you continue to enjoy your tasty beverage.

FIGURE 12.14
Setup Wizard Property Page DLL message

When it's all done, you've got a lovely Setup application on your disk, along with a couple of disks' worth of compressed support files.

Many (if not all) of these files do not actually need to be installed on your users' machines with each control you distribute. This is because most of these files are shared components that get installed into the user's Windows system directory. If your users already have a copy of the files you're distributing, the Setup program is smart enough to know not to litter their hard drives with additional copies. So if you're worried about dumping megabytes of junk on your users' disks, don't be.

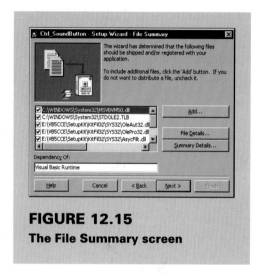

FIGURE 12.15
The File Summary screen

Binary Licensing

Controls that support licensing enable you to restrict the use of your control. When your control is licensed, programmers are permitted to write code to access the interface of your controls within a development environment (such as Visual Basic's), and they can distribute the control to their end users. But those end users cannot access the control in a development environment unless they, too, have a licensed copy of the control.

Usually it's necessary to install a control (using the setup diskettes created by the developer of the control) to license the control. In the past, Visual Basic controls used tiny binary files stored in the Windows system directory as license files. ActiveX controls use registry entries for this purpose. Neither scheme will prevent a dedicated software pirate from making unauthorized copies of your controls, but adding support for licensing will slow down less technical (and less dedicated) users.

Controls that are destined for commercial distribution should always support licensing. You can add support for licensing to your control by doing the following:

1 In your control project, select the Project, <your project name> Properties menu.

2 In the Project Properties dialog box, select the General tab.

3 Select the Require License Key checkbox. The dialog box will look like Figure 12.16.

If you have compiled your control already, you'll need to compile it again in order for the licensing requirement to take effect. Once you have done this, your users will have to install your control using a setup application you provide for them; simply placing a copy of the .OCX file on their system will not suffice.

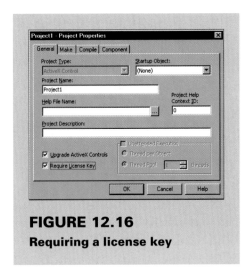

FIGURE 12.16
Requiring a license key

When to License

It's a bad idea to require licensing when you're creating a control that you don't plan to sell. For example, if you wrote a control that acted as the interface for an expense account tracking system for your company, adding licensing support would be pointless; nobody (except a certifiable weirdo) would attempt to surreptitiously copy your control without your authorization. Also consider that, in this scenario, licensing adds an additional set of steps for your user. Instead of simply asking your network system administrator to blast a copy of your .OCX onto every computer on your LAN, you'd have to ask each user to install your control using a setup program you'd have to author.

Localization

A *localized* application is an application that has the ability to display text in different languages. Localization requires first and foremost a top-down planning effort. It is much easier to implement as you're building your application rather than after the fact (believe me).

The national language used by a piece of software is referred to as its *locale*. The locale of an ActiveX control is embedded into it by Visual Basic at compile time; if you're using the U.S. English version of VB, for example, your controls will have the U.S. English Locale ID.

You can determine the locale of the program in which your control is being used by inspecting the LocaleID property of the Ambient object. This property tells a localized control which language to display text in. If your control displays different text based on the LocaleID of its container, you should inspect the LocaleID in the InitProperties and AmbientChanged events of the UserControl.

> **Note** *Most localized applications make use of resource files to store string data displayed in the user interface. That way, when the application needs to be localized, all you need to do is take out the English string resource file, replace it with the international file, and recompile. For more information on resource files, see Chapter 11.*

Registering and Unregistering Controls

You may run into a situation of having to register your control manually without running a setup application. For example, if you compile a control, then move the control to another folder on your computer (to reflect the fact that the control has moved from development to production, for example), you need to re-register the control so that your system knows where to find the relocated .OCX file.

You can manually register a control using a utility called Regsvr32. For example, to register the SoundButton OCX manually, do the following:

1 Locate the utility regsvr32.exe on your disk. On my Windows NT machine, it's located in \windows\system32. The utility regsvr32.exe is installed by a number of applications, including Visual Basic and Microsoft Internet Explorer.

2 Using the Start menu in the Windows task bar, select **Run**. Enter the following command line:

```
c:\windows\system32\regsvr32.exe c:\windows\system32\sndbtn.ocx
```

3 The confirmation dialog box shown in Figure 12.17 is displayed.

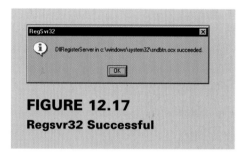

FIGURE 12.17
Regsvr32 Successful

You may find it useful to unregister a control, particularly in situations where you mistakenly registered a control or you simply want to clear a few controls off your system.

You can manually unregister a control by using the Start menu in the Windows task bar to select Run. Then enter the following command line:

```
c:\windows\system32\regsvr32.exe /u c:\windows\system32\sndbtn.ocx
```

Using Regclean

Regclean is a utility that checks your OLE registry and insures that all of the registered files actually exist on your computer. If it doesn't find the file that corresponds to the registry entry, it blows the registry entry away. This can be a great help when you're testing the ActiveX control registry. It's also nice to get rid of applications you installed years ago but have long since deleted. (Did I *ever* have Lotus Approach installed on my system? Yeees.) The latest version of Regclean is available on the Microsoft Web site at http://www.microsoft.com/kb/softlib/mslfiles/REGCLN.EXE. (An older version shipped with Visual Basic 4.0; I would imagine they'll ship it with VB5 as well.)

A nice thing about the way that Regclean works is that it leaves an *undo file* that tells you exactly what registry entries it removed. This file, undo.reg, is created in the same folder in which Regclean resides.

A Word of Caution about Regclean

I recently used Regclean on my Windows NT 4.0 machine. It came up with so many things wrong with my registry I permitted it to clean up all the problems it found without notifying me of what it was doing. It wound up hosing the registry of the Data Access Object (DAO) library used by Microsoft Access 95. It wasn't hard to fix–I just had to figure out which library it had un-registered, which took a few minutes, and then re-register it using the registration utility Regtlb32. I could have also simply re-installed Access 95. Not a huge deal, but do bear in mind that over-zealous use of Regclean can cause these kinds of problems.

Summary

This chapter discussed some of the more common methods of distributing controls to users. In addition to compiling the control into an .OCX and applying compiler-related properties to your control, the chapter covered a number of ancillary topics such as localization, the system registry, and licensing support.

The next chapter addresses a new way to distribute your controls to users–through a World Wide Web page.

Chapter 13
Deploying Your Control on the Web

This chapter will discuss methods of getting your control on the World Wide Web. We'll cover not only the method of distributing your controls to Web users, but also the basics of the VBScript, the scripting language that enables you to program ActiveX controls that you've embedded in your Web pages.

> **Note** *Appendix A gives information on online references pertaining to Visual Basic that you might want to check out, including a Web page for this book.*

Hosting a Web Site

In order to have a place where users can view your Web pages (and download ActiveX controls), you need access to a *Web server*, a computer connected to the Internet that runs software designed to send Web pages to other users' computers.

For individuals, the easiest way to locate a Web page on a Web server is to obtain an Internet Service Provider (ISP) that offers space on their Web server as part of their basic service package. With this kind of setup, you don't have to worry about maintaining the technical details of the Internet connection; the ISP does it all for you. However, you may have to pay the ISP extra if your site is very large or very popular; check with your service provider for details on that.

If you have more sophisticated requirements, you may wish to set up your own Web server. Microsoft gives its Web server software away free as a part of the Windows NT Server operating system; there are a number of other Web server packages available from a variety of vendors.

Note that your Web server need not be hooked up to the Internet-at-large to be effective. Web servers designed to serve the needs of individuals within a department or organization are gaining popularity as a way to distribute information within corporations.

This chapter assumes that you have access to some kind of Web server and that you have the ability to place files on it.

For the Net-Impaired

If you're not hooked up to the Internet already, this chapter still has relevance to you. Much of what is discussed in this chapter has relevance both to the Internet and to

181

intranets (defined as private networks using technology standards developed on the Internet).

> **Note** *I personally can't stand the term intranet, since to a software developer, there is no such thing as an intranet. Your software either adheres to Internet standards and makes use of Internet technologies, or it doesn't. So this book won't make much of a distinction between the greater Internet and your intranet. Bear in mind that essentially anything having to do with Internet technologies is also applicable to intranets.*

Even if you're totally Net-impaired, you should be able to use and test most of the demonstrations in this chapter using a stand-alone machine. If you use Windows NT Server 3.51 or 4.0, you can use the free Internet Information Server (IIS) software; if you're on Windows 95, you'll want to investigate the Personal Web Server that comes with Microsoft FrontPage 97.

Obtaining the ActiveX Control Pad

You start your ActiveX Web odyssey by obtaining a copy of ActiveX Control Pad. This is a tool you can use to put together Web pages; it's specifically geared toward building pages that contain ActiveX controls controlled with the VBScript language. I use this tool to test ActiveX controls in Web pages because it's free, it's fast, and it's no-nonsense. It also has some nice features for automatically inserting VBScript code into your HTML Web pages.

You can, of course, use other tools (including Microsoft FrontPage and plain old Windows Notepad) to build Web pages containing ActiveX controls, if you like. And while the Web page examples in this chapter were created with the ActiveX Control Pad, you shouldn't have too much trouble tailoring the discussion to your development tool of choice, since the underlying HTML code is the same.

> **Note** *You can obtain a free copy of the ActiveX Control Pad from the Microsoft Web site at http://www.microsoft.com/workshop/author/cpad/.*

Crash Course on HTML and VBScript

Once you've obtained and set up the ActiveX control pad, you're ready to get started sticking your control into a Web page and writing code to make it do its magic.

In this demonstration, you'll use a combination of two Web technologies–HTML and VBScript–in order to embed a SoundButton control in a Web page.

About HTML

Hypertext Markup Language (HTML) is the language that defines the appearance of World Wide Web pages. You don't have to know much of anything about HTML to get through this chapter, but you will need to know something about it to set up and maintain a Web site. Fortunately, it's not hard to learn.

> **Note** *The greatest books on how to get started with HTML are written by Laura Lemay. Her Teach Yourself Web Publishing with HTML 3.2 in 14 Days (Sams.net, 1996) and Teach Yourself Web Publishing with HTML 3.2 in a Week (Sams.net, 1996) are essential. (The "In a Week" title is a lighter-weight version of the "In 14 Days" book, which is comprehensive.) If you have not done so already, go acquire one or the other immediately.*

About VBScript

VBScript is a Microsoft extension to HTML. You can use VBScript to program ActiveX controls inside a Web page, among other things.

VBScript is a subset of Visual Basic. It lacks many of the features of the Visual Basic language, because it is optimized for speed and safety over the public Internet. (See the section titled "Safety Considerations" later in this chapter for more about safety on the Internet.)

> **Note** *This section is (obviously and necessarily) an extremely limited discussion of the capabilities of VBScript. For more information on how to use VBScript, check out the Microsoft VBScript Web site at http://www.microsoft.com/vbscript, or check out the title Teach Yourself VBScript in 21 Days by Keith Brophy and Timothy Koets (Sams.net, 1996). It didn't actually take me 21 days to get through their book, and if you know Visual Basic already, it shouldn't take you that long, either.*

Using the ActiveX Control Pad

Now that you have the two-bit backgrounder on HTML and VBScript, here's a brief demonstration of how to use an ActiveX control in a Web page. This demonstration assumes that you have Microsoft Internet Explorer 3.01, the ActiveX Control Pad, and the SoundButton control installed on your machine. (If you didn't compile and install the SoundButton control back in Chapter 12, there is an installable version of the control on your CD-ROM.)

> **Note** *The current version of Microsoft Internet Explorer for Windows 95 and Windows NT is 3.01. This update is supposed to fix some ActiveX-related problems, but Microsoft is a little cagey on exactly what those problems are. At any rate, if you have an older version, download the update. It ain't exactly the most expensive software in the world.*

In this demonstration, you'll create an HTML Web page that will contain an embedded SoundButton control. The point of this demonstration is not to have a fully functional Web page right off the bat, but just to make the control appear in the browser. To do this:

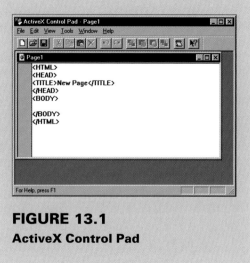

FIGURE 13.1
ActiveX Control Pad

1 Launch the ActiveX Control Pad. (By default, the ActiveX Control Pad is installed to c:\program files\ActiveX Control Pad\ped.exe on your computer.) The application displays an untitled page, as illustrated in Figure 13.1.

What you're looking at is a skeletal HTML page. It contains the minimal elements of a Web page, comprised mostly of *tags* denoting page structure and formatting elements. (For example, <BODY> is a tag that exists in most HTML pages; it denotes the start of the main body of text in a Web page.)

The text that appears between the <TITLE> and </TITLE> tags will appear in the browser's title bar when the page is viewed. To customize this default page, begin by changing this text:

2 Click-drag across the text **New Page** to select it. Overtype it with the words **SoundButton Example**.

3 Next, insert some text in the body of the Web page. To do this, click between the <BODY> and </BODY> tags. Type the text:

```
<p>This page demonstrates the SoundButton control.
Not only does the SoundButton control emit a pleasant sound,
but it can perform useful actions in a web page.</p>
```

Be sure to remember to type the <p> tag at the beginning and the </p> at the end of the sentence. This tag pair indicates that this is a paragraph, so that a paragraph break will be inserted after the text. The HTML should look like Figure 13.2.

Next you'll insert the SoundButton control in the page you're editing. To do this:

1 At the end of the document, press **Enter** a few times to open up some space.

2 From the ActiveX Control Pad menu, select **Edit, Insert** ActiveX Control.

3 Scroll through the list until you find MySoundButton.SoundButton. Click on it, then click on **OK**.

4 A visual design form (similar in appearance to a Visual Basic form) and a property sheet appear.

5 In the Properties sheet, change the SoundButton's Caption property to **Click Me!**, then click on **Apply** (or press **Enter**). The screen should look like Figure 13.3.

6 Click on the Properties window's close button in its upper right corner, then close the Edit ActiveX Control window the same way.

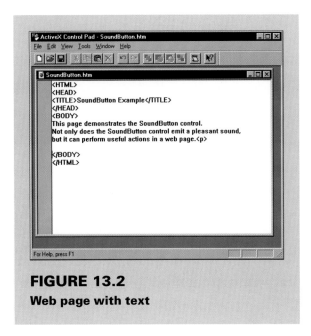

FIGURE 13.2
Web page with text

FIGURE 13.3
SoundButton properties

7 Save the page using the menu command **File, Save**. Give the page the file name SoundButton.htm.

The ActiveX Control Panel has inserted the following code in your document:

```
<OBJECT ID="SoundButton1" WIDTH=84 HEIGHT=36
 CLASSID="CLSID:7E0B5DF2-576C-11D0-9A3B-204C4F4F5020">
    <PARAM NAME="_ExtentX" VALUE="2223">
    <PARAM NAME="_ExtentY" VALUE="953">
    <PARAM NAME="Caption" VALUE="Click Me!">
</OBJECT>
```

This is the code that makes the ActiveX control show up on the Web page. Here's a brief description of the lines of code that were inserted:

▶ The <OBJECT> tag is an HTML tag that directs the Web browser to embed a software component into the page.

▶ The ID parameter is similar to the Name property of a Visual Basic control.

▶ The WIDTH and HEIGHT parameters dictate the dimensions of the control.

▶ The CLASSID tag is the GUID of the control. (The concept of the GUID was introduced in Chapter 12.)

▶ The PARAM tags set initial values for the control's properties; they are the equivalent of design-time properties. (The only settable property of the SoundButton control is Caption; the _ExtentX and _ExtentY properties are internal to the ActiveX Control Pad.)

That's it. At this point your control is ready for testing (even though it doesn't really do anything yet). Leave the ActiveX Control Pad open for now; in the next section you'll bring up Microsoft Internet Explorer and try out your HTML page.

Testing Your Control in a Web Browser

Now that you have a minimal HTML test page with a copy of your ActiveX control embedded into it, you can see how it looks in a Web browser. To test the Web page you're developing:

1 Leave the ActiveX Control Pad open and launch Microsoft Internet Explorer.

2 In Internet Explorer, choose the menu command **File, Open**.

3 The Open dialog box appears. Click on **Browse** and locate the file SoundButton.htm you saved in the first step, then click on **Open**.

4 In the Open dialog box, click on **OK**. The Web page opens, displaying the Potential Safety Violation dialog box illustrated in Figure 13.4.

> **Note** *The exact message you see when loading a control is dependent on your Web browser's security settings. The message displayed here is what you'd see when your browser's security is set to Medium. To change your browser's security settings, in Internet Explorer choose the menu command View, Options, then select the Security tab, then click on the Safety button.*

FIGURE 13.4
Potential safety violation dialog box

5 If you were opening a page on the Internet, this would be a problem, but because you're opening your own control, it's no big deal. (We'll deal with this warning, what it means, and how to resolve it later in the chapter.) For now, click on **Yes to All** to proceed.

6 The Web page opens, as Figure 13.5 illustrates.

This page doesn't do much of anything, but if you click on the Click Me! button, you will be treated to the pleasant clicking sound you've grown so accustomed to.

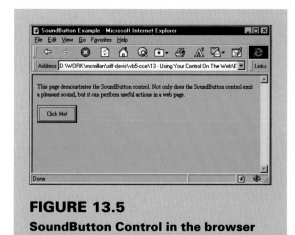

FIGURE 13.5
SoundButton Control in the browser window

In the next demonstration, you'll return to the ActiveX Control Pad to make the page do something more useful.

Adding VBScript Code to the Web Page

Now that you have a rudimentary Web page, it's time to make it more functional. To do this, you'll add a VBScript procedure to it using the ActiveX Control Pad. To do this:

1 Leave Microsoft Internet Explorer running. Switch back to the ActiveX Control Pad. You should still have the file Soundbutton.htm open in the ActiveX Control Pad.

2 From the ActiveX Control Pad Tools menu, select Script Wizard.

3 The Script Wizard appears, as illustrated in Figure 13.6.

4 You'll use the Script Wizard to create an event procedure in the SoundButton control's Click event. This code will execute whenever a user clicks on this SoundButton. To do this, double-click on SoundButton1 in the Select an Event panel of the Script Wizard, then select Click.

5 In the Insert Actions panel on the right side of the Script Wizard, double-click on Go To Page...

6 The Enter A Page dialog box appears. Type the following URL:

```
http://www.mcp.com/zdpress/
```

7 Click on **OK**. The Script Wizard looks like Figure 13.7.

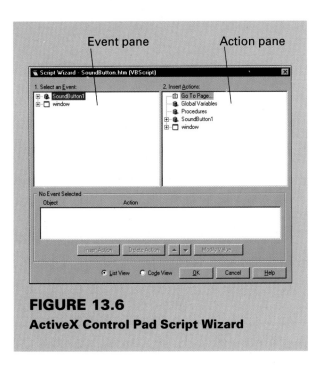

FIGURE 13.6
ActiveX Control Pad Script Wizard

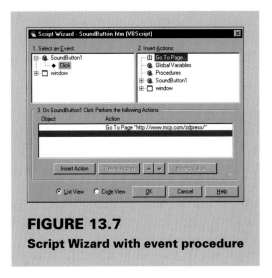

FIGURE 13.7
Script Wizard with event procedure

8 Click on **OK** to close the Script Wizard. The following code is added to your document:

```
    <SCRIPT LANGUAGE="VBScript">
<!—
Sub SoundButton1_Click()
Window.location.href = "http://www.mcp.com/zdpress/"
end sub
—>
```

You can see that with the exception of the <SCRIPT> tag and HTML comment tags (the <!— and —> tags), the code is quite similar to a Visual Basic event procedure.

> **Note** *The <!— and —> tags are HTML comment tags. In a normal HTML Web page, these tags mark the beginning and end of a comment; normally they are not interpreted by a browser. However, when a Web page contains a script, the body of the script is usually placed inside comment tags in order to keep Web browsers that don't understand the script (in this case, every browser in the world except Microsoft Internet Explorer 3.0) from displaying the lines of code that comprise the script as literal text in the Web page. The ActiveX Control Pad inserts these comment tags for you, but if you ever get to the point where you can hand-code VBScript, be sure not to forget these tags, or else your page will look goofy in non-Microsoft browsers.*

To test this procedure, do the following:

1 In the ActiveX Control Pad, re-save the Web page by choosing the **File, Save** command (or by using the keystroke shortcut **Ctrl+S**).

2 Leave the ActiveX Control Pad open. Switch to Internet Explorer.

3 In Internet Explorer, reload the page by selecting the menu command **View, Refresh**.

4 When the Potential Safety Violation dialog appears, ignore it by clicking **Yes to All**. The Web page refreshes.

5 Click on the **Click Me!** button. It looks the same as before, but this time when you click it, you not only hear the pleasant clicking sound, but the Web browser also loads the stylish and engaging Ziff-Davis Press home page.

Well, that's it. You've created a test page that successfully tests the two elements of the SoundButton control's interface (its Click event and its Caption property) as well as its feature-set enhancement (the pleasant clicking sound).

Note *A script debugger for VBScript Web pages is available free from Microsoft. You can use this tool to check the syntax of Web pages you create that include VBScript code. You can download this tool from the Microsoft Web site at http://www.microsoft.com/workshop/prog/scriptie.*

Extra Credit

If you want, you can insert a few more lines of HTML code in your page to enhance it. To do this, replace the <BODY> tag with the following HTML code:

```
<BODY bgcolor=CCFFCC>
<FONT FACE="Trebuchet MS, Ariel, Helvetica">
<h1>SoundButton Control Test</h1>
```

Here's a brief explanation of what the new HTML code does:

▶ The new BODY tag now has a bgcolor component that instructs the browser to render this page with a soothing green background color. (The CCFFCC value is a hexadecimal triplet that works similar to Visual Basic's RGB function; it provides a color by specifying red, green, and blue values. For example, pure red is FF0000, blue is 0000FF, and white is FFFFFF.)

▶ The FONT FACE tag tells the browser to display the page's text in one of the fonts indicated. (The reason why it lists three fonts is because not everyone has the same fonts installed on their computers. So the browser tries Trebuchet MS first, then Ariel, then Helvetica. If none of these three fonts are available on the client machine, or if the browser is not capable of displaying fonts, the browser will display a default font.)

▶ Finally, the <H1> tag indicates that the following text is a header and should accordingly appear larger and more emphasized on the page. The </H1> tag shuts off the display of the header font.

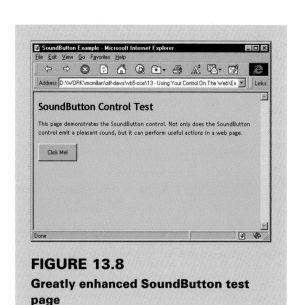

FIGURE 13.8
Greatly enhanced SoundButton test page

To test this, save the HTML file, switch to MS Internet Explorer, and refresh the page. It should look something like Figure 13.8 (although the exact color and font you see will depend on what you have installed on your system).

From here, you could go on to build a complete Web site based on SoundButton controls, clicking yourself silly in short order. But there are a few enhancements you need to make to the distribution of the SoundButton control–specifically, addressing the issue of the Potential Safety Violation warning, but also handling the actual installation of the control over the Net. I'll address those issues later in this chapter.

Making It Work with Netscape

I know what you're saying. You're saying, "Well, Jeffrey, this may be all well and good, but the minute a Netscape user hits my page, the whole thing is going to go kablooey." Am I right? Well, friends, gather 'round, because I'm going to show you a way to display an ActiveX control that will look like an ActiveX control to a Microsoft Internet Explorer user and like a hyperlink to a Netscape Navigator user (or a user of any one of a number of other fine browsers).

The home page for this book (http://www.well.com/user/jeffreyp/activex/) contains a list of links to ActiveX-related resources. Originally, this list was a conventional list of hypertext links. But the more I worked with the pleasant-sounding SoundButton control, the more I liked the idea of a clicky hypertext button. So I decided to replace the hyperlinks with SoundButtons. Here's how I did it.

Originally, the HTML code that produced hypertext links on the book's home page looked like this:

```
<a href="author.html">About the Author</a><br>
<a href="errata.html">Errata</a><br>
<a href="xlinks.html">ActiveX Resources</a><br>
<a href="vblinks.html">Visual Basic Resources</a><br>
<a href="../vbscript/index.html">VBScript Links</a><br>
<a href="http://www.mcp.com/zdpress">Ziff-Davis Press</a>
```

But that was boring, and I'm a novelty freak, so I started replacing the hyperlinks with buttons. Here's what this looks like for the first hyperlink:

```
<OBJECT ID="sbnAuthor" WIDTH=83 HEIGHT=24
CLASSID="CLSID:7E0B5DF2-576C-11D0-9A3B-204C4F4F5020">
        <PARAM NAME="Caption" VALUE="Author">
<a href="author.html">About the Author</a>
</OBJECT><br>
```

Although most of this could have been done with the ActiveX Control Pad, there is one extra twist that makes the page compatible with non-Microsoft browsers: the hyperlink tag embedded *inside* the OBJECT tag. This works because whenever a browser can't figure out what to do with a particular tag, it generally tosses the tag out, ignoring it completely. In the case of the OBJECT tag, non-Microsoft browsers can't figure out what to do with the SoundButton control, so it displays the part of the OBJECT tag it *does* understand: the hyperlink. Microsoft browsers get the ActiveX control interface, other browsers get the conventional hyperlink interface, and your Web page is, once again, safe for democracy.

Note *You can view the underlying HTML of any Web page by going to the page, then choosing the menu command View, Source. This is a great way to get information on real-world usage of HTML and to answer the question "How'd they do that?" when you're viewing a page.*

Using the Setup Wizard in an Internet Context

In order to distribute your control over the Internet, you must create a special type of compressed installable file. The Setup Wizard (introduced in Chapter 12) has an option that enables you to build such files. To see how this works:

1 Launch the application Setup Wizard the same way you did in Chapter 12 (by closing VB5 and selecting the Setup Wizard from the Windows Taskbar's VB5 program group).

2 The Introduction screen appears. Click on **Next**.

3 Click on **Browse** to locate the project file for the SoundButton project, Ctrl_SoundButton.vbp.

4 In the Options panel, click on **Create Internet Download Setup**. The What's New icon appears, providing you with a hypertext jump to information on downloadable software from Microsoft. (This hypertext jump is actually just a link to http://www.microsoft.com/vbasic/.)

5 Click on **Next**. A disturbing momentary delay takes place, after which the Internet Distribution Location screen appears. If you have direct access to a Web server from your LAN (or if your local machine is itself a Web server), then select a public directory you have access to. If you don't have access to a Web server at this point, don't worry. Select a directory that's convenient, and you can move the downloadable file into place later.

6 Click on **Next**. The Internet Package screen appears, as illustrated in Figure 13.9. In this screen, you do two important things. You designate the server from which users will download support files (such as the dreaded Visual Basic Virtual Machine). And you mark your components as safe for initialization and scripting.

Note *For more information on component safety, see the topic Safety Considerations later in this chapter.*

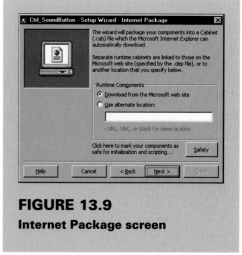

FIGURE 13.9
Internet Package screen

7 For now, leave the Download from Microsoft Web Site option button selected. This will enable users to download support files (such as the Visual Basic Virtual Machine) from Microsoft's Web site rather than yours, thereby conserving bandwidth and disk space on your Web server. (The down side to this is that every user of your control must be connected to the Internet; in a corporate intranet situation, you might instead choose to distribute these support files from an intranet Web server.)

Note *You can get information on locally hosting Visual Basic support files on the Microsoft Web site at http://www.microsoft.com/vbasic/controls/webmastr/cabs.htm. You would want to look into this information if you are planning to deploy your controls across a corporate intranet or if your users are otherwise restricted from downloading the Visual Basic distributables from www.microsoft.com.*

8 To mark your components as safe for initialization and scripting, click on the **Safety** button.

9 The Safety dialog box appears. Select the Safe for initialization and Safe for scripting checkboxes, as illustrated in Figure 13.10.

10 Click on **OK**. You are returned to the Internet Package screen. Click on **Next**.

11 The ActiveX Components screen appears. Since your control does not make use of any constituent controls, there is nothing to do here. Click on **Next**.

12 The File Summary screen appears, displaying a list of files that will be distributed with your control. Click on **Next**, then click on **Finish**.

13 The Setup Wizard compresses the files and displays a dialog box indicating that it has finished.

FIGURE 13.10
Safety dialog box

In the directory you selected to serve as the repository for your controls, you should have a .CAB file, as well as a few other files I'll describe in the next section.

CAB Files and CODEBASE Tags

You should now be able to see that the directory you selected back in step 5 of the Setup Wizard process has been filled with files–specifically, a .CAB file and an .HTM file, as well as a subdirectory called Support that contains the original, uncompressed version of the control along with a few other files.

The .CAB file is the important one. This is a compressed file that contains your .OCX file and any other files required for your control to run. (Absent from this file are support files, such as the Visual Basic Virtual machine, for reasons discussed in the demonstration.) Because they're compressed and they don't include Visual Basic and Windows support files, .CAB files tend to be fairly small. They're perfect for placing on a Web page without slowing the download process too much, although the exact size of your control's .CAB file will obviously depend on the size and complexity of your control.

The .HTM file is important, too, because it shows you exactly what HTML code needs to be written in order to embed your control in a Web page. This is going to be old hat to you, assuming you followed the ActiveX Control Pad demonstration earlier in this chapter. But just for your edification, here are the contents of SNDBTN.HTM:

```
<HTML>
<!- If any of the controls on this page require licensing,
you must create a license package file.
        Run LPK_TOOL.EXE in the tools directory to create the
required LPK file.

<OBJECT CLASSID="clsid:5220cb21-c88d-11cf-b347-00aa00a28331">
        <PARAM NAME="LPKPath" VALUE="LPKfilename.LPK">
</OBJECT>
->

<OBJECT
        classid="clsid:7E0B5DF2-576C-11D0-9A3B-204C4F4F5020"
        id=SoundButton
        codebase="sndbtn.CAB#version=1,0,0,0">
</OBJECT>
</HTML>
```

Since SoundButton isn't a commercial file, you don't need to worry about the licensing part (see the section later in this chapter about distributing licensed controls). The other code should be familiar to you, except for the CODEBASE tag, which I'll explain next.

Using the CODEBASE Tag

When you deploy your ActiveX control on the Internet, you need to provide a way for the Web browser to find the binary .OCX file in situations where the user's machine doesn't already have it.

You use a <CODEBASE> tag to do this. A <CODEBASE> tag is part of the <OBJECT> tag; it tells the Web browser where to download the software component. The value of a CODEBASE tag can be an .OCX file, but it's more commonly a .CAB file. The location of a file in a CODEBASE tag can be on a disk drive on your LAN, or it can be a URL.

> **Note** *This may seem obvious, but it's worth stating explicitly: If your Web browser runs across a Web page that contains an ActiveX control that is already installed on your system, it won't bother to re-download the control. This is a great thing, because it means that Web browsers don't have to re-download your ActiveX component each time they visit your page. This behavior is in contrast to Java components, which must be downloaded fresh each time you hit the page into which they are embedded. There is an emerging Java technology specification called Java Beans that seeks to make Java applets behave like ActiveX controls in this respect.*

You can see that at the end of the CODEBASE tag, the VERSION parameter was added. This is important because it directs the Web browser to download the latest version of the ActiveX control if it needs to.

For example, let's say you make enhancements to the SoundButton control, releasing version 2.0. You update all the HTML files on your Web site so the CODEBASE tag refers to version 2.0 of the control. Later, a user who has version 1.0 of the SoundButton control on her computer hits one of your Web pages. Because the CODEBASE tag indicates that the HTML page requires SoundButton 2.0, her browser knows to download the new version before rendering the Web page.

Note that when a browser downloads and installs a new version of a control, it overwrites any previous version the end user has installed on his or her computer. This is one reason why it's important that your control maintain a consistent, backward-compatible interface across versions, so that upgrading to a newer version of the control doesn't break existing applications.

GUIDs

The GUID used as an argument to the CODEBASE tag is generated at the time the control is compiled. The GUID of a particular control should never change after the control is released, even if you release a new version of the control. (To enforce this, you turn binary compatibility on when compiling the control; for more information on this, see Chapter 12.)

It goes without saying that to avoid transcription errors, you should avoid typing a GUID directly into the OBJECT tag. Use the ActiveX Control Wizard, or copy and paste the OBJECT tag in from the sample HTML file generated by the Setup Wizard.

Safety Considerations

Safety refers to a control's ability to cause harm to an end-user's computer. A control is said to be safe if it is incapable of performing such actions as filling the user's hard drive, shutting down the user's computer, and filling memory.

It is your responsibility as the control's author to devote mental resources to determining if your control is safe. This is particularly the case if your control is signed, because signed controls include your or your company's name. If you certify a control as safe and it's really not, end users can figure out who you are through your code signature, find you, hunt you down, and gnaw on your limbs.

Script-safe

Script-safe controls are certified by the control author (you) to be incapable of damaging a machine no matter what the script does. Put another way, when you certify a control as script-safe, you're saying that no scripting command can possibly cause your control to harm someone's computer.

Initialization-Safe

Controls that are initialization-safe are certified to not cause problems on an end user's machine no matter what wacky values the control's initial properties (in its PARAM tags) are set to.

For example, consider a control that has a Picture property. If you permit a user to assign the Picture property of your control to a 9GB picture file, it's going to download that file and hang the user's machine. If your control has the ability to save to a file (something that isn't possible to do using scripting, but *is* possible to do using Visual Basic and is therefore possible to do using an ActiveX control), you need to make sure that the control can't overwrite a file (such as a vital operating system file) or fill the end user's hard drive with files.

Does safety mean you can't build ActiveX controls with properties that can be freely set? No, it just means you can't distribute such controls on the Net and mark them as safe. Does safety mean that you can't use unsafe constituent controls in your ActiveX control? Again, no. The degree of safety provided by your control is a function of the elements its interface provides.

Licensing Issues on the Web

When you distribute licensed controls over the Web, you must contend with additional issues, most of which stem from the fact that on the Web, there is no such thing as design-time.

The solution to this problem is to create a license package file that temporarily checks out a license to the Web browser. This license is held in memory, enabling the Web browser to display the control, but it does not permit the user to then use your control in a development environment such as Visual Basic (unless, of course, the user has purchased a licensed version of your control and installed it on his computer).

> **Note** *For your control to support licensing, you must specify a licensing option at the time the control is compiled. See Chapter 12 for information on how to do this.*

You'll recall from the previous section that the Setup Wizard put the following license package-related code in the SoundButton control's sample HTML file:

```
<!-   If any of the controls on this page require licensing,
you must create a license package file.
        Run LPK_TOOL.EXE in the tools directory to create the
required LPK file.

<OBJECT CLASSID="clsid:5220cb21-c88d-11cf-b347-00aa00a28331">
        <PARAM NAME="LPKPath" VALUE="SoundButton.LPK">
</OBJECT>
->
```

If the SoundButton control were a licensed control, you would be required to include this HTML at the top of any Web page in which a SoundButton control resided. You'd also be required to create and store the file SoundButton.LPK (the SoundButton control's license package file) on the Web server along with the .CAB file for your control. The following section describes how to create a license package file.

Using the Lpk_tool Utility

The Lpk_tool utility enables you to create a license package (.LPK) file. To create an .LPK file for the SoundButton control, do the following:

1 Locate and run the Lpk_tool utility, Lpk_tool.exe. If you have the ActiveX Software Development Kit, you'll find this file in the \inetsdk\bin\i386 directory.

> **Note** *The Lpk_tool utility used in this book was taken from the ActiveX Software Development Kit because the beta version of Visual Basic used for testing the examples in this book did not contain it. However, it is likely that the Lpk_tool utility will be included with the final, shipping version of Visual Basic 5.0.*

2 The utility runs, displaying a list of all the controls that are registered on your system. Select the SoundButton control, then click on **Add**. The screen should look like Figure 13.11.

3 The control moves to the Controls in license package list. At this point, you could move additional controls to the

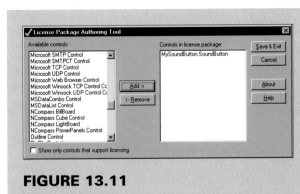

FIGURE 13.11

Lpk_tool utility

list if you wish; this is necessary if you plan to add additional licensed controls to the Web page you wish to design, because you must include all the controls on a given Web page in a single .LPK file.

4 For now, this is the only control you need to add to create this .LPK file, so click on **Save & Exit**.

5 A file dialog appears, prompting you to save the .LPK file. Name the file SoundButton.lpk and save it into the same directory as you saved sndbtn.cab earlier.

6 After you save the file, a message box appears informing you that the license package file was successfully created and that the utility is terminating. The license package file, SoundButton.lpk, is created on your disk.

Signing Your Code

So you've got a compiled control, you've marked it as safe for scripting and safe for initialization, you've made it into a .CAB file, you've put it on a Web server, and you've purchased it the cutest little pair of footed jammies with bunny ears. You may think your life is complete, but there's something missing–you *still* don't have everything you need to put your control on the public Internet.

In order to distribute your controls over the Web, you must digitally *sign* your control. Signing your control embeds information that connects you, the software developer (or software development company), with the file you're distributing. The theory here is that if your name is associated with the software you write, it's less likely that you'll write controls that will reformat people's hard drives, shut down their computers, or stomp through downtown Tokyo crushing buildings and breathing fire. Digital signing, then, is a way of keeping ActiveX control developers from unleashing destructive control abominations upon the Internet landscape.

The process of digitally signing code is known as *Authenticode*. In order to digitally sign a control created in Visual Basic, you must go through the following steps:

▶ Obtain a Software Publisher's Certificate. This is an electronic signature you apply to your binary files that marks you as its author. Microsoft does not issue these certificates; you must go to a third party (known as a certificate authority, or CA) to obtain one. Check out the page http://www.microsoft.com/ intdev/ security/authcode/certs.htm for the latest information on certificate authorities.

▶ Use the Signcode utility to apply your digital certificate to your downloadable .CAB file.

Obtaining a Software Publisher's Certificate

The first step to getting your signed controls on the Web is to sign up with a certificate authority. As of this writing, there is only one certificate authority, Verisign, although there may be more authorities by the time you read this book. The Verisign page is at http://digitalid.verisign.com/.

The starting point to obtain a digital ID is http://digitalid.verisign.com/codesign.htm. If you're an individual software developer, you want to get a Class 2 certificate, which as of this writing costs $20 a year. If you're registering a company that produces software, you'll need to obtain a Class 3 certificate, which costs $400 a year. Also, if you are based outside of the U.S. or Canada, you can't get a Class 2 certificate.

The Verisign Web pages tell you exactly what you need to get signed up. The process to receive a digital ID is arranged in a series of steps; each Web page tells you what's required in detail, and it's pretty hard to mess up. The steps are:

1   Choose which kind of digital ID you want. If you're an individual, choose Class 2; if you're representing a business, choose Class 3.

2   Supply some information about yourself. If you're an individual, you just need to give them some information about yourself. If you're registering a company, you'll need to supply information about your organization.

3   Pay the annual fee. You can do this online by supplying your Visa or Mastercard number.

4   Confirm that the information you entered is correct.

5   Read and agree to the Software Publisher's Pledge. (Placing your right hand over your heart at this stage is, I believe, optional.)

6   Submit the information to Verisign.

After you've supplied this information, Verisign will e-mail you a digital ID personal identification number (PIN) that you'll need to activate your digital ID. (Doing it this way verifies that the e-mail address you gave them is valid.) When you receive this PIN, you return to Verisign's Web site, enter the PIN, and your digital ID request is complete.

At this point, the request process generates two files on your machine: a *credential file* and a *private key*. Because it can be made to work like a signature, you should store the private key on a disk that is not connected to the Net. (I keep mine on a floppy, with a backup in my safe deposit box at my bank.)

The credential file contains information about who you are, such as whether you're an individual or a business and what your e-mail address is. Both the credential file and the private key are used by the signing utility when you sign your file.

> **Note** *Authenticode should not be looked at as an airtight security system for ActiveX objects. Instead, it's a way to make developers more accountable*

for the effects of the software they create. The premise is that a developer will devote more effort into debugging and safety verification if that developer can be identified through Authenticode. Authenticode is based on two concepts: integrity and authenticity. The premise of authenticity dictates that if your name is attached to the code you're distributing, it's less likely to contain a virus or other destructive code. The principle of integrity covers situations where your code might be altered by a malicious third party. But just because the code is authentic doesn't mean it doesn't contain bugs, for example.

Using Signcode to Sign Your .CAB File

Once you've obtained a software publisher's certificate, you can use the Signcode utility to digitally sign your files. Signcode is a utility that comes with the ActiveX SDK (on my machine, it's installed into the \inetsdk\bin\i386 directory).

> **Note** *The Signcode utility used in this book was taken from the ActiveX Software Development Kit because the beta version of Visual Basic used for testing the examples in this book did not contain it. However, it is likely that this utility will be included with the final, shipping version of Visual Basic 5.0.*

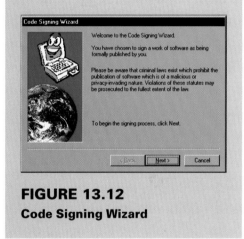

FIGURE 13.12
Code Signing Wizard

When you run Signcode, it launches the Code Signing Wizard, as illustrated in Figure 13.12.
To sign your code using Code Signing Wizard, do the following:

1 Click on **Next** to move past the initial screen. The second Code Signing Wizard screen appears.

2 In the field "Which program would you like to sign?" enter the path and filename to your control's .CAB file. Use the Browse button if you don't feel like typing the full path.

3 In the "What would you like to call this program?" field, type the full name of the control.

4 In the "Where can people find more information about it?" field, type the name of the control's URL, if one exists. The screen should look like Figure 13.13.

5 Click on **Next**. The next screen asks you how you want to sign your control. In this screen, you need to specify the location of your credentials file and your private key. Enter

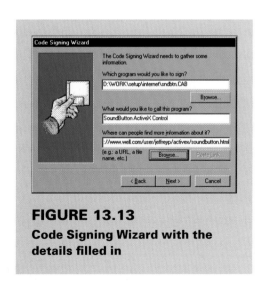

FIGURE 13.13
Code Signing Wizard with the details filled in

this information. The screen should look like Figure 13.14.

6 Click on **Next**. The Code Signing Wizard will display a screen verifying the information you supplied. Make sure everything is correct, click on **Next**, then click on **Sign**.

The wizard will read the files it needs to read, then it will alter your .CAB file to accommodate the digital signature. When it's done, it will display a message saying that it successfully signed the program.

Testing the Signed .CAB File

The easiest way to test a signed ActiveX control is to load it through Microsoft Internet Explorer. If the control hasn't been installed on your computer before and it has been signed properly, your digital certificate will appear after the control is downloaded, as Figure 13.15 illustrates.

When this certificate appears, it confirms your identity to the end users of your control.

> **Note** *If the control has been installed on your computer before and you want to uninstall it for the purpose of testing a Web installation, use the Regsvr32 utility. This utility is described in Chapter 12.*

Summary

In this chapter you learned how to embed an ActiveX control into an HTML Web page using the ActiveX Control Pad. You also saw how to create a .CAB file, a compressed file that enables Web users to seamlessly download your ActiveX control with a Web browser.

In the next chapter, you'll take this crazy Internet thing one step further, creating Internet-aware controls that transmit data over the Net and have the ability to remotely download their properties.

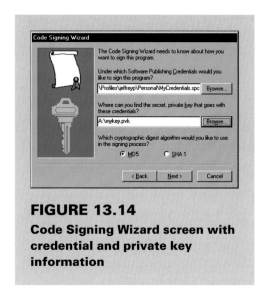

FIGURE 13.14
Code Signing Wizard screen with credential and private key information

FIGURE 13.15
SoundButton control certificate

Asynchronous
Download of
Property Values

Internet Controls
as Constituent
Controls

Adding Web-
Browsing Features
to Your Control

Chapter 14
Controls That Interact with the Internet

This chapter discusses how to add Internet features to your control. The Internet features I address fall into two broad categories:

▶ Using Internet technologies in the context of a compiled EXE application; for example, writing a Visual Basic application that sends e-mail based on a control you provide

▶ Creating ActiveX controls that are destined for use in the context of a Web browser; for example, a control that sends the user to a different Web page based on the user's input

Whether your control is appropriate to use in an EXE or a Web page context, or both, will depend on its functionality, as well as safety issues discussed in Chapter 13. This chapter will discuss both types of controls. In addition, we'll tie in the topics of distributing your control and using your ActiveX control in a Web context that we covered in Chapters 12 and 13.

> **Note** *A few of the examples in this chapter require Microsoft Internet Explorer. You can download Internet Explorer free from the Microsoft Web site at http://www.microsoft.com/ie/download/.*

Asynchronous Download of Property Values

One of Visual Basic 5.0's new features is the ability of ActiveX controls to asynchronously download property values. This feature enables your control to read a property from a remote source–generally, the Internet. The fact that the download is asynchronous means that your application does not have to wait for the download to complete before proceeding with other processing. Because files can take a while to be transmitted over the Internet, the asynchronous download feature is very useful indeed.

The HappyHour control, comprised of a constituent PictureBox and Label controls, was introduced earlier in this book. Because it is designed to display a different picture and text message depending on the time of day, it is an ideal demonstration of the power of asynchronous download over the Internet.

This new version of the HappyHour control has the following programmable interface:

▶ The HappyHourChanged event, triggered when the happy hour status changes. This event is passed a Boolean argument–True if it's currently happy hour, and False if it isn't. This event is only triggered if the HappyHourBegin and HappyHourEnd properties have been set.

▶ The Caption property, a string set by the user.

▶ The HappyHourBegin property that stores the beginning of happy hour. This property is stored as a Date.

▶ The HappyHourEnd property, which stores the end of happy hour. This property is also stored as a Date.

▶ HappyHourYesURL, a string that stores a local filename or an Internet URL that points to a graphic. The graphic located at this URL is loaded by the control at the beginning of happy hour.

▶ HappyHourNoURL, a string that stores a filename or a URL; the graphic located at this URL is loaded by the control when happy hour is over.

Using the AsyncRead Method

In order to access the graphics denoted by the HappyHourYesURL and HappyHour-NoURL properties, your control will need to download them. You use the UserControl object's AsyncRead method to do this. Because AsyncRead is an asynchronous process, as soon as you call this method, processing continues while the property downloads in the background. This processing could include, for example, additional input by the user or even the download of additional data from another source, since you can have a hypothetically unlimited number of downloads going at the same time. Even if you don't plan on enabling your control to perform other actions while it's asynchronously downloading a property value, it's a good idea to asynchronously download properties your control gets from the Internet, since you often have no control over how long something takes to download over the Internet.

The syntax of the AsyncRead method is:

```
UserControl.AsyncRead strURL, lngAsyncType, [Property]
```

The argument strURL is the target URL from which to download the property. The lngAsyncType argument is an enumeration that specifies what kind of property is being downloaded. The legal values for this argument are:

▶ vbAsyncTypeByteArray. A byte array is a way of storing binary data of indeterminate size. (Chapter 11 gives a demonstration of using a byte array in this manner.)

▶ vbAsyncTypeFile. The downloaded property is a file.

▶ vbAsyncTypePicture. The downloaded property is a Picture object.

The *Property* argument is an optional identifier. It does not assign the download to a property, as you might think it would. Instead, it gives a name to the download so you can cancel it later if you need to. (You would use the CancelAsyncRead method to cancel the download.) The property name you assign here is also used to assign the downloaded data to a property; this is done in the AsyncReadComplete event, which is fired after the download is complete.

To see how this works, begin by opening the version of the HappyHour control in the Chapter 14\HappyHour4\Before folder in the CD-ROM that accompanies this book. The project group file is HappyHour.vbg.

The HappyHour Control's URL Properties

In the previous iteration of this control, the HappyHour control raised a HappyHour-Changed event when it was time for happy hour. This new iteration of the control continues to raise this event but also adds two new properties, HappyHourYesURL and HappyHourNoURL. These two URLs point to graphic files on the Internet that are loaded when the HappyHourChanged event is triggered. When it's happy hour, the graphic located at HappyHourYesURL is loaded. When it's not happy hour, the graphic located at HappyHourNoURL is loaded.

To enable these new properties, do the following:

1 Add the two new properties to the happy hour control. The complete list of private property declarations should look like this:

```
' Properties (in declarations section)
Private mdatHappyHourBegin As Date
Private mdatHappyHourEnd As Date
Private mstrHappyHourYesURL As String
Private mstrHappyHourNoURL As String
```

2 Declare the internal variable mvHappyHour as a Variant. This private variable is used by the control as a flag to determine whether it is currently happy hour or not. (It is declared as a Variant instead of a Boolean so the control can perform a test to determine whether the variable was initialized or not; this is an enhancement to this version of the HappyHour control.)

```
' Internal variables
Private mvHappyHour As Variant
```

3 The existing event declaration for the HappyHourChanged event should remain as-is, as shown below. The declarations for this control are now complete.

```
' Events
Public Event HappyHourChanged(HappyStatus As Variant)
```

4 Next, to save the control's properties' design-time values, add code for them in the ReadProperties and WriteProperties events of the UserControl. The code in events (including the code that was there previously) should now look like this:

```
Private Sub UserControl_ReadProperties(PropBag As PropertyBag)
On Error Resume Next
    mstrHappyHourYesURL = PropBag.ReadProperty("HappyHourYesURL", "")
    mstrHappyHourNoURL = PropBag.ReadProperty("HappyHourNoURL", "")
    Caption = PropBag.ReadProperty("Caption", Extender.Name)
    mdatHappyHourBegin = PropBag.ReadProperty("HappyHourBegin")
    mdatHappyHourEnd = PropBag.ReadProperty("HappyHourEnd")
End Sub

Private Sub UserControl_WriteProperties(PropBag As PropertyBag)
    PropBag.WriteProperty "HappyHourYesURL", mstrHappyHourYesURL, ""
    PropBag.WriteProperty "HappyHourNoURL", mstrHappyHourNoURL, ""
    PropBag.WriteProperty "Caption", Caption, Extender.Name
    PropBag.WriteProperty "HappyHourBegin", mdatHappyHourBegin
    PropBag.WriteProperty "HappyHourEnd", mdatHappyHourEnd
End Sub
```

5 Enter Property Get and Property Let procedures for these new properties:

```
Public Property Get HappyHourYesURL() As String
    HappyHourYesURL = mstrHappyHourYesURL
End Property

Public Property Let HappyHourYesURL(ByVal strNewValue As String)
    mstrHappyHourYesURL = strNewValue
    If mvHappyHour Then
        HappyHourLoadGraphic True
    End If
    PropertyChanged "HappyHourYesURL"
End Property

Public Property Get HappyHourNoURL() As String
    HappyHourNoURL = mstrHappyHourNoURL
End Property
```

```
Public Property Let HappyHourNoURL(ByVal strNewValue As String)
    mstrHappyHourNoURL = strNewValue
    If Not(mvHappyHour) Then
        HappyHourLoadGraphic False
    End If
    PropertyChanged "HappyHourNoURL"
End Property
```

The LoadHappyHourGraphic subroutine, called from the Property Let procedures of the new properties, initiates the asynchronous download. The code for this subroutine looks like this:

```
Private Sub LoadHappyHourGraphic(HappyStatus)
' Loads the appropriate happy hour graphic

If HappyStatus = True Then
    AsyncRead mstrHappyHourYesURL, vbAsyncTypePicture, _
    "asyncHappyHourYes"
Else
    AsyncRead mstrHappyHourNoURL, vbAsyncTypePicture, _
            "asyncHappyHourNo"
End If

End Sub
```

Putting the AsyncRead in its own subroutine helps you to avoid duplicating code in your project, since (as you'll see) the AsyncRead method must be called in several different places. Although the AsyncRead method reads the property from the Net, the property can't be assigned until the download is complete. This assignment takes place in the AsyncReadComplete event.

In order to assign the downloaded data to a property, the AsyncReadComplete event of the UserControl is passed an AsyncProperty object. The AsyncProperty object represents the property that was downloaded. This object has three properties of its own:

▶ Value. The value of the property that was just downloaded.

▶ PropertyName. The name of the property as established by the parameter you gave to the AsyncRead method. Again, this is just an identifier and is not necessarily the name of a property of your control.

▶ AsyncType. The type of the download (also established by you when you called AsyncRead method). This is either a byte array, a file, or a Picture object.

To handle an incoming asynchronously downloaded property, enter the following code:

```
Private Sub UserControl_AsyncReadComplete(AsyncProp As AsyncProperty)
    If AsyncProp.AsyncType = vbAsyncTypePicture Then
        Picture1.Picture = AsyncProp.Value
    End If
End Sub
```

This code is simple because there are only two types of asynchronous downloads handled by the HappyHour control–one that downloads the Happy Hour graphic, the other that downloads the "Get back to work" graphic–and they are both assigned to the same thing (the Picture property of Picture1).

However, if your control had to download many different kinds of files over the Net, you'd have to set up a Select Case based on AsyncProp in the AsyncReadComplete event. The code would look like this:

```
Private Sub UserControl_AsyncReadComplete(AsyncProp As AsyncProperty)
    Select Case AsyncProp.PropertyName
        Case "asyncHappyHourYes"
        ' assign AsyncProp.Value to the property

        Case "asyncHappyHourNo"
        ' assign AsyncProp.Value to the property

        Case "asyncSomethingElse"
        ' and so forth

    End Select
End Sub
```

Finally, in order to cause the control to download the property at happy hour, change the Timer event of the constituent Timer control to call the same LoadHappyHourGraphic subroutine you called in the control's Property Let procedures. The code for the Timer event should look like this:

```
Private Sub Timer1_Timer()
' Raise the appropriate event based on
' whether it's happy hour or not

' happy hour hasn't been set yet
    If mdatHappyHourBegin = 0 Or mdatHappyHourEnd = 0 Then
```

```
        Exit Sub
    End If

Select Case mvHappyHour
    Case Empty   ' i don't know whether it's happy hour or not
        If Time > mdatHappyHourBegin And _
            Time < mdatHappyHourEnd Then
            mvHappyHour = True
        Else
            mvHappyHour = False
        End If
        LoadHappyHourGraphic mvHappyHour
        RaiseEvent HappyHourChanged(mvHappyHour)

    Case True    ' it was happy hour a second ago
        If Time > mdatHappyHourBegin And _
            Time < mdatHappyHourEnd Then
        ' it's still happy hour; do nothing
        Else
            mvHappyHour = False
            LoadHappyHourGraphic (False)
            RaiseEvent HappyHourChanged(False)
        End If

    Case False   ' it was not happy hour now a second ago
        If Time > mdatHappyHourBegin And _
            Time < mdatHappyHourEnd Then
        ' it's now happy hour
            mvHappyHour = True
            LoadHappyHourGraphic (True)
            RaiseEvent HappyHourChanged(True)
        Else
        ' do nothing
        End If

End Select

End Sub
```

There's nothing particular tricky about this event procedure; all of the work is done in the subroutines you entered previously.

What the Timer Event Does

The code in the Timer event first checks the variables that store happy hour's begin and end times. If either of these is set to zero (that is, it has not yet been initialized), then the event bails out, because it would make no sense to proceed if the control didn't know when happy hour is. Note that if mdatHappyHourBegin and mdatHappyHourEnd were Variant instead of Date values, you'd instead use the IsEmpty function to determine if the variables had not yet been initialized.

Once the procedure has determined when happy hour is, it compares that value to one of three previous states for happy hour: True, False, or uninitialized (Empty). This comparison takes place in the Select Case in the Timer event.

Based on this comparison, the procedure either raises the HappyHourChanged event and downloads the appropriate graphic, or (if the state of happy hour has not changed), does nothing.

Testing the Code

Now that you've set up the new asynchronous download properties, you can test the control. To do this:

1 Close the code window and close the HappyHour control's designer. Switch to the EXE test form frmHHTestForm.

2 Click on the HappyHour control on the EXE project test form to select it.

3 In its HappyHourYesURL property, type the URL of a graphic, either on your local machine or on the Internet. Type the URL of a different graphic in the HappyHourNoURL property. (If you don't have Net access or you just don't want to come up with a URL of your own, you can use the files happy.bmp and work.bmp on the CD-ROM that accompanies this book.)

4 Enter time values for HappyHourBegin and HappyHourEnd. Make HappyHourBegin a few minutes from now (according to your computer's clock). The Properties window should look like Figure 14.1.

5 Depending on whether it's happy hour or not, one of the graphics will appear. (This may take a moment, depending on the size of the file, whether you selected a local file or an Internet file, and the speed of your Internet connection.)

FIGURE 14.1

Properties window for HappyHour control

6 Wait a few minutes for the state of the control to change from non-happy hour to happy hour. When it becomes time for happy hour, you should be able to see the control download the happy hour graphic you specified in its HappyHourYesURL property, as illustrated in Figure 14.2.

FIGURE 14.2
Downloaded HappyHourYesURL property

Internet Controls as Constituent Controls

You can include an Internet control as a constituent control in order to give your project Internet capabilities. Internet controls handle such tasks as sending e-mail and transferring files (using file transfer protocol, or FTP). There are also Internet controls that give you direct access to Net connections, so-called *socket controls* that enable you to build your own Internet-aware application from scratch without having to worry about how the network transport works.

In this demonstration, you'll build a control that will act as a custom technical support request interface. This control could be used in situations where you need to deploy one or more applications that supply a tech support e-mail feature. Providing an ActiveX control to enable users to send e-mail to tech support would not only be useful in a number of different applications, but it would also provide a consistent interface across those different apps.

> **Note** *The Internet control I used for this demonstration is a shareware mail control produced by Mabry Software. There are a few suites of Internet controls on the market; I chose Mabry's because I like their liberal shareware policy–and they make good stuff. You can find Mabry on the web at http://www.mabry.com.*
>
> *In 1996 Microsoft briefly made a set of Internet controls available called Internet Control Pack. These controls have since been "transferred" to Net-Manage, and you can find them on the Web at http://www.netmanage.com.*

Obtaining the Mabry Mail Control

You can obtain a shareware version of the Internet mail control used in the following demonstration. This control is available as part of the Mabry Internet Pack, downloadable from Mabry Software's Web site at http://www.mabry.com. Information on the Internet Pack is at http://www.mabry.com/ipack.htm; the downloadable shareware version of the controls are at ftp://ftp.mabry.com/ipack.exe.

Once you've obtained ipack.exe and installed it on your system, the complete set of Mabry Internet controls is available on your system. You'll use one of these controls in the following demonstration.

Building the TechSupport Control

To build the TechSupport control, do the following:

1 Create a new control project. Open the UserControl's designer. Give the UserControl the name TechSupport.

2 Add a list box, command button, and text box control to the control designer. Give the command button the name cmdSend. Give the text box the name txtMessage. Give the list box the name lstDepartment.

3 Set the Caption property of cmdSend to **Send**.

4 Set txtMessage's MultiLine property to **True**.

5 Set the Text property of txtMessage to **Type your message here, then click on the Send button**. The control designer should look like Figure 14.3.

Next you'll add code to initialize the control. The idea here is to give the user the ability to send a tech support request to any one of a number of tech support departments. To do this:

1 Double-click on the control designer to open its code window.

2 In the Initialize event of the UserControl, type the following code:

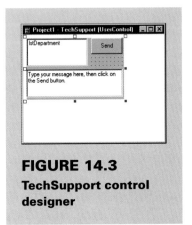

FIGURE 14.3
TechSupport control designer

```
Private Sub UserControl_Initialize()
    lstDepartment.AddItem "Hardware Support"
    lstDepartment.AddItem "Software Support"
    lstDepartment.AddItem "Athletic Support"
End Sub
```

Next, you'll put code in the command button's Click event to validate that the tech support message has been created correctly. To do this:

1 In cmdSend's Click event, type the following code:

```
Private Sub cmdSend_Click()
    If lstDepartment.ListIndex = -1 Then
        MsgBox "Please choose a tech support department " & _
                "from the list.", vbExclamation, "Tech Support"
        lstDepartment.SetFocus
        Exit Sub
    End If
```

```
    If txtMessage.Text = "" Then
        MsgBox "Please type a message.", vbExclamation, "Tech Support"
        txtMessage.SetFocus
        Exit Sub
    End If


    ' OK to send the message
    SendMessage
End Sub
```

2 The SendMessage subroutine, called at the end of the Click procedure, is the procedure that actually sends the mail; you'll write that procedure in a later step. First, to make the SendMessage work, type the following enumeration and module-level declaration in the Declarations section of the code window:

```
Private State As EmailState


Enum EmailState
    StateSending = 1
    StateConnecting = 2
    StateDisconnecting = 3
End Enum
```

Now you're ready to add the mail control and write the code that will drive it. To do this:

1 Select the menu command **Project**, **Components**. In the list of available components, check Mabry Internet Mail control. The Components dialog box should look like Figure 14.4.

2 Click on **OK**. The Mabry Mail control appears in the Toolbox, as illustrated in Figure 14.5.

3 Using the Toolbox, add an instance of the mail control to the control designer. If you're using the shareware version of the mail control, an information window (popularly known in the downscale world of shareware as a *nag screen*) pops up. Wait a few seconds, then click on the nag screen to make it go away.

Note *The nag screen appears because this control, like many ActiveX controls, is distributed as shareware. Shareware means that you can try the software before you purchase it; if you use it, you're expected to pay the author for it. Additionally, if you*

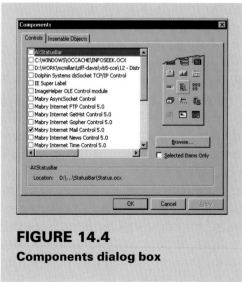

FIGURE 14.4
Components dialog box

register the control by purchasing it, the nag screen goes away. Mabry Software has a very liberal shareware policy; all of their controls are available for download as shareware.

4 An instance of the Mabry Mail control appears on your control designer. Don't worry about where this control is positioned on the designer; it will be invisible at runtime.

5 The code that will send the mail message exists in two places: the SendMessage subroutine and the Done event of the mail control. The following code implements the SendMessage subroutine.

Note *The best way to test an application like this is to set it up to send e-mail messages to yourself (as opposed to, for example, me). Be sure to replace those bogus e-mail addresses with your own, so that when you're testing this control you'll actually get some mail.*

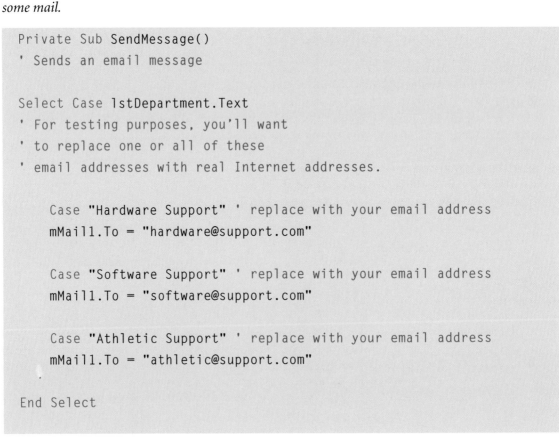

Mabry Mail control

FIGURE 14.5
Mail control in Toolbox

```
Private Sub SendMessage()
' Sends an email message

Select Case lstDepartment.Text
' For testing purposes, you'll want
' to replace one or all of these
' email addresses with real Internet addresses.

    Case "Hardware Support" ' replace with your email address
    mMail1.To = "hardware@support.com"

    Case "Software Support" ' replace with your email address
    mMail1.To = "software@support.com"

    Case "Athletic Support" ' replace with your email address
    mMail1.To = "athletic@support.com"

End Select
```

```
    mMail1.Subject = "Tech Support Request"
    mMail1.From = "Hapless User <hapless@user.com>"


' Replace the value in the next line with your
' internet service provider's email server; usually
' "mail.yourisp.com".
    mMail1.Host = "mail.your_internet_service_provider.com"


' Replace the value in the next line with the
' name of your email account. This value will not
' appear in the email message; it's used to log in
' to your outgoing email server (if the server
' requires such a login).
    mMail1.EMailAddress = "<your_account@yourisp.com>"


    mMail1.Body(Ø) = txtMessage.Text


    Screen.MousePointer = 11
    State = StateConnecting
    mMail1.Action = MailActionConnect


    If (mMail1.Blocking = True) Then
        mMail1_Done
    End If


End Sub
```

The important part of this code is toward the end of the procedure. This code calls
the Done event of the mail control three times, once for each stage of the e-mail session
(sending, connecting, and disconnecting).

To finish the project, put the following code in the mail control's Done event:

```
Private Sub mMail1_Done()
    Screen.MousePointer = Ø


    Select Case State
        Case StateConnecting
            State = StateSending
```

```
                mMail1.Flags = MailDstIsHost
                mMail1.Action = MailActionWriteMessage
                If (mMail1.Blocking = True) Then
                    mMail1_Done
                End If
        Case StateSending
                State = StateDisconnecting
                mMail1.Action = MailActionDisconnect
                If (mMail1.Blocking = True) Then
                    mMail1_Done
                End If
        Case StateDisconnecting
                'do nothing; let it finish
        End Select

End Sub
```

You can see that this event procedure can do three things depending on the state of the session with the mail server. If the event is raised after the control has finished connecting with the server (the StateConnecting case), the procedure changes the State flag to Sending, then sends the message. If the event is raised after the control has sent the message (the StateSending case), the event procedure changes the State flag to Disconnecting and disconnects from the server. If the event is raised after the control has disconnected (the StateDisconnecting case), then the procedure does nothing, because its work is done.

This control project now has all it needs to blanket the world (or you, at least) with useless e-mail. To test the control, do the following:

1 Close the code window and the control designer.

2 Open the test EXE project form.

3 Place an instance of the control on the form.

4 Run the project by choosing the menu command **Run, Start,** or by pressing the function key **F5**.

5 The project runs. Select a tech support department from the list box, then type a message in the text box. Click on **Send** to send the message.

6 If you modified the code so it sends e-mail to yourself, wait a few minutes, then check your mail (using whatever application you normally use to check your mail). The mail message should appear in your incoming e-mail.

Although this is an extremely simple example of sending Internet e-mail, the fact that you have programmable control over the process opens up a number of interesting possibilities. You could write a control that polls a database once per hour, notifying a system administrator when a query retrieved a particular set of results. Or you could modify the control to generate a mass mailing to everyone in your company once per day, thereby introducing you to the exciting and dynamic world of independent consulting.

About the Winsock API

Any Windows application that does anything with the Internet does so through a net-working API known as Winsock. Winsock implementations have existed for every version of Windows since 16-bit Windows 3.1.

In this chapter, I wanted to include an example of how to write a Winsock control using native Winsock API calls, but I quickly realized that such a project could very well take up a book of its own—and, in fact, somebody else has already written that book. The book is Michael Marchuk's *Building Internet Applications With Visual Basic* (Que, 1995), and it's definitely one of a kind. This book will really give you an insight into how to get to the Internet from Visual Basic. Its only problem from the perspective of a Visual Basic control creator is that all the examples and API declarations are geared toward the 16-bit implementation of Winsock.

What's Going On under the Hood

In order to appreciate how much functionality is encapsulated by the mail control, you might find it helpful to see the actual text of the conversation it has with the server when it sends your e-mail message. You can get a look at the conversation the mail control has with the mail server by activating its debug mode. To do this:

1 Open the control designer and click on the mail control. In the Properties window, set the control's Debug property to 1.

2 Double-click on the mail control to bring up its code window. Using the Procedure combo box, switch to the mail control's Debug event.

3 In the Debug event, write the following code:

```
Private Sub mMail1_Debug(ByVal Message As String)
    Debug.Print Message
End Sub
```

4 Close the code window and the control designer. Go back to the EXE test form, launch it, and send yourself another e-mail message.

5 In the Immediate window, the following conversation appears:

```
OnSend
220-mail.sirius.com Sendmail 8.6.12/960710 ready at Mon, 23 Dec 1996
12:10:50 -0800
```

```
220 ESMTP spoken here

HELO bedrock

250 mail1.sirius.com Hello ppp011-sf1.sirius.com [205.134.227.11],
pleased to meet you

MAIL FROM:"Skippy" <skippy@sirius.com>

250 "Skippy" <skippy@well.com>... Sender ok

RCPT TO:skippy@sirius.com

250 skippy@sirius.com... Recipient ok

DATA

354 Enter mail, end with "." on a line by itself

250 MAA19061 Message accepted for delivery

quit

221 mail1.sirius.com closing connection
```

Note *This is roughly what I get when I send mail through my Internet service provider (ISP), anyway. The exact words you'll see will depend on how your ISP's mail server is configured.*

From looking at the debug information, you can see that the mail control really works on two levels. It handles the Winsock connectivity behind the scenes, acting as a wrapper around the Winsock API calls and encapsulating the Internet mail protocol, known as Simple Mail Transfer Protocol (SMTP). This protocol governs the way applications send mail through Internet mail servers. Again, it isn't strictly necessary for you to know how this works to add Internet mail functionality to your application, but it might prove helpful if you ever wanted to write your own Internet mail control.

Adding Web-Browsing Features to Your Control

Although there are a few ActiveX controls on the market that enable Web browsing and downloading of Internet data, none are likely to have an interface as rich (or well-supported) as that of Microsoft Internet Explorer. So it's fortuitous that Internet Explorer is a free download. Someday (hopefully soon) ActiveX will be supported on all operating system platforms, so you'll be able to activate Web browsers everywhere.

Internet Explorer's object interface can be used by Visual Basic applications in two ways: as an ActiveX control (the WebBrowser control) and as an Automation object. We'll take a look at both of these techniques in the remainder of this chapter. Then, in Chapter 16, "Object-Oriented Programming," you'll see how to put these technologies to work in the form of a custom Web-browsing Hotlist control.

Using Internet Explorer as a Constituent Control

One of the neat things about Microsoft Internet Explorer is the fact that it is built around an ActiveX control. This means you can use Internet Explorer as a constituent control in your applications; the only requirement is that your users have Internet Explorer installed on their computers–not a particularly steep requirement, since it's a free download.

> **Note** *The full documentation of the object model of the WebBrowser control is available on the Microsoft Web site at http://www.microsoft.com/int-dev/sdk/docs/iexplore/. It's definitely worth downloading if you plan on building a control based on the WebBrowser object. There are separate versions of the documentation geared toward Visual Basic and C/C++ developers.*

The ActiveX implementation of the WebBrowser control is in a file called shdocvw.dll; it is registered in the list of ActiveX components as Microsoft Internet Controls.

> **Note** *In order to keep you on your toes, Microsoft did not give the WebBrowser ActiveX control an .OCX extension as you'd expect; it is a .DLL file. But you knew already from your diligent reading of the previous chapters of this book that .OCX files are really just special types of .DLL files. You weren't confused by that, were you? Of course not.*

In order to see an example of the WebBrowser control in a control project, you'll build a control that will display Web pages automatically, one after the other, in a slide show format. To do this:

1 Start a new control project. Give the UserControl the name NetSlideShow.

2 Add a Timer control to the control designer.

3 From the Project menu, select Components. Scroll through the list until you find Microsoft Internet Controls, then check it. The dialog box will look like Figure 14.6.

4 Click on **OK**. The WebBrowser control is added to the Toolbox, as illustrated in Figure 14.7.

5 Add an instance of the WebBrowser control to the control designer.

Note *In the beta version of Visual Basic 5.0 used to develop the examples in this book, the WebBrowser control did not repaint itself or display its borders correctly at design time. This was probably just a quirk in the beta of VB 5.0; it's likely that this will have been fixed by the time you read this. This problem does not affect the control's functionality, at any rate.*

6 Add the following code to resize the WebBrowser control to the dimensions of the UserControl. In addition to resizing the control, this code also displays a Web page; it exists in the Resize event so the control will display something as soon as it is instantiated at runtime.

```
Private Sub UserControl_Resize()
    WebBrowser1.Move 0, 0, ScaleWidth, ScaleHeight
    If mstrFirstURL > "" Then
        WebBrowser1.Navigate mstrFirstURL
    End If
End Sub
```

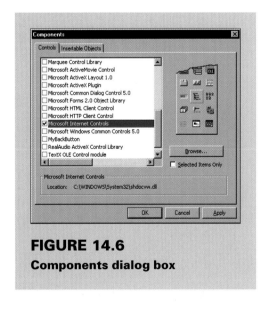

FIGURE 14.6
Components dialog box

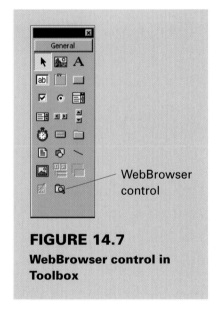

FIGURE 14.7
WebBrowser control in Toolbox

7 Your control needs to expose a TimerInterval property that enables the user to specify how many seconds to display each Web page. Unlike the constituent Timer's Interval property, this property is measured in seconds, instead of milliseconds; your control will perform the conversion seamlessly. Additionally, the Property Let needs to include validation code to ensure that the user does not set the TimerInterval property to an unreasonable value. To implement this property, enter the following code:

```
Public Property Get TimerInterval() As Integer
    TimerInterval = Timer1.Interval / 1000
End Property


Public Property Let TimerInterval(ByVal lngNewValue As Integer)
    If lngNewValue > 0 And lngNewValue < 60 Then
        Timer1.Interval = lngNewValue * 1000
    End If
End Property
```

8 Next you'll implement two properties, FirstURL and SecondURL. These properties store the URLs of the Web pages that the control will display. To do this, enter the following code:

```
' Declarations
Private mstrFirstURL As String
Private mstrSecondURL As String
Private mbURLFlag As Boolean  ' specifies which URL is current

Public Property Get FirstURL() As String
    FirstURL = mstrFirstURL
End Property

Public Property Let FirstURL(ByVal strNewValue As String)
    mstrFirstURL = strNewValue
    WebBrowser1.Navigate strNewValue
End Property

Public Property Get SecondURL() As String
    SecondURL = mstrSecondURL
End Property


Public Property Let SecondURL(ByVal strNewValue As String)
```

```
        mstrSecondURL = strNewValue
        WebBrowser1.Navigate strNewValue
End Property
```

9 The Timer event of the constituent Timer control performs the work of down-loading the appropriate URLs at runtime. To make it work, enter the following code:

```
Private Sub Timer1_Timer()


' Only rotate slides at run time.
If Ambient.UserMode = True Then
    If mbURLFlag Then
        If mstrFirstURL > "" Then
            WebBrowser1.Navigate mstrSecondURL
            mbURLFlag = False
        End If
    Else
        If mstrSecondURL > "" Then
            WebBrowser1.Navigate mstrFirstURL
            mbURLFlag = True
        End If
    End If
End If
End Sub
```

10 Finally, add code to the ReadProperties and WriteProperties events of the UserControl so the values of its design-time properties are stored:

```
Private Sub UserControl_ReadProperties(PropBag As PropertyBag)
    mstrFirstURL = PropBag.ReadProperty("FirstURL", "")
    mstrSecondURL = PropBag.ReadProperty("SecondURL", "")
    Timer1.Interval = PropBag.ReadProperty("TimerInterval", 0) * 1000
End Sub


Private Sub UserControl_WriteProperties(PropBag As PropertyBag)
    PropBag.WriteProperty "FirstURL", mstrFirstURL, ""
    PropBag.WriteProperty "SecondURL", mstrSecondURL, ""
    PropBag.WriteProperty "TimerInterval", Timer1.Interval / 1000, 0
End Sub
```

11 Now you can test the control. To do this, close the code window, close the control designer, and open the text EXE project form.

12 Place an instance of the NetSlideShow control on the form. The control appears, but no URL opens, because you haven't set any of the control's properties yet.

13 Set the control's FirstURL property to http://www.field-guide.com. The Web page for the *Field Guide to North American Males* appears, as illustrated in Figure 14.8.

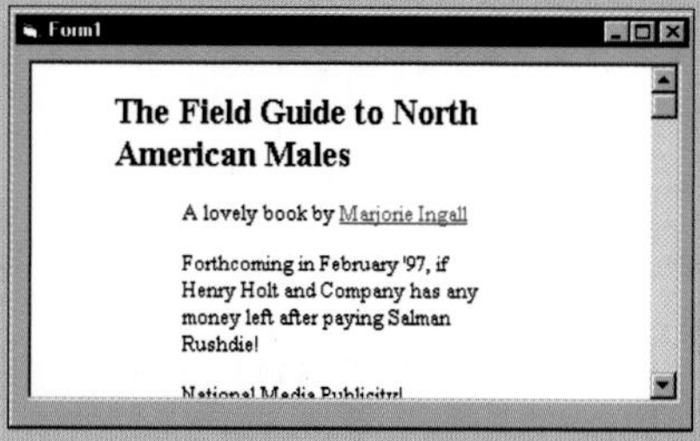

14 Set the control's SecondURL property to http://www.well.com/user/jeffreyp/activex/. The home page for this book appears.

15 Set the control's TimerInterval property to 20. (The trick here is to set the interval to a number high enough that the user can see the current picture fully loaded before the next one starts loading.)

FIGURE 14.8
NetSlideShow control with Web page

16 Launch the EXE project by choosing the menu command **Run, Start**, or by pressing the function key **F5**. Wait twenty seconds; the URL should change automatically.

> **Note** *A more elegant way to implement the URL properties of this control might be through the use of a collection. That way, rather than limiting the number of Web pages to two, you could display a (theoretically) unlimited number of Web pages by adding each new Web page to a collection of URLs. For more information on how to implement collections, see Chapter 16, "Object-Oriented Programming."*

Controls That Act as Hyperlinks

You can use the Internet Explorer object model to control a Web browser from an ActiveX control contained in the browser.

For example, consider a large Web site with large pages containing lots of links. Such sites often contain HTML hyperlinks that say Back, which is the link that takes you back to the page where you came from. But how does the page know exactly which page you came from? The answer is: it doesn't. It assumes you followed the hierarchy the Web site designer set up for you. But we all know the Web doesn't always work that way. You could have come to the site from a search engine or typed in the URL manually.

In order to have a true Back button, your control would need information about which URL the user had been previously viewing. Internet Explorer conveniently stores that information in a place called the *history list*. You can move through the URLs in the browser's history list by using the GoForward and GoBack methods of the WebBrowser control.

To see how this works, you'll set up a custom command button that acts as a Back button. The advantage of this control over a Back hyperlink is that it will always take the user back to the previous URL viewed. Another advantage is that it will always work, no matter which Web page you use it in. To set up this control:

1 Create a new control project. Give the UserControl the name BackButton.

2 Add a constituent command button to the control designer.

3 In the command button's Click event, enter the following code:

```
Private Sub Command1_Click()
On Error Resume Next
    Hyperlink.GoBack
End Sub
```

Note *You include the On Error Resume Next in case some wisenheimer tries to put the control in a Visual Basic form; since only Web pages support the GoBack method, this control is only appropriate for use in a Web page.*

In the Click event procedure, you use the Hyperlink object (an element of the UserControl object) to navigate through the Web browser container's history list. The Hyperlink object has three methods:

▶ GoBack sends the Web browser to the previous URL viewed, backing the browser through the history list. If you continue executing the GoBack method, the browser continues to be sent backward through the history list.

▶ GoFoward sends the Web browser to the next URL in the history list (this presumes that you previously used GoBack to move backward in the history list).

▶ NavigateTo sends the Web browser to a URL you specify. This method takes a string argument (the name of the URL).

To finish this control and prepare it for testing, include the standard code for resizing and initializing the control's Caption property:

```
Private Sub UserControl_InitProperties()
On Error Resume Next
    Caption = Extender.Name
End Sub


Private Sub UserControl_Resize()
    Command1.Move 0, 0, ScaleWidth, ScaleHeight
End Sub
```

```
Public Property Get Caption() As String
    Caption = Command1.Caption
End Property


Public Property Let Caption(ByVal strNewValue As String)
    Command1.Caption = strNewValue
End Property
```

Now you're in a funny situation, because at this point you want to test the control. But you don't want to go to the trouble of testing the control on a Web page, because then you'd have to compile it and write an HTML test page for it. I thought about creating an EXE test form with a Web browser control on it, then making the Web browser control the container of the BackButton control. But that doesn't work (because the Web browser control doesn't contain controls in the traditional sense; it can contain controls, but only if those controls are embedded into the HTML).

So for now, you're stuck with compiling and writing an HTML test page for the BackButton control in order to test it. To do this:

1 In the Project Explorer, give the control project a name, such as MyBackButton. This name will show up when you compile the control.

2 Select the menu command **File, Make MyBackButton.ocx**. The Make Project dialog appears. Click on **OK**.

3 Launch the ActiveX Control Pad. Insert an instance of MyBackButton.BackButton in the HTML page that's automatically generated, then save the page as BackButton.htm.

> **Note** *See Chapter 13 for more information on how to use the ActiveX Control Pad.*

4 Close the ActiveX Control Pad and launch Microsoft Internet Explorer. The browser will launch and open to the default page.

5 In Internet Explorer, select the menu command **File, Open**. Click on Browser to locate the file BackButton.htm you saved previously.

6 The Web page containing the BackButton control appears. Click on it and you'll be sent back to the default page.

> **Note** *If at this point you wish to go back and enhance the control you're working on, be sure to check the Binary Compatibility option (in Project Properties) before you recompile. If you don't do this, you'll need to recreate your test HTML page, because the control's GUID will change when it is recompiled.*

Using the Internet Explorer Automation Object

You can launch an instance of Microsoft Internet Explorer using a technology known as Automation (formerly known as OLE Automation). Automation is an object technology, related to but different from ActiveX control objects. Automation objects have the following distinguishing characteristics:

▶ They exist primarily in code and do not always include a visual interface.

▶ They have a programmable interface comprised of properties, methods, and collections.

▶ They are generally related to an application, known as an Automation server. For example, all of the Microsoft Office applications, including Word and Excel, are Automation servers; Internet Explorer is an Automation server as well.

▶ They are accessed as variables of type Object and instantiated through the CreateObject function.

You can use Internet Explorer as an Automation server to provide additional Internet features to your control project in situations where you would rather not use the WebBrowser control. To see an example of how to do this:

1 Start a new control project. This project will provide the user with a list of choices from which to obtain online help in an application; selecting a choice will launch an instance of Internet Explorer and display an online help topic.

2 Give the UserControl the name OnlineHelp.

3 Add a constituent list box control to the project. Give the list box the name lstURL.

4 Double-click on the control designer to open its code window. In the control's Initialize event, populate the list box by adding the following code:

```
Private Sub UserControl_Initialize()
    lstURL.AddItem "General Help Topics"
    lstURL.AddItem "Printing"
    lstURL.AddItem "Saving Your Work"
End Sub
```

5 Make the constituent list box resize to fit the dimensions of the UserControl by adding the following code to the UserControl's Resize event:

```
Private Sub UserControl_Resize()
    lstURL.Move 0, 0, ScaleWidth, ScaleHeight
End Sub
```

6 Finally, place the following code in the constituent list box's DblClick event:

```
Private Sub lstURL_DblClick()
    Screen.MousePointer = vbHourglass

    Dim objExplorer As Object
    Set objExplorer = CreateObject("InternetExplorer.Application")


    Select Case lstURL.Text
        Case "General Help Topics"
        objExplorer.Navigate "http://www.microsoft.com/kb/"

        Case "Printing"
        objExplorer.Navigate "c:\work\print.html"

        Case "Saving Your Work"
        objExplorer.Navigate "c:\work\save.html"

        Case Else
        ' whoops! do nothing
        Exit Sub

    End Select


    ' Setting explicit Left and Top values
    ' ensures that IE will always appear in
    ' a full window even if the user has an
    ' existing instance minimized
    objExplorer.Left = 10
    objExplorer.Top = 10
    objExplorer.Visible = True
    Screen.MousePointer = vbArrow

End Sub
```

As you've probably surmised, this code launches Internet Explorer, tells it to navigate to a particular URL, then makes the application visible. (Most Automation servers are initially invisible by default.)

The code creates an instance of Internet Explorer by using the CreateObject function. Using the CreateObject function to create an instance of an Automation server is not unlike creating a control on a form in Visual Basic, except that Automation takes place in code; there is no visual component to it. Once you've created an instance of Internet Explorer (represented in this code by the object variable objExplorer), you can execute its methods (such as its Navigate method) and alter its properties (such as its Left, Top, and Visible properties).

Once the instance of Internet Explorer is visible, users are free to use Internet Explorer's user interface to do whatever they want, saving you a heap of trouble in the area of user-interface design and event handling.

To test the capabilities of the code you just entered, do the following:

1 Close the code window and the control designer.

2 Switch to the text EXE project form, Form1.

3 Place an instance of the OnlineHelp control on Form1.

4 Launch the project using the menu command **Run, Start** (or the function key F5).

5 Double-click on the first item in the list. After a short delay, Internet Explorer should pop up, displaying the Microsoft Knowledge Base Web page.

If this were a real control project, you'd want to insert an error trap to handle the situation where a URL didn't exist or couldn't be opened by Internet Explorer. See Chapter 15 for more information on how to do this. A more elegant version of this control will be presented in Chapter 16, as you learn how to use Visual Basic's object-oriented programming features to create a working Internet Hotlist control project.

> **Note** *There is an article on the Microsoft Web site that gives a code example of how to launch Internet Explorer from Visual Basic. The code example provided in the Microsoft article is incorrect, at least as of this writing. This article is in the Microsoft Knowledge Base; its article ID is Q160976. You can access the Microsoft Knowledge base on the Web at http://www.microsoft.com/kb/.*

Summary

In this chapter, we explored a number of Internet-related topics, including downloading property values, sending Internet mail and controlling Microsoft Internet Explorer. It's good to get a handle on these technologies–even if you're not doing Internet stuff right now, chances are in the coming years you'll be called upon to do so.

In the next chapter, we'll jump into the infinitely sublime topic of handling errors and debugging your control projects.

Debugging

Error-Handling

Chapter 15
Debugging and Error Trapping

Control creation presents new challenges in the area of debugging. It can sometimes seem as if you're debugging two programs at once–the ActiveX control and the Visual Basic application in which it resides.

The key, as you've seen already from the previous examples in this book, is to keep your control project separate from your EXE project until you're fairly sure your control is ready for prime time. The fact that Visual Basic now enables you to keep multiple projects in the same development environment is a great help in this area; it enables you to keep a "throwaway" EXE project lying around any time you need it.

Planning ahead can also give you an edge when it comes to dealing with problems in your code. For example, if you start your project by making a list of your control's properties, their data types, and whether those properties are to be delegated or stored in variables, it's less likely that you're going to forget the name of an obscure variable or property.

Good planning leads to fewer bugs. But you knew that already. This chapter deals with what happens *after* you've planned and coded and adjusted your expectations and you discover that things are still messed up.

Debugging

Debugging is the practice of taking care of problems in your code after you've written it. Whether these problems are comprised of *bugs* (you committed a syntactical mistake in your code) or *errors* (your code doesn't come up with the correct result), the debugging features of Visual Basic can help you figure out what's wrong.

This section describes all of the debugging features of the Visual Basic IDE, highlighting the new features of Visual Basic 5.0 where appropriate. Because VB's debugging features have only a tangential bearing on control creation, I tried to keep the demonstrations succinct. This was so I could leave more room for the second half of this chapter, which covers error-handling, and which has more of a bearing on control creation.

The Immediate Window

In previous chapters, you used the Immediate window as a place to view the results of the Debug.Print method. But you can also issue commands to Visual Basic through the Immediate window. This is useful when you want to execute individual lines of code to see what they'll do at the point the program is currently at.

Typing code into the Immediate window works only when you've paused program execution. When a program has been paused as the result of a pre-programmed break-point or as a result of the programmer pressing Ctrl+Break, it is said to be in *break mode*. The following example shows how to enter break mode–pausing a program while it's running–by using Ctrl+Break.

To see how to issue commands to a running program through the Immediate window:

1 Start a new EXE project.

2 Add a command button to the form. In the form's Click event, enter the following code:

```
Private Sub Command1_Click()


For x = 1 To 1000000
    Debug.Print x
    y = 3.14159
    z = y * x


Next x
```

This code simulates the code you'd normally see in a real program.

3 Run the code by using the function key **F5**.

4 Click the command button on the form. You should be able to see the Immediate window fill up with all kinds of meaningless numbers.

5 Press **Ctrl+Break** on your keyboard. The program stops. The currently active line is highlighted, as illustrated in Figure 15.1.

6 Position your mouse pointer on top of one of the variables in the code (but don't click). After you hold the mouse pointer over a variable for a second or so, Visual Basic displays the value of that variable, as displayed in Figure 15.2.

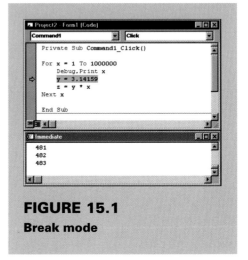

FIGURE 15.1
Break mode

7 Now click in the Immediate window. Type the code:

```
x = 999999
```

and press Enter.

8 Run the program by pressing the function key **F5**. You should be able to see that the program picks up from where it left off, but because you increased the value of the counter x to 999,999, it only goes through the loop once more before exiting the Click event procedure.

> **Tip** *To exit break mode and resume running your code, press F5.*

Using the Immediate window is helpful when you're trying to track down the source of a bug. But using Ctrl+Break can be a bit tricky when you're trying to break the program at a particular line of code. It's doubly so when you're trying to get at your control project's running code from the EXE project. That's where breakpoints come in.

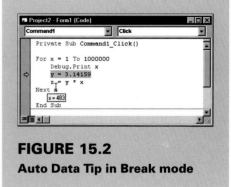

FIGURE 15.2
Auto Data Tip in Break mode

Breakpoints

A breakpoint halts program execution when your application comes to a certain line of code. You can set as many breakpoints in your project as you want, except for lines of code that aren't executed–such as variable declarations, comments, and blank lines.

You can use breakpoints in control projects just as you do in normal Visual Basic code. To place a breakpoint, you must have a code window open and have the insertion point on the line of code where you want your breakpoint to be. There are four ways to place a breakpoint in a line of code:

▶ Choose the menu command **Debug, Toggle Breakpoint.**

▶ Use the function key shortcut **F9.**

▶ Right-click on a line of code, then from the context menu, select **Toggle**, then from the submenu, select **Breakpoint.**

▶ Use the mouse shortcut by clicking in the left margin of the code window. This is a new shortcut in Visual Basic 5.0, illustrated in Figure 15.3. The red circle that appears in the margin of the code window is called a *breakpoint margin indicator*; it appears whenever a breakpoint is set on a particular line.

> **Tip** *By far, the mouse shortcut is the easiest way to set a breakpoint.*

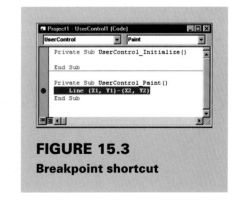

FIGURE 15.3
Breakpoint shortcut

To resume running your code after you're done examining it in break mode, press F5. Since you can have as many breakpoints as you want in your code, the code will run until it reaches another breakpoint, or otherwise pauses or terminates.

The Stop Statement

Inserting a Stop statement in your code is the same as placing a breakpoint there. In some ways, a Stop statement is more convenient, since you can type it without having to fool around with the mouse, or a function key, or any of that other hoo-hah. To insert a Stop statement in your code, simply type the statement

```
Stop
```

on a line by itself. When your code runs, Visual Basic will stop execution as if there were a breakpoint there.

Stepping through Code in Break Mode

Once your program is in Break mode, you can step through the lines of code that follow the breakpoint, one line at a time. Stepping through the code enables you to see the effect of each line of code as it is executed. While you're stepping through each line of code, you can use the Immediate window to execute additional lines of code, or use Auto Data Tips to inspect the values of variables at any point (as described in the preceding section).

The easiest way to step through code is to use the function key F8, although you can also use the menu command Debug, Step Into. To see how to step through code, do the following:

1 Open the code snippet from the previous demonstration. Using your favorite method from the list above, set a breakpoint on the next-to-last line of code, so that the code looks like Figure 15.4.

2 Run the EXE project and click on the command button. The code runs, pausing at the line where you set a breakpoint, as illustrated in Figure 15.5.

3 Press the function key F8 a few times. You should be able to see the code execute one line at a time.

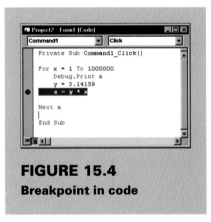

FIGURE 15.4
Breakpoint in code

Stepping over Code

While you're stepping through code, you can step over code that you know doesn't need to be scrutinized. For example, say you're debugging a subroutine that contains code of its own, as well as calls to other subroutines. If you've already verified that the other subroutines are bug-free, you'd probably want to step over them rather than stepping through them for the hundredth time. You might also want to step over a line of code to see what happens when it is omitted.

You step over code in Break mode by using the keystroke shortcut Shift+F8 or by choosing the menu command Debug, Step Over. This ignores the current line of execution; stepping

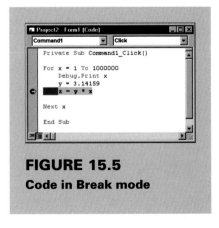

FIGURE 15.5
Code in Break mode

over a subroutine or function in this manner prevents the subroutine or function from executing.

> **Tip** *You can step over only one line at a time. To step over multiple lines at a time, use the Set Next Statement command described later in this chapter.*

Running to Cursor

Run to Cursor is another new feature of Visual Basic 5.0 used in Break mode. The command instructs Visual Basic to start running code up to the point where you've placed the cursor. When execution hits the line where the cursor is at, VB returns the program to Break mode. In a sense, the Run to Cursor command is sort of like a temporary breakpoint, because it doesn't persist after you've run the command. To see how run to cursor works:

1 Run the EXE project code. Execution stops at the break point.

2 Click on the line that contains the Debug.Print statement.

3 Select the menu command **Debug**, **Run to Cursor** (or use the keystroke shortcut **Ctrl+F8**). The code runs up to the point where your cursor is, then goes back into Break mode.

Stepping Out

You use the Step Out command to tell Visual Basic to finish executing a particular subroutine, then return to Break mode. This is another Break mode command that is new to Visual Basic 5.0.

For example, say you're stepping through code and you inadvertently step into a subroutine you've already debugged. You can use the Step Out command to whiz through the remainder of the already debugged subroutine and return to stepping through the original code. To see how this works:

1 Modify the example code so it contains a subroutine. The code should now look like this:

```
Private Sub Command1_Click()

For x = 1 To 1000000
    Debug.Print x
    Spoon
    y = 3.14159
    z = y * x

Next x
```

```
End Sub

Private Sub Spoon()
    For a = 1 To 10
        Debug.Print "Spoon!"
    Next a
End Sub
```

2 Run the code. Execution is paused at the break point.

3 Step through the code one step at a time until execution moves to the Spoon subroutine, as illustrated in Figure 15.6.

4 Choose the menu command **Debug, Step Out**. The remainder of the Spoon subroutine is executed and control returns to the Click event procedure.

Setting the Next Statement to Be Executed

In Break mode, you can designate the next line of code to be executed. This is helpful when you want to skip a number of lines or when you want to execute a number of lines again.

You set the next statement to be executed by following these steps:

1 In Break mode, click on the line of code you want to be executed next.

2 Select the menu command **Debug, Set Next Statement**, or use the function key shortcut **Ctrl+F9**, then restart execution by choosing the command **Run, Continue** (or use the function key **F5**). The program immediately resumes running at the point you set.

In Visual Basic 5.0, there is a new and easier way to set the next statement to be executed. In Break mode, you can click-drag the margin indicator that designates the next line to be executed. To see how this works:

1 While in Break mode, use the mouse to click-drag on the yellow arrow in the margin; this margin indicator shows which line of code will execute next. Drag the indicator to the last line of code, as illustrated in Figure 15.7.

2 Continue execution by choosing the menu command **Run, Continue**, or by pressing the function key **F5**. You

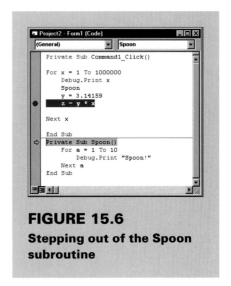

FIGURE 15.6
Stepping out of the Spoon subroutine

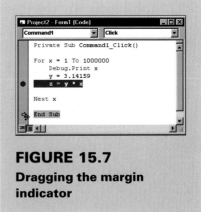

FIGURE 15.7
Dragging the margin indicator

should be able to see that you've broken out of the loop by moving the next line of execution to the last line of the subroutine.

Note *You can clear all the breakpoints in your project at any time by choosing the menu command Debug, Clear All Breakpoints, or by using the keystroke shortcut Ctrl+Shift+F9.*

Using Option Explicit

When you want to use a variable in Visual Basic, you simply make a reference to it. There are very few restrictions on what variables you can use or how many or how they need to be declared.

This is a good thing if you're new to Visual Basic or if you're brainstorming. (See the note at the end of this section for my thoughts on that.) But if your program has a lot of variables, or if you change the names of variables around quite a bit, you'll sooner or later run into a situation where you make reference to an uninitialized variable. In Visual Basic, an uninitialized variable is equivalent to zero, so this represents a problem if you thought you were referring to a variable that contained some meaningful value.

The Option Explicit statement forces you to declare all the variables you use. When you use explicit variable declaration, the program warns you when you make reference to a variable you haven't explicitly declared. To turn explicit variable declaration on, you type the code:

```
Option Explicit
```

in the declarations section of a code module. All of the procedures in that module will then be subject to explicit variable declaration.

For example, consider the following code:

```
Private Sub cmdCalcVolume_Click()
    theVolume = intHeight * intWidth * intDepth
    MsgBox "The volume is" & theVolume
End Sub
```

The assumption here is that the variables intHeight, intWidth, and intDepth were declared and initialized elsewhere (possibly at the module level). But if you forgot to declare these variables, or if you named them something other than intHeight, intWidth, and intDepth, they'll be uninitialized when this code runs. The volume calculation will always be zero.

If you use explicit variable declaration, Visual Basic spots this problem as soon as you attempt to run the application. The undeclared variable is highlighted and the error message in Figure 15.8 appears.

FIGURE 15.8

Variable not defined error

To resolve this problem using Option Explicit, you'd modify the code as follows:

```
' Declarations
Option Explicit


Private Sub cmdCalcVolume_Click()
    theVolume = intHeight * intWidth * intDepth
    MsgBox "The volume is" & theVolume
End Sub
```

The Locals Window

The Locals window, a new feature to Visual Basic 5.0, lets you see the state of all of the variables and properties in your project.

To see how the Locals window works, select the menu command View, Locals from an application that's in Break mode. The Locals window appears, as illustrated in Figure 15.9

As you can see, in addition to showing the value of each variable, the Locals window also shows you the data type of each variable, including the Variant type, if applicable.

The Locals window also shows you the current value of all the properties in the active form. To see this information, click on the plus to the left of the Me item in the Locals window (Me always refers to the active form). The list of properties expands into an outline, as illustrated in Figure 15.10.

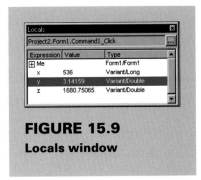

FIGURE 15.9
Locals window

Should You Be Explicit?

Although every book on professional Visual Basic programming ever written emphatically espouses the use of Option Explicit in every code module you ever write, I'm here to say that I don't use Option Explicit when I first start writing code. This is because I go through a brainstorming phase (right after I scrupulously plan out my project's feature set on a sheet of graph paper). In this phase, I add and remove variables willy-nilly.

When I'm at this point in the project, I don't like to be slowed down by having to return to the top of the procedure to declare a new variable when I need one. When my procedure is close to doing what it needs to do, I throw an Option Explicit into the code module and start debugging. This method may not work for you; it's one man's approach, submitted for your consideration.

You can also use the Locals window to inspect the relationship between your UserControl and its container. If you place a UserControl on an EXE project form and open the Locals window in Break mode, you'll see an entry in the outline for your UserControl. Click on the plus to the left of the UserControl in the list to expand the outline, and you'll see something like Figure 15.11.

The Locals window also enables you to change the value of a variable or property while in Break mode. To see how this works:

1 Run an EXE project, then put it in Break mode by pressing **Ctrl+Break**.

2 Open the Locals window by choosing the menu command **View, Locals**.

3 Click on the plus sign to the left of Me. The outline expands to display a list of properties for the current form.

4 Click in the Value column to the right of the BackColor property.

5 Change the BackColor value to 255. You should be able to see that the form's background color has turned red.

Monitoring Expressions Using Watches

You can use watches to monitor the state of a variable or expression. You can also use a watch to pause program execution when a variable expression changes.

When you set a watch, it appears in the Watches window. From there, you can monitor the state of the variable or expression. To see how this works:

1 Click-drag to select the variable x in your example code. (This code exists in the Spoon project on the CD-ROM that accompanies this book; the project group filename is Spoon.vbg.)

2 Choose the menu command **Debug, Add Watch**. The Watches window appears, displaying the watch you've just set, as illustrated in Figure 15.12

3 Remove any breakpoints you may have set up in the code (by using the menu command **Debug, Remove All Breakpoints** or the keystroke shortcut **Ctrl+Shift+F9**).

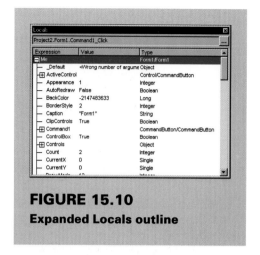

FIGURE 15.10
Expanded Locals outline

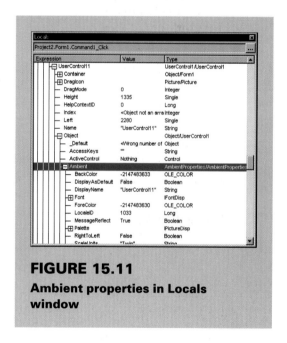

FIGURE 15.11
Ambient properties in Locals window

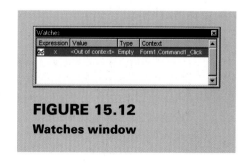

FIGURE 15.12
Watches window

4 Run the code, then use **Ctrl+Break** to pause it. The Watches window displays the current value of x, as illustrated in Figure 15.13.

Just as you can change the value of a property or variable in the Locals window, Visual Basic 5.0 now lets you change the value of a variable in the Watches window. To see how this works:

1 In Break mode, click on the value of x in the Value column of the Watches window.

2 Type in the value 999999.

3 Continue program execution by using the menu command **Run, Continue** (or by pressing the function key **F5**). The code should iterate once more, then complete.

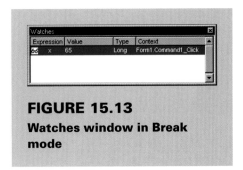

FIGURE 15.13
Watches window in Break mode

To delete a watch, right-click on the watch you want to delete in the Watches window, then from the pop-up menu, choose Delete Watch.

Quick Watch

The Quick Watch feature is a holdover from the Instant Watch feature of previous versions of Visual Basic. You use a quick watch to inspect the value of a variable or expression in Break mode.

This feature is essentially supplanted by the Auto Data Tips feature, which enables you to see the value of a variable or expression by simply positioning the mouse pointer over your code in Break mode. But the Quick Watch feature is helpful if you think you might attach a formal watch to the variable you're inspecting. To see how this works:

1 Run your code example, then put it in Break mode.

2 Click-drag to select any instance of the variable y in your code.

3 Select the menu command **Debug, Quick Watch**, or use the keystroke shortcut **Shift+F9**. The Quick Watch dialog box appears, displaying the current value of the variable, as illustrated in Figure 15.14.

4 Click on **Add**. Notice that the Watches window appears and your quick watch has been converted into a formal watch.

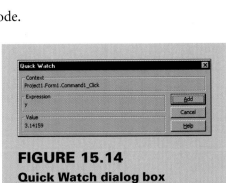

FIGURE 15.14
Quick Watch dialog box

Using Assertions

You can use the Assert method of the Debug object to test whether an operation succeeded or not. If the test is False (that is, the operation was unsuccessful or the expression returned zero or the value False), execution is paused on the line that contains the assertion. So in a sense, an assertion is like a conditional breakpoint.

Let's say you've encountered a bug in the sample application. You've determined that if the variable z goes above a value of 32,000, the bug is triggered. But you're not sure where in your code z exceeds 32,000, or why that causes an error to occur. You can use an assertion to find out. To do this:

1 Change the code of the Click event in the Spoon project as follows:

```
Private Sub Command1_Click()
Dim x As Long, y As Single, z As Single


For x = 1 To 1000000
    Debug.Assert (z < 32000)
    y = 3.14159
    z = y * x
Next x


End Sub
```

2 Run the code. The code will run, then break when the value of z equals 32,000.

> **Note** *You can also use a watch to accomplish the same thing as the assertion described in this example. However, watches can only be set to break when an expression is True, as opposed to assertions, which always break when an expression is False. Additionally, watches are not saved along with your code; when you close a project and re-open it, the watches you've set are lost. Assertions, in contrast, stay with your code and are saved along with it.*

Error-Handling

Error-handling, sometimes referred to as *error-trapping*, is a vital component of any programming project; it's particularly important in an ActiveX control. It refers to the process whereby a program attempts to deal with unexpected problems–anything from a mismatched variable data type to a full hard drive.

In a conventional Visual Basic project, when you fail to include an error-handler in a procedure, any error your program encounters causes the program to stop executing. When your ActiveX control generates an unhandled error, the error is passed along to the host application.

Writing Error-Handlers

You use the On Error statement to handle errors in procedures you write. When you initiate error-handling through the use of an On Error statement, that error-handler remains in effect for the duration of the procedure, unless it is superseded by another error-handler you enable or it is shut off by you. There are three forms of the On Error statement:

▶ On Error GoTo *line*

▶ On Error Resume Next

▶ On Error GoTo 0

On Error GoTo *line* jumps program execution to another point in the procedure (by convention, at the end of the procedure). On Error Resume Next tells the procedure to ignore any errors generated by the procedure and proceed as if nothing has happened; the implication is that your code is either going to ignore the error or handle it on the line immediately following the error. On Error GoTo 0 disables the current procedure's error-handler. It is used very infrequently; in fact, the only situation in which I'd use it is in an error-handler, in order to prevent an endless loop. (An endless loop is where the procedure encounters an error and hands control to an error-handler, which then encounters an error and then attempts to hand control to an error-handler, *ad infinitum.*)

Here's an example of the various incarnations of the On Error statement. In previous examples in this book dealing with controls designed for use in Web pages, we included the minimal error-handler

```
On Error Resume Next
```

in the control's InitProperties event. We did this to avoid problems with the Extender object, since you're not supposed to rely on the Extender object's availability.

On Error Resume Next used in this way isn't really an error-handler at all, since it tells the procedure to eat any error it may encounter, no matter how heinous. (In the SoundButton example in Chapter 13, for example, we used this as a cheap way to get around the fact that a control in a Web page can't get the same Extender properties as a control in a VB project.)

Now that you know all about error-handlers, you can write more adept error-handlers for your controls. Consider the following modification to the InitProperties event of the SoundButton control:

```
Private Sub UserControl_InitProperties()
    On Error GoTo InitPropErr


    Caption = Extender.Name


Exit Sub


InitPropErr:
```

```
MsgBox "InitProperties: " & Err & " - " & Error$
Resume Next

End Sub
```

This is an example of an extremely rudimentary placeholder error trap I use when I'm in the process of figuring out what errors my procedure is likely to encounter. The code you see here is better than On Error Resume Next, but not much better. (You can see that as a result of the Resume Next in the error-handler, any error encountered by the procedure is ignored anyway.)

Also, the MsgBox statement in the error-handler violates the guideline that your control raise errors rather than display message boxes. But this is just a placeholder, so humor me for a few minutes while I get through this demonstration.

The most likely error this procedure will encounter has to do with the nefarious Extender object. For example, Access 95 can't deal with the concept of Extender.Name; if you place the control in a Microsoft Access form, the control displays the error message illustrated in Figure 15.15. Access then proceeds to insert the control anyway, even though your control encountered an error. Go figure.

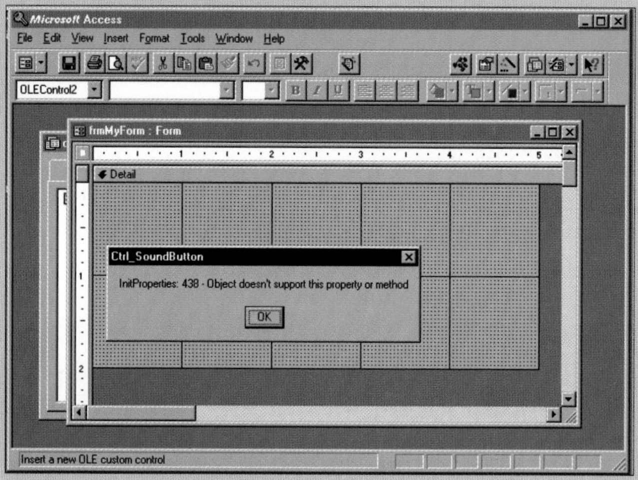

Instead of just generating an error message, it's better if your control attempts to do something intelligent to resolve the error condition. Because you inserted a rudimentary error trap in the control's InitProperties event, you now know in which procedure the error took place, as well as what error number was triggered.

FIGURE 15.15
SoundButton error message

Because the whole point of the code in the InitProperties event is to give the SoundButton control a default caption, the resolution of the problem is simple. When the control encounters error 438 in its InitProperties event, supply some generic default caption (like SoundButton, rather than SoundButton1).

But what happens when a totally unexpected error happens, something you couldn't have planned for? In a Visual Basic EXE project, you'd write code to gracefully abort out of the subroutine, or perhaps even shut down the application if the error took place in a critical spot. But in an ActiveX control, the appropriate response to an unexpected error is to raise it to the level of the host application. You raise an error to the host application by using the Raise method of the Err object, as explained in the next section.

Error-Handling Options

You have the ability to control the conditions under which Visual Basic will halt your application in situations where the application encounters an error. You do this in the General tab of the Tools, Options dialog box, as illustrated in Figure 15.16.

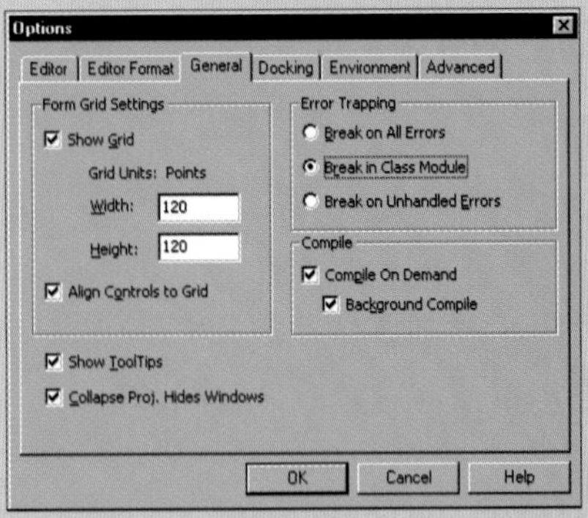

Here is what the different levels of error-handling mean:

FIGURE 15.16
Options dialog box

▶ Break on All Errors–Every error encountered by your project will place the project into Break mode. You might use this setting when you're testing newly developed code and writing error-handlers in order to determine which errors your code is likely to encounter.

▶ Break in Class Module–Unhandled errors in a class module place the project in Break mode. You use this setting when you're debugging a control project and you want errors in the control project to put the EXE project in Break mode. If you don't use this mode when you're debugging a class module, Break mode displays the code in the EXE project that called the class module's procedure that encountered the error, not the code in the class module itself. This setting is the default setting for error-trapping in Visual Basic.

Note *Class modules are covered in Chapter 16. For the purposes of this setting, your ActiveX control projects are not considered to be class modules, even though they have a number of attributes in common with class modules.*

▶ Break on Unhandled Errors–Errors that are handled by your code do not put your project into Break mode. Unhandled errors put the project into Break mode. Unhandled errors in class modules break at the point where the class procedure was called (not in the class module's code).

Err Statements versus Objects

In the previous examples of error-handling in this chapter, you saw that you could get the number of the error by using Err. Once upon a time, Err was a Visual Basic statement, but now that Err is an object, when you refer to Err, you're really making a reference to the default property of the Err object. The default property of Err is Number, so references to Err.Number and Err are really the same thing.

Similarly, references to Error$ and Err.Description really refer to the same thing. It's probably better (from the viewpoint of clarity, correctness, and all that) if you use the new, improved, object-style references to Err properties, but the old style works, and old habits die hard, and Err is easier to type than Err.Number. It's obviously up to you which style you use.

Note *Be aware that when you change the level of error-handling, the change becomes a part of the Visual Basic IDE, not part of the current project, so the change you make will be reflected in all the projects you work with until you change the setting back.*

The Err Object

In Visual Basic, information about errors is handled through the Err object. Err is a system-provided object that contains information about the last error that took place in your code. In addition, you can use the Raise method of the Err object to cause your application (or, more likely, your control project) to signal that an error condition has arisen.

When your control raises an error, it's sending a message to the host application. This is distinguished from error-*handling*, which attempts to deal with an error condition. *Raising* an error means that your control has encountered an error and is passing that information on to the host application. Table 15.1 shows a complete listing of the properties of the Err object, and Table 15.2 covers its methods.

Raising Errors

Although you're probably accustomed to seeing ActiveX controls display message boxes when they encounter error conditions, your control shouldn't display such message boxes with the MsgBox statement. Instead, your control should raise an error, sending a message back to the host application that an error has taken place and enabling the host application to deal with the error.

TABLE 15.1   PROPERTIES OF THE ERR OBJECT

Property	Description
Description	The textual description of the error
HelpContext	The Help Context ID of a help topic that describes this error
HelpFile	The Windows Help file that contains a help topic that describes this error
LastDLLError	The error code returned from a DLL call. (This property is only relevant if the error was raised as the result of a call to a DLL.)
Number	The number of the error. If no error exists, Number equals zero.
Source	The object or process that generated the error.

TABLE 15.2   METHODS OF THE ERR OBJECT

Clear	Clears the properties of the Err object
Raise	Raises an error to the host application

When your control raises an error, one of two scenarios takes place:

▶ If the host application does not handle the error, then Visual Basic will display a message box telling the user what happened (and, in all likelihood, the host application will then terminate).

▶ If the host application does handle the error, then control passes to the host application's error-handler. Whatever action the host application takes to resolve the error or inform the user of its existence is up to the host application.

You can modify your control's error-handler so it will react more intelligently to this error condition, raising an error instead of displaying a message box. Here's a basic example of a procedure that does this:

```
Private Sub UserControl_InitProperties()

    On Error GoTo InitPropErr

    Caption = Extender.Name

Exit Sub

InitPropErr:

    Select Case Err
        Case 438   ' Obj doesn't support this property
        Caption = "SoundButton"

        Case Else"
        Err.Raise Err, "SoundButton", Err.Description

    End Select

End Sub
```

Tip *Notice that the Select Case in the error-handler uses the error number (438), rather than the textual description of the error ("Object doesn't support this property"). This is because error numbers are guaranteed not to change from one version of Visual Basic to the next, while descriptions can change.*

You may want to consider declaring and using constants for error numbers so you don't have to sit around wondering what "438" means. Using a constant like ERR_OBJECT_DOESNT_SUPPORT can make much more

*sense, depending on your programming style. I like using the numbers and
commenting them, as in the above example, so I don't have to remember
what I named my constants.*

Having a single error-handler for a procedure is nice because all the error-handling
code is in the same place. However, this may not give you the granularity you need to
handle the many things a particular procedure may be called upon to do. As an alternative, you can handle potential errors line-by-line, in this way:

```vb
Private Sub UserControl_InitProperties()

    On Error Resume Next


    Caption = Extender.Name


    If Err Then
        Select Case Err
            Case 438  ' Obj doesn't support this property
            Caption = "SoundButton"


            Case Else
            Err.Raise Err, "SoundButton", Err.Description


        End Select
    End If


End Sub
```

In this case, there is no On Error Goto; instead, the value of Err is inspected after
any line that might cause problems. If Err is nonzero, the error is handled immediately.

Handling errors line-by-line requires more work on your part, but it's vital if you
have a procedure that may need to handle the same error in several different ways depending on where in the procedure the error comes up.

Summary

In this chapter we talked about debugging and error handling, particularly with respect
to control creation. We covered error-handling as well as raising errors encountered by
your control project to the level of the host application.

In the next chapter we'll take a look at object-oriented programming concepts in
Visual Basic, and how to put them to work in your control projects.

Object-Oriented
Concepts

Classes

Collections

Incorporating a
Class in a Control

Building Interfaces
Using the Implements
Keyword

Using Friend Methods

Chapter 16
Object-Oriented Programming

The Basic programming language began as a *procedural* language, based on variables, function calls, and statements. It is evolving toward an *object-oriented* language, based on objects, properties, methods, and collections.

Visual Basic has always had support for objects, even though you couldn't always create objects in VB. The ability to create objects from classes was added in VB 4.0, while the ability to create an ActiveX object is new in VB 5.0.

But while purists would argue that Visual Basic isn't a fully object-oriented language (mainly because it doesn't have all the object-oriented features of C++, the 800-pound gorilla of object-oriented languages), it has become more object oriented over time.

You have already seen a number of object-oriented concepts at work in Visual Basic; indeed, ActiveX control creation itself demonstrates a number of object-oriented concepts, such as encapsulation. In the remainder of this chapter you'll see examples of Visual Basic's object-oriented features as they apply to control creation.

Object-Oriented Concepts

An object-oriented system focuses on the elements of the problem (the objects) rather than the method of getting there (the procedures).

When designing an object-oriented system, you often find yourself working backward from the solution (for example, a fully functional inventory system for an ice cream factory) to the objects involved in that solution (a tub of ice cream, a freezer, a truck) to the business rules that govern those objects (a truck can hold 50 tubs of ice cream, a freezer must be kept at 0 degrees Celsius). You may find that working backwards in this way represents a bit of a stretch if you're accustomed to procedural programming, but in time you'll probably find that focusing on the problem rather than the solution is a more natural way to program.

An object-oriented system contains language elements that provide the following:

▶ Abstraction, which entails reducing the complexity of a problem to an easy-to-understand metaphor instead of getting bogged down with the details of how the problem is solved.

▶ Polymorphism, which involves enabling an object to expose multiple interfaces. Polymorphism exists as a new feature in Visual Basic 5.0.

▶ Encapsulation, which entails grouping data and program logic together to minimize complexity and avoid having to track which functions access which data. You always know which functions access which data because the functions and data are encapsulated in the same construct. Data stored in properties accessed by Property Let and Property Get procedures is an example of encapsulation.

▶ Inheritance, the ability to create a new object from existing objects. It means that the new object you build inherits the properties and other elements of the existing object. You get a taste for inheritance with constituent controls in Visual Basic 5.0; they let you create new ActiveX controls out of existing controls. But inheritance as implemented in the Visual Basic language is limited.

So far in this book, you've seen how to build ActiveX controls that act as the basis for user-interface objects. In this chapter, you'll see how to use *classes*, elements of code that enable you to apply these object-oriented principles to your VB applications.

Classes

When you create a class, you're giving yourself the ability to instantiate objects in your application. But unlike ActiveX controls, objects created from classes:

▶ Generally do *not* have a user-interface component. Instead, classes are geared toward data processing and storage rather than user interface.

▶ Are not targeted at other developers. When you create a class in your application or control project, it's generally for your use somewhere else in that project. (The most notable exception to this is when you use a class to build an ActiveX DLL.)

Consider the ice cream factory example introduced earlier in this chapter. If you get a job as a programmer for an ice cream factory, there are certain elements of the business you know will change very infrequently, if ever: the freezing point of orange sherbet, or the number of quarts in a gallon, for example. These concepts are referred to as *business rules*. It makes sense to abstract these concepts into objects early in the game. If you do this, you'll be more efficient. You'll also suffer fewer (ice cream) headaches, because you won't have to rewrite the code that converts quarts to gallons in each new program you write; you'll simply add a reference to your already existing business rules contained in the classes you've authored. This goal of *code reuse* is another prime goal of object-oriented programming.

Much of the programming of classes in Visual Basic will be familiar to you from your work with ActiveX controls. For example, when you create a public subroutine in your class, it is exposed as a method of your object. You can also include Property Let and Property Get procedures in your class in order to expose properties of the objects created from the class.

Although you may get the impression that classes are a watered-down version of ActiveX controls, it happens that classes are a very relevant part of control creation. Many controls (such as the Data control, for example) expose their own object models. In order to implement such object models, you must understand how classes work.

Creating a Class

Every class you create exists in its own file, known as a *class module*. In this example, you'll create a class that will store and process Internet uniform resource locators (URLs). Later, we'll incorporate this class into a collection, and finally, you'll see how to incorporate the collection of URLs into an ActiveX control.

To create the class, do the following:

1 Start a new project. In the Project Explorer, click on the project to which you wish to add a class.

2 Select the menu command **Project, Add Class Module**. A new class module appears in the Project Explorer, as illustrated in Figure 16.1.

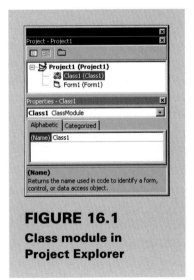

FIGURE 16.1

Class module in Project Explorer

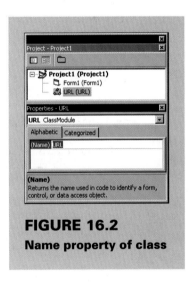

FIGURE 16.2

Name property of class

3 After creating a class, you should give the class a name. Do this in the Properties window, the same way you'd create a name for any other object. The example class we're going to build will store the properties of an Internet URL, so give the class the name URL, as illustrated in Figure 16.2.

4 Double-click on the class in the Project Explorer to open its code window.

5 You'll add properties to this class—a process astoundingly similar to adding properties to an ActiveX control. To do this, add the following code. Note that the DateCreated property is read-only, so in its Property Let procedure, instead of assigning the value to the variable mdatDateCreated, you raise an error.

```
' Declarations

Private mstrDescription As String
Private mdatDateCreated As Date
Private mstrURL As String
```

```
Public Property Get Description() As String
    Description = mstrDescription
End Property

Public Property Let Description(ByVal strNewValue As String)
    mstrDescription = strNewValue
End Property

Public Property Get URL() As String
    URL = mstrURL
End Property

Public Property Let URL(ByVal strNewValue As String)
    mstrURL = strNewValue
End Property

Public Property Get DateCreated() As Date
    DateCreated = mdatDateCreated
End Property

Public Property Let DateCreated(ByVal datNewValue As Date)
    ' this value is read-only; raise an error
    Err.Raise 512 + vbObjectError, "URL", "Property is read-only"
End Property
```

6 This variable should be initialized automatically at the time the object is created; the Initialize event of the class enables you to do this. Enter the following code:

```
Private Sub Class_Initialize()
    mdatDateCreated = Now
End Sub
```

7 Finally, add a public subroutine to your class; this procedure will be exposed as a method of your object. This method will launch Internet Explorer, displaying the URL stored by your class:

```
Public Sub Navigate()


    If mstrURL <> "" Then
```

```
            Dim objExplorer As Object
            Set objExplorer = CreateObject("InternetExplorer.Application")
            objExplorer.Navigate mstrURL
            objExplorer.Left = 20
            objExplorer.Top = 20
            objExplorer.Visible = True
        Else
            Err.Raise 1025 + vbObjectError, "URL", _
                    "No URL has been specified."
        End If


End Sub
```

Now that you have a minimal class defined, you can test it in an application. To do this:

1 Close the class's code window and switch to Form1.

2 Place a command button on Form1. Double-click on the button to open its code window.

3 In the command button's Click event, enter the following code:

```
Private Sub Command1_Click()
    Dim MyURL As New URL

    MyURL.Description = "The News Babe Page"
    MyURL.URL = "http://www.well.com/user/jeffreyp/newsbabe1.html"
    Debug.Print "Created: " & MyURL.DateCreated
    MyURL.Navigate
End Sub
```

The Dim statement at the beginning of this procedure declares the object variable that will store the instance of the object defined by the URL class. (The rule in Visual Basic is that all object variables must be declared explicitly, even if your code has no Option Explicit.)

You can see that once the URL object has been instantiated, you can address its properties and methods just as you would any other object. The complexity involved in calling Internet Explorer as an Automation object has been abstracted behind your class' Navigate method; by placing the Automation code in a method of your class, you've essentially reduced the lines of code required to display a Web page from ten to three.

Collections

A *collection* is a group of related data elements. In Visual Basic, a collection represents a group of variables or objects. You use collections as a handy way to organize program data.

If you're accustomed to using arrays to store data in Visual Basic, you may want to consider using collections instead. Collections have a number of built-in tools that make manipulating data easier–and, in some cases, more efficient–than manipulating arrays.

Using collections is easier than using arrays because collections provide a predefined set of methods for manipulating data. For example, when you have an array of 10 elements and you want to add an 11th element, you have to write several lines of code, redimensioning the array and then adding the new element. The collection, in contrast, has an inherent Add method. You don't have to write any code to implement this method, so adding a new element to the collection requires a grand total of one line of code.

In the next sections, you'll get a look at how to add new usefulness to your URL class by building a class that contains a collection.

How Collections Work

You use the inherent methods of the collection to manipulate its members. (I know that sounds perverse; stick with me, it gets even better later on.) Collections have the properties and methods listed in Table 16.1.

If your collection is wrapped in a class module, you can extend the set of properties and methods of your collection, making it even more flexible (we'll do that later on in this chapter). For now, we'll implement a simple collection and expand upon it.

In this example, you'll take your first stab at using a collection to store a number of URLs. This first example won't be perfect, but it will demonstrate the rudiments of how collections work; we'll refine the example in the following sections of this chapter.

TABLE 16.1	**PROPERTIES AND METHODS OF COLLECTIONS**
Element	**Description**
Add method	Adds an item to the collection
Delete method	Removes an item from the collection
Item method	Returns an element of the collection
Count property	The number of items in the collection

To set up your collection, modify the demonstration code in Form1 so that rather than launching a browser, it adds a few URLs to a collection of URLs called colBookmarks. To do this, modify the existing code so it looks like this:

```
' Declarations
Dim colBookmarks As New Collection
```

```
Private Sub Command1_Click()
    Dim MyURL1 As New URL, MyURL2 As New URL, MyURL3 As New URL

    MyURL1.Description = "The News Babe Page"
    MyURL1.URL = "http://www.well.com/user/jeffreyp/newsbabe1.html"
    'Debug.Print "Created: " & MyURL1.DateCreated
    'MyURL.Navigate

    colBookmarks.Add MyURL1

    MyURL2.Description = "Electric Minds"
    MyURL2.URL = "http://www.minds.com/"

    colBookmarks.Add MyURL2

    MyURL3.Description = "The Onion"
    MyURL3.URL = "http://www.theonion.com/"

    colBookmarks.Add MyURL3

    Debug.Print colBookmarks.Count

End Sub
```

You declare the collection colBookmarks in the Declarations section of the form for two reasons: first, because it is an object variable, it must be explicitly declared somewhere; second, because it is a collection, you want its lifetime to be that of the form, not of the procedure. Declaring the variable in the Declarations section of the form, then, causes the collection to persist throughout the lifetime of the form.

Experimenting with the Collection

At this point, try a few experiments to see how to use the methods of the collection. To do this:

1 Run the project and click on the command button to execute your code.

2 The collection is created, and the three URL objects are added to it. The Immediate window displays the number 3–the count of the collection, as illustrated in Figure 16.3.

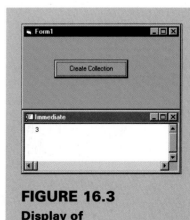

FIGURE 16.3

Display of colBookmarks.Count in Immediate window

3   Pause execution by selecting the menu command **Run, Break**.

4   In the Immediate window, type the code:

```
? colBookmarks.Item(1).URL
```

> **Note**   *The question mark character is shorthand for the Print method.*

The Immediate window prints the value of the URL property of the first member of the collection, as illustrated in Figure 16.4.

5   Because the Item method is the default method of a collection, you can refer to items in the collection using a shorthand syntax, omitting the Item method. To see how this works, enter the code below. The Immediate window should return the same URL value as in the previous example.

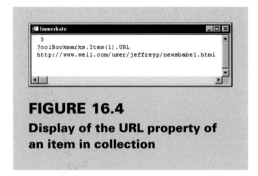

FIGURE 16.4
Display of the URL property of an item in collection

```
?colBookmarks(1).URL
```

> **Note**   *Unlike arrays in Visual Basic, collections are one-based, which means that the first item in the collection is numbered 1. (In contrast, the first item in a default array is numbered 0.) There is a problem with using a collection in this manner, however. To see this problem, type the following code in the Immediate window:*

```
colBookmarks.Add "Yadda yadda yadda."
?colBookmarks.Count
```

No error is returned, and the Immediate window reports the count of items in the collection to be four. This is a problem, because this is supposed to be a collection of URL objects, not a collection of random gibberish text strings.

You can avoid this problem by wrapping your collection in a class. Among the benefits of classes we've discussed earlier in this chapter is that putting collections in classes enables you to enforce *type-safety*. This prevents procedures in your code from incorrectly adding the wrong data types to your collections.

Creating a Collection Class

In order to type-safe your collection, you can place it in a class. To do this:

1   Create a new class. Give this class the name Bookmarks. (Classes that act as collections are conventionally given a plural name, although you don't have to name your classes this way.)

2   Double-click on the class in the Project Explorer to open its code window.

3 Enter the following code:

```
' Declarations
Private mcolBookmarks As New Collection

Public Property Get Count() As Long
    Count = mcolBookmarks.Count
End Property

Public Function Add(theURL As URL)
    mcolBookmarks.Add theURL
End Function

Public Function Item(ByVal varKey As Variant) As URL
    Set Item = mcolBookmarks.Item(varKey)
End Function
```

Note that if you were building a real Bookmarks class, you'd also include code to wrap the collection's other methods, such as Remove. But this code will do for our demonstration.

You can see that these procedures access the private collection mcolBookmarks in much the way that an ActiveX control delegates properties and methods of its constituent controls. The difference in this method of accessing the collection, though, is that the Add and Item methods of the collection are strongly typed. That is, they will only accept URL objects as their input.

Also, note that at no time does the user of this class have direct access to the data stored in mcolBookmarks; she must instead go through the class's interface to get to that data. This is a good thing, because it provides your collection with a simple and safe interface. If something changes down the road (such as the addition of a new property of the URL object), you can be fairly certain that the change will not break existing code.

Making the Item Method the Default

You'll want to make the Item method of your collection class the interface default of the class. This is so the following two lines of code will be the same:

```
Bookmarks.Item(1).Navigate
Bookmarks.(1).Navigate
```

In other words, you're adding another feature of the default collection object to your collection class.

You've seen this kind of thing before, when you set methods and properties of your control projects as the default. However, the way to do this for classes is slightly different than for controls. To set the Item method as the default procedure for your collection class:

1 Make sure the code window for the Bookmarks class is open.

2 Click in the code anywhere in the Item function.

3 Choose the menu command **Tools, Procedure Attributes**. The Procedure Attributes dialog box appears.

4 Click on the **Advanced** button.

5 In the Procedure ID combo box, select (**Default**).

6 Click on **OK**.

Testing the Bookmarks Collection Class

The Bookmarks collection class is now ready to test:

1 Close the Bookmark class's code window and return to Form1.

2 Create a new command button on the form. In the command button's Click event, type the following code:

```
Private Sub Command2_Click()
    Dim myMarks As New Bookmarks
    Dim myURL As New URL


    With myURL
        .Description = "The News Babe Page"
        .URL = "http://www.well.com/user/jeffreyp/newsbabel.html"
    End With


    myMarks.Add myURL
    Stop


End Sub
```

3 Run the code and click the command button. The code executes, then pauses at the Stop statement.

4 In the Immediate window, type the following code. The Immediate window displays the Description property of the item in the collection.

```
?myMarks.Item(1).Description
```

Performance Considerations

Programmers often cast a wary eye on certain elements of object-oriented programming because they fear they're going to spend time adopting a new paradigm only to find their applications run dog-slow.

It is true that collections require more memory overhead than conventional arrays. This is because collections are variants, and variants always consume 16 bytes, no matter which type of data is stored in them. For example, if you use a variant to store a lowly integer–a data type that normally requires two bytes of storage–the variant still requires 16 bytes to store it. However, this increased memory consumption may not necessarily lead to a performance degradation, depending on how you use collections.

When comparing collections vs. arrays, the real measure of performance comes when you consider that you don't have to iterate through an entire collection to retrieve a particular value. Instead, you can use a For Each block, which is always more efficient than iterating through an array.

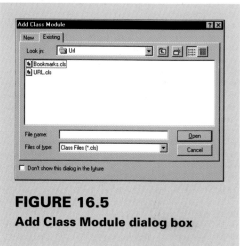

FIGURE 16.5

Add Class Module dialog box

Incorporating a Class in a Control

Now that you have functional URL and Bookmarks classes, you can incorporate them into a control. Not only will this example demonstrate how you can use a class module as a component of a control project. It will also demonstrate how easy it is to re-use code in class modules. To do this:

1 Save the files in the demonstration application you're working on. Give the URL class the filename URL.cls and give the Bookmarks class the filename Bookmarks.cls.

2 Start a new control project. Give the control the name Hotlist.

3 Add a constituent ListBox control to the control designer. This list box will store a list of Web pages.

4 Right-click on the control project in the Project Explorer. The Project Explorer context menu appears.

5 From the context menu, select **Add, Class Module**. The Class Module dialog box appears. Select the Existing tab. The dialog box looks like Figure 16.5.

6 Use the dialog box to add the Properties and URL classes to your control project. After you've done this, the Project Explorer should look like Figure 16.6.

Note *Make sure you add these classes to your control project, not to the EXE test project.*

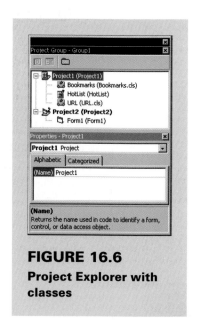

FIGURE 16.6

Project Explorer with classes

7 In the Properties window, change the Instancing properties of the two classes to 2–PublicNotCreatable. This will allow you to instantiate objects defined by these classes from within your control project.

8 Double-click on the code designer to open its code window. Add the following code:

```
' Declarations
Private mbkmBookmarks As New Bookmarks

Private Sub UserControl_Resize()
    List1.Move 0, 0, ScaleWidth, ScaleHeight
End Sub

Public Sub AddURL(strDescription As String, strURL As String)
    Dim urlNew As New URL

    With urlNew
        .Description = strDescription
        .URL = strURL
    End With

    mbkmBookmarks.Add urlNew
    List1.AddItem urlNew.Description

End Sub

Private Sub List1_DblClick()
    mbkmBookmarks.Item(CLng(List1.ListIndex) + 1).Navigate
End Sub
```

You can see that the AddURL subroutine (which, because it is public, is exposed as a method of the HotList control) adds the URL to the Bookmarks collection and displays the description of the URL in the constituent list box.

In the DblClick event of the constituent list box, you can see that the ListIndex property of the list box has to be converted into a long integer and incremented by 1 before it can be used to retrive an item from the collection. The reasons for this are:

▶ The ListIndex property is 0-based, while a collection's index is 1-based.

▶ When you're referring to the elements of a collection by number, you should always explicitly convert that reference to a number. This is because there is a way to refer to a member of a collection by key (not covered in this book). A key can be a string or other data type. When you use a numeric index, the collection knows you're referring to the ordinal number of the item in the collection rather than its key.

Note *Although the user doesn't have access to the URL object in this example, there's no reason why you couldn't give the user access to a URL object similar (or identical) to the URL object in the UserControl project. That way, instead of adding items to your HotList procedurally (using the AddURL method) your control would have a more fully object-oriented interface. I chose to provide access to the Bookmarks collection through a method rather than by adding an object because it greatly simplified this example.*

To test your control, place an instance of the HotList control on the EXE project form, then place the following code in the form's Load event:

```
Private Sub Form_Load()
    HotList1.AddURL "The News Babe Page", _
                    "http://www.well.com/user/jeffreyp/newsbabel.html"
    HotList1.AddURL "The Onion", "http://www.theonion.com/"
    HotList1.AddURL "Home Page", _
                    "http://www.well.com/user/jeffreyp/activex/"
End Sub
```

Then run the EXE project. When the project runs, double-click on one of the items in the hot list. Internet Explorer should launch, displaying the page you chose. Because it stores URLs in a collection, the HotList control should support a hypothetically unlimited number of URLs.

Note *If you're looking for more information on object-oriented programming in VB, you might want to check out Deborah Kurata's Doing Objects In Microsoft Visual Basic 4.0. This unique book covers not only the nuts-and-bolts of programming using classes in Visual Basic, but the just-as-important design principles behind object-oriented programming that every programmer should know about.*

Building Interfaces Using the Implements Keyword

An *interface*, as you know, is the set of properties and methods exposed by an object. You've learned that the interface of a programmable software component can't be changed for fear of losing backward compatibility with existing code. If you developed an enhanced version of a control or class that omitted support for a particular property or method, code based on that component would break.

So how, then, do you modify or enhance the interface of an existing component? One way is to build multiple implementations of an interface based on a type library or abstract class.

A *type library* is created with a utility called mktyplib, which is found in the ActiveX Software Development kit. (The mktyplib utility, like most of the ActiveX SDK, is targeted primarily at developers using C++.)

As a Visual Basic developer, you will probably find it easier to create abstract classes. An *abstract class* is a class module that contains declarations for the class's interface but no code to implement the interface elements. The particulars of how each interface element is implemented are left to the classes that implement the abstract class.

Once you have an abstract class in your project, you can refer to it in other classes by using the Implements keyword. For example, let's say you need to build a class to handle your ice cream factory. You know you're going to transport ice cream to customers in vehicles (ice cream trucks). There are different kinds of ice cream trucks, but all ice cream trucks have a number of common properties, such as size, carrying capacity, and number of wheels.

The Implements statement, which is new to Visual Basic 5.0, enables your object to exercise the object-oriented property of *polymorphism*. Polymorphism means that an object can be manipulated using more than one interface–a useful thing, because it means that you can build new interfaces for your objects without disturbing the old ones. Leaving old interfaces in place means that new versions of your object won't break the old versions.

In this example, you'll build an abstract class to represent an ice cream truck, then build classes that implement the abstract class. This example will demonstrate how easy it is to write multiple interfaces to a single abstract class. To do this:

1 Create a new EXE project. Add two class modules to the project. Name the first class ITruck and the second class SmallDeliveryTruck.

> **Note** *The letter "I" prefixing the name of an abstract interface class is an ActiveX convention; it's done this way to remind the programmer that this class is designed to provide an interface for other classes. You are free to call your classes anything you want, but for this example we'll stick with the convention.*

2 Declare the extremely abbreviated interface of the ITruck class by entering the following code:

```
Public Sub LoadTruck()

End Sub
```

3 You're done with the ITruck class for now. Close the code window and open the code window for the SmallDeliveryTruck class.

4 Use the Implements keyword to designate that this class is an implementation of the ITruck class. Do this by typing the following code into the SmallDeliveryTruck class's code window:

```
' Declarations
Implements ITruck
```

5 Next, you have to write the code to implement each element of the ITruck interface. The rule here is that you have to implement every element of the ITruck class, or Visual Basic will scold you and refuse to run your program. This should not be particularly difficult in this demonstration application, since ITruck has only one interface member, the LoadTruck method. Enter the following code:

```
Private Sub ITruck_LoadTruck()
    Debug.Print "Truck Loaded."
End Sub
```

Note *This simplified example prints to the Immediate window when the LoadTruck method is called; your real-world implementation of the LoadTruck method would obviously include code that performed whatever processing that needed to be done to implement the loading of a truck.*

6 Now that you've got an abstract class and an implementation of that class, you can take a stab at using the class in an application. Close the SmallDeliveryTruck class's code window and open the code window for Form1.

7 In Form1's Load event, type the following code:

```
Private Sub Form_Load()
    Dim MySmallTruck As New SmallDeliveryTruck
    Dim TruckAtLoadingDock As ITruck

    Set TruckAtLoadingDock = MySmallTruck
    TruckAtLoadingDock.LoadTruck

End Sub
```

8 Run the code. The LoadTruck event of the ITruck object is executed, displaying text in the Immediate window.

We're now at the point, finally, where you can begin to see the usefulness of multiple interfaces. Let's say that your ice cream factory has started using a new, larger kind of delivery truck. Your application must represent the new kind of truck with a class that is a new implementation of the ITruck interface. To do this:

1 Add a new class module to your project. Call this class BigDeliveryTruck.

2 Double-click on the class module to open its code window.

3 In its code window, enter the following code:

```
' Declarations
Implements ITruck


Private Sub ITruck_LoadTruck()
    Beep
    MsgBox "Attention! The big truck is now being loaded!"
End Sub
```

4 Close the code window and return to the Load event of Form1. Modify the code so it looks like this:

```
Private Sub Form_Load()
    'Dim MySmallTruck As New SmallDeliveryTruck
    Dim MyBigTruck As New BigDeliveryTruck
    Dim TruckAtLoadingDock As ITruck

    Set TruckAtLoadingDock = MyBigTruck
    TruckAtLoadingDock.LoadTruck


End Sub
```

5 Run the code. You can see that this time, when your procedure executes the code TruckAtLoadingDock.LoadTruck, the BigDeliveryTruck version of the LoadTruck method is executed.

You can see from this example that by implementing multiple interfaces of classes, you enable your application to grow and change without the intense level of grief that is usually associated with changing a software design after it has been initially written.

Using Friend Methods

You can declare methods as Friend so private data members can be accessed from other objects that know how to access them safely. Friend procedures are not an object-oriented concept as much as they are an exception to object-oriented rules.

A Friend method can be executed by another procedure in the same class as the method, but not by a procedure outside the class. But unlike a private procedure (which also can't be accessed from outside the class in which it resides), a Friend procedure has access to data that exists in other objects of the same type.

For example, say you have a MidsizedDeliveryTruck class. Because your fleet of mid-sized delivery trucks has a special loader device that enables a driver to dump all the tubs of ice cream into another truck at the flick of a switch, you decide to write a software class to emulate the behavior of the mid-sized ice cream truck. To see an example of how you might write such a class, do the following:

1 Create a new EXE project.

2 Add a class module to the project. Name the class MidsizedDeliveryTruck.

3 Type the following code in the class's code window:

```
' Declarations
Private mlngTubs As Long


Public Property Get Tubs() As Long
    Tubs = mlngTubs
End Property


Public Property Let Tubs(ByVal lngNewValue As Long)
    mlngTubs = lngNewValue
End Property


Public Sub SwapTubs(TargetTruck As MidsizedDeliveryTruck)
    ' Takes all the tubs in the current
    ' truck and moves them to a new truck.


    If mlngTubs > 0 Then
        TargetTruck.Transfer mlngTubs, TargetTruck
    End If


End Sub
```

```
Friend Sub Transfer(lngTubs As Long, Truck As MidsizedDeliveryTruck)
    ' Can be called from another BigDeliveryTruck
    ' object, but not from a form or another
    ' type of object.

    Debug.Print "Transferred " & lngTubs & " tubs."
    mlngTubs = 0
    Truck.Tubs = lngTubs

End Sub
```

In this code, the public subroutine SwapTubs (exposed as a method of the MidsizedDeliveryTruck class) performs validation only; it hands off the actual work of swapping tubs to the Friend procedure called Transfer. Transfer is not a publicly accessible method of this class; it can only be called from other procedures in the class.

The Transfer subroutine, meanwhile, takes responsiblity for setting the number of tubs in the current truck object to 0 while setting the number of tubs in the target truck object to the appropriate number. To see how this code works:

1 Close the class and open Form1.

2 In Form1's Load event, type the following code:

```
Private Sub Form_Load()
    Dim RedTruck As New MidsizedDeliveryTruck
    Dim BlueTruck As New MidsizedDeliveryTruck


    RedTruck.Tubs = 20
    RedTruck.SwapTubs BlueTruck
    Debug.Print "BlueTruck now has " & BlueTruck.Tubs & " tubs."

End Sub
```

3 Run the code, then look at the Immediate window. You should be able to see that the SwapTubs method moved all the tubs from RedTruck to BlueTruck by means of the Friend subroutine Transfer.

Of course, instead of using a Friend procedure, you could instead place the code that performed the work of transferring tubs into the public SwapTubs method–or simply make the Transfer method public instead of a Friend procedure. But this would mean that the user of this class would have more control over exactly how many tubs were transferred, something you might want to prohibit. You can see that by using a

Friend procedure in this way, you get more control over the contexts in which your code can be used.

> **Note** *Although we used a class module in this example for the sake of simplicity, you can use Friend procedures in your ActiveX control projects as well. There is no syntactical difference between Friend procedures in classes and ActiveX control projects.*

Summary

In this chapter, we covered the object-oriented features of Visual Basic 5.0. We discussed object-oriented programming in conceptual terms, then demonstrated them with an ActiveX project that contained its own object model created with Visual Basic classes.

In the next chapter, we'll take a look at some of the database features of Visual Basic 5.0 and demonstrate how you can make your ActiveX control project database-aware.

Visual Basic Data Access

Providing Data Awareness in Your ActiveX Control

Chapter 17
Database Access

For business users, database access is one of the most compelling—and easy-to-implement features of Visual Basic. Even if you're not a captain of industry, using VB as a way to display and edit information in a database is easy and powerful.

This chapter is split into two sections. The first section deals with how data access works in Visual Basic. The second deals with how to set up your ActiveX control to connect to a database.

Visual Basic Data Access

There are a number of ways to connect your application to a database in Visual Basic. This chapter is concerned with the simplest: connecting ActiveX controls to a database using the Visual Basic Data control.

But if you've never used Visual Basic before, you should know that there are a number of other database programming topics not directly related to control creation. Briefly summarized, they are:

▶ Data Access Objects (DAO)—An object model for referring to databases in Visual Basic code. Using DAO, you can create Recordset objects, which can then be manipulated programmatically. For example, you might use DAO to create a custom database report in Visual Basic or perform regular automated queries based on preprogrammed criteria.

▶ Remote Data Objects (RDO)—A way of accessing client-server data from Visual Basic. Remote data objects are geared toward data processing rather than the user-interface. Visual Basic provides a custom control, the RemoteData control, for accessing client-server databases; the Data control is to the RemoteData control as DAO is to RDO.

Using a Microsoft Access Database

Database access has been a part of VB's feature set for quite some time. Since VB 3.0, Visual Basic has included the Microsoft Access database engine, which gives you a number of benefits:

▶ You can use Access's powerful and intuitive development environment to develop a database.

▶ Both Microsoft Access and Visual Basic users can access your database simultaneously.

▶ If you're an experienced Access developer, you will find that much of the code you've written in Access is usable in Visual Basic. This is because Access includes a dialect of Visual Basic known as Visual Basic for Applications. In many cases you can copy and paste code directly between Access and Visual Basic.

As of the time you're reading this, the current version of Access is Microsoft Access 97; it is part of the Microsoft Office 97 suite. Visual Basic has the ability to access Microsoft Access databases created with versions of Access as early as Access 2.0.

Other Data Sources Accessible to the Data Control

If for some reason you can't or don't wish to use a Microsoft Access database, you have a plethora of other options. The Access engine supports a number of other database formats as well, such as Paradox and the dBASE format used by FoxPro and a number of other database management applications.

You use the Connect property of the data control to designate which type of database you wish to connect to. Choices of database formats provided by the Connect property include:

▶ Microsoft Access (the default)

▶ dBASE III, IV, or 5.0

Database Access and the Control Creation Edition

Although the Visual CCE enables you to create controls that are data-aware, it doesn't include database access. This can put you in the unamusing position of being able to create a control that you cannot test. The control may work fine; you just can't connect it to a data control to prove this fact for yourself, at least not in the CCE.

Database access is available in the Professional and Enterprise editions of Visual Basic. If you're a user of the Professional or Enterprise editions of Visual Basic 4.0 and you haven't upgraded yet,

you're in luck, because you can use those editions of VB to test your control. (And, of course, you can use the control in any of the retail editions of Visual Basic 5.0.) It is a hassle, yes, because you have to switch back and forth between two different versions of VB, but whaddya want for nothing?

Even if you don't have an edition of VB that can test your data-aware control, you can still follow along through this chapter to learn how to create such a control. You'll just need to skip over the parts where you test your control.

▶ Excel versions 3.0 to 7.0

▶ FoxPro versions 2.0 through 3.0

▶ Lotus WK1, WK3, and WK4 formats

▶ Paradox versions 3.0 through 5.x

▶ Text files

> **Note** *These data sources are the sources that were supported natively by the Visual Basic 4.0 data control. It's likely that this list will expand somewhat in the shipping version of VB 5.0, possibly (for example) to include data files created by Microsoft Excel 97.*

More Choices: Using Open Database Connectivity

If the native database formats available to you aren't enough, you can also connect to a database using a Windows technology called Open Database Connectivity (ODBC). ODBC provides a set of drivers that enables your application to access a data source no matter what format that data source is in. You can access any ODBC data source from a Visual Basic Data control.

If your application needs to access a client-server database (such as Oracle or Sybase), an ODBC driver is one part of the equation that connects your application to the database. But ODBC isn't just for client-server connections; there are ODBC drivers for many applications that store and process data—even for applications that are not relational databases. For example, there is an ODBC driver for Microsoft Excel, enabling you to access data stored in an Excel spreadsheet as if it were stored in a relational database. (The Microsoft Excel format is also supported natively by the VB data control as well.)

The good news is that from the control creation perspective, none of this matters. This is because the data source is abstracted at such a high level that your control only sees a record source and a field, as you'll see in the sections that describe data-aware controls later in this chapter.

Data-Aware Controls in Visual Basic

Visual Basic comes with a number of data-aware controls. You can use these controls as examples of how data-aware controls behave; you can also use these controls as constituent controls of your control project. The data-aware controls that come with all versions of Visual Basic are:

▶ TextBox

▶ PictureBox

- ▶ Label

- ▶ CheckBox

The Professional and Enterprise editions of Visual Basic include these additional data-aware controls:

- ▶ RichTextBox

- ▶ DBGrid

- ▶ DBList

- ▶ DBCombo

There are also a number of data-aware third-party controls. For example, data-aware grids, which can display two-dimensional lists of data displayed in rows and columns, are particularly abundant.

How Database Access Works

You connect an ActiveX control to a database through the Data control. The Data control handles the connection between the application and the database, while the ActiveX control displays the data and permits the user to edit the data that it displays.

The Visual Basic Data control is illustrated in Figure 17.1.

You only need to set two properties of the Data control to connect it to a data source: the DatabaseName and RecordSource properties. These properties are outlined in Table 17.1.

In addition to providing a connection to the database, the Data control provides a user interface for a form that contains data-aware controls. The four buttons in the Data control are illustrated in Figure 17.2.

When the user is navigating through the recordset using the Data control, she has the ability to edit records (unless the Data control's ReadOnly property has been set to True). When an edit occurs, the edit is saved to the database as soon as the user moves to a different

FIGURE 17.1
Visual Basic Data control

TABLE 17.1	PROPERTIES OF THE DATA CONTROL
DatabaseName	The name of the database. This can be a file on disk (for a Microsoft Access database), a directory (for a dBASE-style database), or an ODBC data source (for a client-server database or other type of database not directly supported by Visual Basic).
RecordSource	The name of the table in the database to which the Data control is connected. For relational databases, this can be the name of a table, a query stored in the database, or a text string in Structured Query Language (SQL).

record or when your application executes the Update method of the Data control's Recordset object.

In addition to navigating through the recordset, you can use the Data control to create a new record. When the Data control's EOFAction property is set to 2–New Record, you can create a new record by clicking on the Move Last button, then clicking on the Move Next button. This behavior mimics the behavior of the navigation buttons in Microsoft Access, which also create new records when the user moves past the last record in a recordset.

Properties of Data-Aware Controls

A control that can be connected to a data control is said to be *bound* or *data-aware*. Data-aware controls expose the DataSource and DataField properties, as shown in Table 17.2.

When a control is bound to a data control, the data displayed is dependent on what's in the database. For example, a bound TextBox control's Text property is almost never set by the developer. Instead, the developer sets the DataSource and DataField properties and the Text property is set by the Data control.

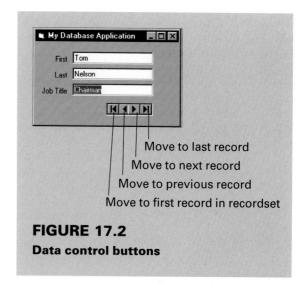

FIGURE 17.2
Data control buttons

Move to last record
Move to next record
Move to previous record
Move to first record in recordset

TABLE 17.2	PROPERTIES OF DATA-AWARE CONTROLS
DataSource	The name of the Data control that maintains the connection to the database
DataField	The name of the field of the table in the database to which the control is bound

So in summary, the steps a developer goes through to create a database application based on the Visual Basic Data control are:

1 Create a Data control on a form.

2 Set the Data control's DatabaseName property to point to the location of the database file.

3 Set the Data control's RecordSource property to refer to the database table or query you wish to use.

4 Create one or more bound controls on the form.

5 Set the controls' DataSource property to refer to the Data control.

6 Set the controls' DataField property to refer to the field in the database.

One of the advantages of setting up a database application in this way is that you can often create an application that requires a grand total of zero lines of code to provide basic functionality.

Providing Data Awareness in Your ActiveX Control

Giving your ActiveX control the ability to connect to a data control is a fairly straight-forward process involving the ever-popular Procedure Attributes dialog box.

To demonstrate this, you'll create a data-aware control that will graphically display the value of a database field. This control will be used by an ice cream factory to provide a visual display of different types of ice cream for a production-tracking database application. To do this:

1 Create a new control project. Give the UserControl the name DataPicture.

2 Add a constituent Picture control to the control designer. Give this control the name picDisplay.

3 Change the AutoSize property of the control to True. Change the BorderSize property of the control to 0 None. Set the Picture control of the property to the file type.bmp, found on the CD-ROM that accompanies this book.

4 Set the Top and Left properties of picDisplay to zero.

5 Add four more Picture controls to the control designer. Name them picChocolate, picIce, picSherbert, and picNull.

6 Set the Picture properties of the four new controls to chocolate.bmp, ice.bmp, sherbert.bmp, and type.bmp, respectively.

7 Set the Visible property of picChocolate, picIce, picSherbert, and picNull to False. This will make the controls invisible at runtime. Your control designer should look something like Figure 17.3.

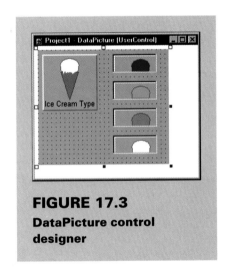

FIGURE 17.3
DataPicture control designer

Next you'll enter code to make the picture displayed by the control change according to the contents of the database field. To do this, enter the following code in the Click event of picDisplay:

```
' Declarations
Private mvDataValue As Variant


Public Property Get DataValue() As Variant
    DataValue = mvDataValue
End Property


Public Property Let DataValue(ByVal vNewValue As Variant)
```

```
        mvDataValue = vNewValue
        Select Case vNewValue
            Case Null
            picDisplay.Picture = picNull.Picture


            Case Ø
            picDisplay.Picture = picChocolate.Picture


            Case 1
            picDisplay.Picture = picIce.Picture


            Case 2
            picDisplay.Picture = picSherbert.Picture


            Case Else
            picDisplay.Picture = picNull.Picture

        End Select

        ' ***** Very important for data-bound properties
        PropertyChanged "DataValue"

End Property
```

You can see that this code simply switches the picture displayed by picDisplay to the appropriate type of ice cream. There are no new concepts in this code, although you'll want to note that the PropertyChanged statement (which you should include in a Property Let statement anyway) is particularly important. This is because it triggers a database update in a data-aware control.

Next, add code that will enable the user to change the value of the field to which the control is bound. For this control, the user can change the value of the field by clicking on the control, so enter the following code in picDisplay's Click event:

```
Private Sub picDisplay_Click()
    Select Case mvDataValue
        Case Ø
        DataValue = 1


        Case 1
```

```
            DataValue = 2

        Case 2
        DataValue = 0

        Case Else
        DataValue = 0

    End Select

    PropertyChanged "DataValue"

End Sub
```

This procedure also contains nothing conceptually new; it simply cycles through the available pictures, changing the value of the database field each time the user clicks on the control until the user has selected the value he wants.

Now enter a Resize event for the UserControl. This procedure will resize the User-Control to conform to the dimensions of the constituent picture control picDisplay:

```
Private Sub UserControl_Resize()
    ' Make the UserControl match picDisplay
    ' because picDisplay is AutoSized
    UserControl.Height = picDisplay.Height
    UserControl.Width = picDisplay.Width
End Sub
```

Finally, to enable your control to connect to a data control, you must designate one of the properties of your control as bindable. Binding a control to a field in the database means that whenever the bound property of your control changes, Visual Basic writes the new value back to the database field to which your control is bound.

To mark the DataValue property as bindable to a database field, do the following:

1 Select the menu command **Tools, Procedure Attributes**.

2 The Procedure Attributes dialog box appears. Click on the **Advanced** button. The dialog box expands.

3 Select the checkbox labeled Property is data bound. Then select the checkbox labeled This property binds to data field. The Procedure Attributes dialog box looks like Figure 17.4.

4 Click on **OK**. The DataValue property is marked as a bindable property.

Note *At this point, if you're going to test your control in a container other than Visual Basic 5.0, you'll need to compile your control using the File, Make menu command.*

Your data-aware control is now complete. To test it:

1 Close the code window and close the control designer.

2 Open the EXE form.

3 Place a Data control on the EXE form. Remember, the Data control is only available in the Professional or Enterprise edition of Visual Basic; if you only have Visual Basic 4.0, that will suffice.

4 Set the Data control's DatabaseName property to icecream.mdb. This Microsoft Access database is on the CD-ROM that accompanies this book.

5 Set the Data control's RecordSource property to tblIceCream.

6 Add three labels and three text boxes to the form so that it looks like Figure 17.5. Name the text boxes txtFactory, txtDate, and txtQuantity.

7 Set the DataSource property of all three text boxes to Data1.

8 Set the DataField property of txtFactory to the field Factory. Set the DataField property of txtDate to the field Date. Set the DataField property of txtQuantity to the field Quantity.

9 Run the application to make sure that everything is hooked up correctly. You should be able to browse data from the database through the interface you've just built, as illustrated in Figure 17.5, above.

10 Now add an instance of the DataPicture control to the form. Set the control's DataSource property to Data1, and set its DataField property to IceCreamType.

11 Run the application. You should be able to see that for each production record, a different type of ice cream appears. The value that is stored in the database field is a long integer, but the value displayed by the control is a type of ice cream, as illustrated in Figure 17.6.

12 In one of the records, click on the DataPicture control to see that you can change the ice cream type. If you click several times, the control cycles through the available types. Any change you make to the data is saved to the database.

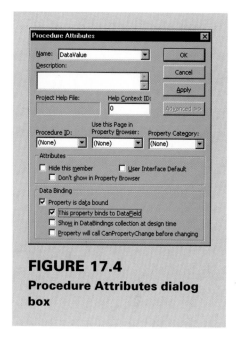

FIGURE 17.4
Procedure Attributes dialog box

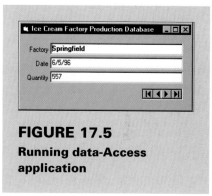

FIGURE 17.5
Running data-Access application

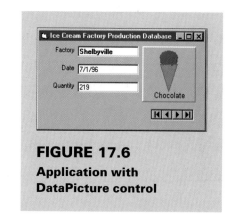

FIGURE 17.6
Application with DataPicture control

Summary

In this chapter, you learned about how database access works in Visual Basic. We went through the various options for hooking up to a database available to the Visual Basic developer and demonstrated how to add database features to your ActiveX control.

Glossary

access key
A keystroke combination that serves as a shortcut for an element of the user interface.

active content
A generic term that refers to the use of such technologies as ActiveX controls, scripting, and database access in Web pages.

ActiveX
A set of component technologies that enables software components to interact with one another in a networked environment, regardless of the language in which they were created. ActiveX controls are 32-bit, which means that they only function under Windows 95 and Windows NT.

ActiveX Control Pad
An application to assist VBScript developers in inserting ActiveX controls into Web pages. The ActiveX Control Pad is downloadable free from the Microsoft Web site at http://www.microsoft.com/workshop/author/cpad/download.htm.

ActiveX gallery
A location on the Microsoft Web site where you can preview and download ActiveX controls from Microsoft and a number of other developers.
http://www.microsoft.com/activex/gallery

ActiveX scripting
A generic term that refers to support in Microsoft Internet Explorer for Visual Basic scripting (VBScript) and Javascript (JScript).

AmbientProperties object
An object provided by a control's container that suggests default properties to the control.

Application Programming Interface (API)
A set of procedures that represents the programmable elements of a software system. For example, your program can issue calls to the Windows API in order to get the

Windows operating system to create windows, draw graphics, open files, and do the other things an operating system does.

argument
A value passed to a procedure.

array
A set of elements storing the same type of data. Each element of an array has a unique identifying number, called an index. In Visual Basic 5.0, many computations requiring arrays are better done with collections instead.

assertion
A programming language feature that conditionally halts your code. You use assertions when testing Visual Basic applications by using the Assert method of the Debug object. If the assertion evaluates to False, your code is paused on the line that contains the Assert method.

asynchronous
A process that performs its work in the background, without preventing the remainder of the application from doing its work. For example, in Visual Basic 5.0, property values of controls can be downloaded asynchronously, enabling the control to continue working even though the property has not finished downloading.

Authenticode
A technology used by Microsoft Internet Explorer to verify that downloaded software (such as an ActiveX control) came from a reputable source. Downloaded files can be verified because they are digitally signed by their creators.

Automation object
An object that is exposed to other applications or programming tools through Automation interfaces. Applications that expose an Automation interface can be programmed just like other types of software objects. Microsoft Word, Microsoft Excel, and Microsoft Internet Explorer are examples of applications that can serve as Automation objects. (They were formerly referred to as OLE Automation objects.)

Boolean expression
An expression that evaluates to either True or False. In Visual Basic, False is equal to 0 and True is equal to -1.

Break mode

A mode of code execution used for debugging. In Break mode, the developer can use the Immediate window, step through code, and use a number of other debugging features of the Visual Basic IDE. To place a running application into Break mode, you use the menu command Run, Break or the keystroke shortcut Ctrl+Break.

bug

A procedure that encounters an unexpected condition that prevents it from carrying out its calculations. Compare with *error*.

by reference

A way of passing the address, rather than the value, of an argument to a procedure. This allows the procedure to access the actual variable. As a result, the variable's actual value can be changed by the procedure to which it is passed.

by value

A way of passing the value, rather than the address, of an argument to a procedure. This allows the procedure to access a copy of the variable. As a result, the variable's actual value can't be changed by the procedure to which it is passed.

CAB file

See cabinet file.

cabinet file

A compressed file that includes software components to be installed on a user's computer over the Internet. You can create cabinet files using the Setup Wizard. Also called *CAB files*.

call

A procedure referring to or executing another procedure.

class

The formal definition of an object. A class is used to create instances of software objects. Classes define the properties of the object and the methods used to control the object's behavior.

code module

A Visual Basic file that can contain code. Typically, code modules end in the file extension .BAS.

collection

An object that contains a set of related objects. In Visual Basic, you can create collections to store data as an alternative to using arrays.

comment

Text within a piece of code that is not interpreted or executed. In Visual Basic, comments are set off with a single apostrophe (') or the Rem statement.

comparison operator

An operator that tests a quantitative relationship between two or more values or expressions.

compile

The process of taking a project's code components and making an EXE or OCX file out of them. You can distribute compiled files to users.

COM

See Component Object Model.

combo box

A list box that drops down when clicked to expose a list of choices. Also referred to as dropdown lists.

Component Object Model (COM)

A specification for reusable software components. ActiveX controls fall under the DCOM, or Distributed Component Object Model specification, which in turn falls under the COM specification.

constituent control

A control that resides in an ActiveX control project. You can place one or more constituent controls in your ActiveX control project in order to use the functionality of those constituent controls.

container

An object that can house another object. For example, a Visual Basic form can be a container to an ActiveX control; a PictureBox can be a container to a CommandButton and ActiveX controls you create can act as containers to other ActiveX controls.

control

A programmable element (usually an element of the user interface). Examples of controls are the text box, the combo box, and the command button. In Visual Basic, "control" also can refer to certain programmable objects that are not part of the visible user interface, such as the timer control or the ActiveX preload control.

control designer
The visual design element of an ActiveX control. You use the control designer in the Visual Basic IDE to build the visual look of your control. Every ActiveX control project built in Visual Basic has a control designer–even controls that are invisible at runtime. Control designers are analogous to forms in Visual Basic EXE projects.

Control Development Kit (CDK)
The software development kit used by C++ programmers to create OCX controls. Superseded by the ActiveX Development Kit.

control project
A Visual Basic project that can be used to make an ActiveX control. Control projects are comprised of a control designer and, optionally, other components such as forms, code modules, and resource files.

custom control
A generic term referring to ActiveX, OCX, or VBX controls.

data ranges
A specific range of allowed values for each Variant subtype.

data types
The different types of variables that can be processed by a programming language. VBScript has only one data type, the Variant, which has many subtypes; variants can contain textual, numeric, or other information. Also see *data ranges*.

date expression
Any expression that can be interpreted as a date. This includes any combination of date literals, numbers that look like dates, strings that look like dates, and dates returned from functions. A date expression is limited to numbers or strings, in any combination, that can represent a date from January 1, 100 through December 31, 9999.

DCOM
See *Distributed Component Object Model*.

declaration

In code, the process of identifying variables or function calls before using them. In Visual Basic, only API calls, arrays, and object variables must be explicitly declared (unless you use Option Explicit, in which case all variables must be explicitly declared).

debug

The process of locating and removing bugs from code.

delegation

The act of assigning a property of your UserControl to one of its constituent controls. Delegating properties keeps you from having to write code to handle property changes. Instead, the inherent functionality of the constituent control is used.

designer

The interface of a control used by a developer at control design time. A control designer is the control creation equivalent of a form.

dialog box

An on-screen message box that conveys or requests information.

dirty

A form or object that has been changed and needs to be saved.

Distributed Component Object Model (DCOM)

A protocol that permits software objects to interact over networks (including the Internet). Previously called Network OLE.

DLL

Dynamic Link Library, a type of Windows file that can be called from an application. DLLs can hypothetically be shared between applications.

download

The process of transferring information from a remote computer to your computer. On the Internet, you can use a file transfer utility (such as FTP) to download or upload files. You also download files using a Web browser.

Dynamic Link Library

See *DLL*.

embedded

An object that resides in another object. ActiveX controls and Java applets, for example, are said to be embedded in HTML pages through the use of the <OBJECT> tag.

Empty

A special value that indicates that a variable has never been initialized. In Visual Basic expressions, Empty can be equivalent of either zero or a zero-length string (“”).

enabled

A control that is capable of receiving user input. You enable or disable controls to reflect the state of the user interface.

enumeration

A method of declaring a related group of constants. You declare an enumeration in Visual Basic using the Enum statement.

error

A procedure that arrives at an incorrect result. Compare with *bug*.

error number

A whole number in the range 0 to 65,535, inclusive, that corresponds to the Number property of the Err object. When combined with the Name property of the Err object, this number represents a particular error message.

error-handler

A procedure that deals with an error condition in a procedure. In Visual Basic, error-handlers are declared with some form of the On Error statement.

evaluate

The process of determining the value of an expression.

event

An occurrence that takes place while an application runs. Events are usually user-initiated. Button clicks, windows opening, and menu commands are examples of events. Code triggered to run when events take place are called event procedures.

event procedure

Code that is run as the result of an event, such as a click on a command button. See *event*.

EXE project

A Visual Basic project that can be made into a stand-alone, executable application. The Visual Basic Control Creation Edition can't create executables; however, you can use EXE projects to test ActiveX components. Compare to *control project*, a Visual Basic project that can be used to make an ActiveX control.

expression

A combination of keywords, operators, variables, and constants that yield a string, number, or object. An expression can perform a calculation, manipulate characters, or test data.

Extender object

An object that enables your ActiveX control to communicate with and manipulate properties of its container.

folder

A list of computer files contained on a disk or drive. May be nested to facilitate organization of data on the disk or drive. Called directories or subdirectories on DOS and Unix systems.

font

One complete collection of letters, punctuation marks, numbers, and special characters with a consistent and identifiable typeface, weight, posture, and font size. Sometimes used to refer to typefaces or font families.

form

A user interface, usually comprised of input controls such as text boxes and buttons. In HTML, *form* refers to a page that takes information inputted into a Web browser and submits it to a Web server. In Visual Basic, a form is the basis of the user interface.

Friend procedure

A procedure that can access private data of procedures declared in the same module as the friend procedure.

function

A procedure that returns a value. Compare with *subroutine*.

Globally Unique Identifier (GUID)

The unique identifier of OLE objects or servers, including ActiveX controls. Your control's GUID is assigned to it by Visual Basic at the time it is compiled.

global variable
A variable that is accessible from any procedure in the application.

Graphic Interchange Format (GIF)
A compressed format for storing graphics.

history list
A list of uniform resource locators stored by a Web browser. The history list stores a list of all the Web pages the user has previously visited.

HTML
HyperText Markup Language, the language that dictates the basic layout of World Wide Web pages. HTML can be extended by various means, including scripting (such as VBScript and JScript) and embedded objects (such as Netscape plug-ins and ActiveX controls).

HTML Layout Control
A Microsoft ActiveX control designed to extend the functionality of style sheets within Microsoft Internet Explorer.

hyperlink
A word or series of words that are clickable. Clicking on a hyperlink enables a user to jump from one document to the next, or from one area of a document to another area in the same document. Also called hypertext.

hypertext
See *hyperlink.*

IDE
See *integrated development environment.*

immediate window
A window in the Visual Basic development environment that enables the developer to issue commands to an application running in Break mode.

index (array index)
A number that uniquely identifies an element of an array.

initialization safety
A principle dictating that an ActiveX control must not be able to harm a user's computer no matter what its initial properties are set to. Compare with *safety, script safety.*

instantiate

To insert a control into a container, either at design time (by drawing the control using the mouse) or in code.

Integrated Development Environment (IDE)

The user interface of a software development environment. When you are developing applications with Visual Basic, you are said to be in Visual Basic's IDE. Other development environments have different IDEs.

interface

The set of functions and data exposed by a programmable software component. For example, the interface of an ActiveX object is comprised of the object's properties, methods, and events.

Internet Explorer

Microsoft's Web browser, available for free download at http://www.microsoft.com/ie/default.asp.

JPEG

A file format that stores images in a compressed format. Support for JPEG files (in the PictureBox control) is a new feature of Visual Basic 5.0.

JScript

A scripting language based on the Java programming language. JScript is comparable to VBScript in its functionality, but uses Java-like syntax.

license

The legal right to use a piece of software. ActiveX controls can support licensing. The license for a control is embedded in the user's system registry when the user installs the control. For licensed controls designed to be distributed over the Web, you must use a special tool to create a temporary license for the control.

lifetime

The period of time a variable exists, depending on the level at which it was declared. Global and static variables persist until the application is done running, while variables declared at the procedural level are only valid while the procedure they were declared in is still running. See also *procedure level, scope.*

locale

The location and language of a user; used for localization purposes. For example, U.S. English, Swiss, German, and Albanian are examples of locales. In Windows, you set your locale through the Regional Settings control panel.

localization

The process of translating software for international use. This entails, among other things, translating the textual elements of the user interface into the local language. In Windows, the operating system is responsible for some elements of localization, such as the format of date and time values. Resource files containing string resources are often used in the process of localization.

loop, looping

A set of program instructions that execute repeatedly until a condition is satisfied. In Visual Basic, the Do...While and For...Next statements are looping structures.

MDI

See *multiple document interface.*

method

A procedure that causes a programmable object to perform an action. Compare with *property*, a characteristic of an object.

module

A Visual Basic file that contains code.

Multiple Document Interface (MDI)

A Windows interface style in which all of an applications' windows are housed in a large window known as the parent window. Compare with *single document interface.*

nested

A code structure that occurs within another identical code structure; for example, an If...Then statement contained inside another If...Then statement.

Network OLE

See *Distributed Component Object Model.*

Nothing

In Visual Basic, a special value that indicates that an object variable is not associated with an object. Evaluates to zero or an empty string ("") in an expression.

Null

A value indicating that a variable contains no valid data. A variable will typically be set to Null in a database context, in situations where a field contains no data or a recordset contains no records.

numeric expression

Any expression that can be evaluated as a number. Elements of the expression can include any combination of keywords, variables, constants, and operators that result in a number.

object

Generally, a self-contained piece of code embedded in another application. Objects provide various interfaces (such as properties, methods, and collections) to permit programmers to access them. VBScript objects are either ActiveX controls or Java applets. Objects are inserted into an HTML page through the use of the <OBJECT> tag.

object browser

A facility that displays the interface of the programmable objects available to your project.

object model

The interfaces made available by an object. The Microsoft Internet Explorer Scripting Object Model, for example, lists the properties and methods of the Web browser accessible from VBScript. You can create objects in your projects that have object models of their own through the use of classes.

OCX

OLE Custom Control, a type of software object designed to be embedded in applications. This term has been supplanted by the term *ActiveX*, but the underlying technology is nearly identical; you can often use most OLE controls in the same contexts you'd use ActiveX controls.

OLE

Originally an acronym for Object Linking and Embedding, it now refers to a broad range of interoperability protocols and standards.

operator

A logical or mathematical symbol that serves as part of an expression in code. Plus and minus signs are examples of math operators; the greater-than symbol (>) is an example of a logical operator.

Paint event

A control event that is triggered when the control needs to redraw itself. Controls need to redraw themselves when they are temporarily obscured by other windows, for example.

painting object

An element of the Visual Basic interface that can use Visual Basic's graphics methods (such as Line and PSet). Examples of painting objects are Forms and PictureBoxes.

PictureBox

An element of the user interface that can store and display a graphic file.

procedure

A collection of statements in a programming language. Examples of procedures are functions, which can return a value, and subroutines, which do not.

program flow

Elements of a program that determine whether a piece of code is executed and, if it is executed, how many times it is executed. The If...Then...Else statement is an example of conditional program flow. The Do While...Loop statement is an example of looping program flow.

project

The collection of all files that comprise a software application's code. A Visual Basic project file contains references to all the forms, code modules, controls, class files, resources used by the application.

Project Explorer

The window in the Visual Basic IDE that enables you to see the components of your project in outline form.

project file

A file that contains references to all the files used in a project. Project files save you time because you don't have to load the individual components of a project separately. Visual Basic 5.0 gives you the new ability to open multiple projects simultaneously.

project group

A file that contains references to one or more Visual Basic projects. Project group files enable you to easily open more than one Visual Basic project at a time; they are new in Visual Basic 5.0.

property

An attribute of a programmable object. Properties define characteristics such as size and color. Compare with *method*, a way to tell a programmable object to perform an action.

property bag

An object that represents the place where design-time properties of an ActiveX control are stored. You write code in the ReadProperties and WriteProperties events of the UserControl so a control can store its design-time properties.

Property Get

The Visual Basic procedure that is executed when a user reads a property of an object. You use Property Get procedures in classes and ActiveX controls.

Property Let

The Visual Basic procedure that assigns a variable to an object. You use Property Let procedures in classes and ActiveX controls.

property page

A dialog box that enables a user to view and set an ActiveX control's properties. Also referred to as a property sheet.

Property Set

The Visual Basic procedure that assigns an object variable to an object. You use Property Set procedures in classes and ActiveX controls.

query

A component of a database that retrieves data from one of more tables.

registry

A system file containing software and hardware information. ActiveX controls must be registered before they can be used on a particular computer. Installing a control that has been packaged with a Setup application registers the control; you can also register a control manually using a utility called Regsvr32.

resource compiler

A utility that takes a resource script and compiles it into a resource file.

resource file

A resource is a piece of data–a string, a bitmap, a sound file–that is compiled along with your control or VB application.

You use resources to avoid having to refer to files on disk; instead, the file resides in the compiled EXE (or OCX) you distribute to users. You create resource files using a resource compiler.

resource script
A text file that gives the resource compiler information on what files to compile into a resource file and how to identify them.

runtime
The time when code is running–as opposed to design time, when you are writing the code. Some object properties can be changed only at runtime, while some can be changed either at design time or runtime.

run-time error
An error that occurs when code is running. A run-time error results when a statement attempts an invalid operation.

safety
The principle that an ActiveX control distributed over the Web must not be capable of harming a user's computer. Safety is divided into *script safety* and *initialization safety*.

ScaleHeight
The Visual Basic property that determines the height of an object in the current measurement system (as determined by the ScaleMode property). For example, the Width of a form might be 4800 twips, but its ScaleWidth might be much smaller if its ScaleMode property is set to pixels. Because the number of twips per pixel is system-dependent, it makes sense to use the ScaleWidth and ScaleHeight properties, rather than absolute Width and Height properties, when computing dimensions of your control.

ScaleWidth
The Visual Basic property that determines the width of an object in the current measurement system. See *ScaleHeight.*

scope
Defines the visibility of a variable, procedure, or object. For example, a variable declared as Public is visible to all procedures in all modules in a project. Variables declared in procedures are visible only within the procedure and lose their value between calls.

script safety

A principle that dictates that an ActiveX control must not be allowed to harm a user's computer no matter how it is used in a scripting language. Compare with *safety, initialization safety*.

SDI

See *single document interface*.

SDK

Software Development Kit. Often, software companies (most notably Microsoft) will distribute SDKs that permit developers to write to application programming interfaces (see *API*). The ActiveX SDK permits Visual C++ developers to create ActiveX controls.

Setup Wizard

A utility used to package software for distribution. The Setup Wizard creates a Setup application. Users run Setup applications to install software on their computers.

signed

A file that has been digitally marked with information about its creator. *Authenticode* is a method of signing a file.

Single Document Interface (SDI)

A Windows interface style in which the application's interface is comprised of a single window with no background parent window. Compare to *multiple document interface*.

Structured Query Language (SQL)

A language for issuing requests to database servers. The RecordSource property of a Data control can be an SQL query.

string

A series of text characters.

subroutine

A procedure that does not return a value. Compare with *function*.

table

A place in a database where data is stored. Tables are comprised of fields, or columns, and records, or rows.

twip

The default unit of measurement in Visual Basic painting objects. There are 1,440 twips to the inch.

Uniform Resource Locator (URL)

Server and path information that locates a document or other file on the Internet; for example, http://www.domain_name.com.

user

The person who uses the software created by a software developer. To an application programmer, a user uses their executable application; to an ActiveX control developer, a user is another programmer.

user-drawn control

A self-contained ActiveX control whose appearance is entirely generated by graphics methods in code, as opposed to a control whose appearance is generated by constituent controls. The appearance of a user-drawn control is generated by graphics methods placed in the UserControl's Paint event.

UserControl

A control you create in Visual Basic. The UserControl object is analogous to the Visual Basic Form object.

user interface

The elements of a software application with which a user can interact. Forms, command buttons, and list boxes are all examples of parts of a user interface; most, but not all, ActiveX controls are designed to serve as part of a user interface.

validation

The process of ensuring that a piece of data is valid before processing that data.

variable

A named storage location that can contain data that can be modified during program execution. Each variable has a name that uniquely identifies it within its level of scope. Variables also have a specific lifetime depending on where and how they were declared (see *lifetime, scope*). Variable names must begin with an alphabetic character, can't contain an embedded period or type-declaration character, must be unique within the same scope, and must be no longer than 255 characters.

variant

A data type unique to Visual Basic. Variants can store nearly any type of data: text, numbers, or object references.

VBScript

Visual Basic Script, a subset of Visual Basic. One of the Web programming languages understood by Microsoft Internet Explorer. You can use VBScript to manipulate ActiveX controls in a Web page.

Visual Basic Extension (VBX)

Visual Basic Extension, a 16-bit component technology that predates OCXs and ActiveX controls. VBXs are usable in the 16-bit versions of Visual Basic only, unlike ActiveX controls, which can be used in a number of development environments.

Windows API

A set of functions and subroutines that enable you to place calls to the Windows operating system. In Visual Basic, you place Windows API calls to perform tasks that are not possible to do using Visual Basic.

winsock

A Windows application programming interface to the TCP/IP networking protocol.

Index

Z